Financial Handbook fo
Sales and Marketing Mana

FINANCIAL HANDBOOK

for
Sales and Marketing
Managers

ANTHONY TAYLOR

KEITH STEWARD

CASSELL

First published 1990 by **Cassell Educational Limited**
Villiers House, 41/47 Strand, London WC2N 5JE, England

© Cassell Educational Ltd 1990

British Library Cataloguing in Publication Data

Taylor, Anthony
   Financial handbook for sales and marketing managers.
   1. Management accounting
   I. Title   II. Steward, Keith
   658.1511

   ISBN 0-304-31672-5

Printed and bound in Great Britain by Page Bros, Norwich

CONTENTS

PREFACE   ix

PART ONE   Basic Accounting for Control   1

1   Objectives, Structure and Principles of Accounting   2

The development of accounting 2;   Objectives of accounting 3;
The balance sheet, financial position and capital employed 5;
The profit and loss account 7;   More detailed analysis 8; Principles
and conventions 9;   Marketing management and accounting 11

2   Interpreting the Corporate Financial Position   12

Part A   Capital Employed: The importance of the subject 12; What
is a balance sheet? 13;   Forms of business organization 14;
Obtaining the capital 16;   An analysis of capital employed 18;
Capital gearing 23; Dividend policy 25
Part B   Net Assets: Introduction 28;   Fixed assets 28;
Net current assets/liabilities 32;   Miscellaneous items 36;
Conclusions for marketing and sales management 37

3   Analysing the Trading Results   39

The stages of profit 39;   Gross profit and cost of sales 40;
Operating profit and operating expenses 41;   Pre-tax profit and
non-trading items 42;   Net profit and tax 42;   The appropriation
account 42;   The manufacturing account 43;   Depreciation in the
accounts 46

4   The Costing System   49

The meaning of cost 49;   The objectives of costing 49;
The mechanics of costing 50;   Costs for different purposes 53;
Standard cost variance analysis 57

PART TWO Financial Analysis for Planning   65

5 Budgeting and Responsibility Accounting   66

Objectives and scope of this chapter 66; The profit target 67;
The 'contribution' approach to profit planning 69; Charting the
figures 70; The allowable cost approach 73; Formulating
departmental budgets 74; Capital expenditure budgets 74;
Responsibility accounting 75; Accounting for divisions 75;
The master budgets 77

6 Economic Stockholding   80

The importance of stock control 80; Main indicators from the
accounts 80; Monitoring work in progress 81; Goods for
sale 81; Economic order quantities 83; Lead time and safety
stock 84; Seasonal trade and fluctuating sales 85; Minimizing
storage cost 85

7 The Availability of Funds   87

The meaning of 'funds' 87; The need for controlling the funds
flow 87; The funds flow statement 88; Appraising the financial
resources of a business 91; Public and private
companies 98; Planning cash requirements 98

8 Economic Evaluation of Investment Proposals   103

Capital budgeting 103; The time value of money 104;
Net present value (NPV) 106; The internal rate of return
(IRR) 107; The payback method 107; NPV versus the IRR 108;
Risk and uncertainty 113

9 The Balance Sheet Capitalization of Brand Names   115

The valuation of brand names 115; Buying international market
share 116; The application – balance sheet repair 116;
The case for capitalization of home-grown brands 119;
The implications of capitalization 119; Capitalization methodology
– the Interbrand plc formula 120; An example of brand
valuation 123; The importance for sales and marketing
management 124

PART THREE Market Planning   127

10 Marketing Measurement, Sales Forecasting and Targeting 128

Market segmentation 128; Bases of segmentation 129;
Measuring the segments and calculating the future demand 133;
Forecasting potential sales 137; Targeting objectives 138

11 Planning Sales Areas and Territories   142

The partitioning of responsibility 142;   Salesforce size 143;
Area and territory management 148;   Meeting budget, monitoring
and control of sales 150

**12 Product Abandonment and New Product Development
Decisions**   151

The product line 151;   Product abandonment and the importance
of the contribution concept 151;   Alternatives to new product
development 154;   New product development in practice 155;
Strategic elements of new product development 161

13 Financial Aspects of Export Marketing   162

Pricing for export markets 162;   Specific country analyses 165;
Sales channel costs 168;   Government support for exporters 171;
Invoicing in foreign currency and foreign exchange procedures 173

14 The Sales and Marketing Plan   176

Corporate objectives and the mission statement 176;   Analysis of
the previous trading year 176;   Interpretation of the previous
year's results 178;   Strengths, weaknesses, opportunities, threats
(SWOT) analysis 180;   Sales and marketing plan 181

PART FOUR Controlling the Performance   187

15 Price Determination and Pricing Policy   188

Standard cost pricing 189;   Cost-plus system of pricing 189;
Market-related pricing tactics 189;   Changes in volume costs and
selling price 190;   The optimum selling price 193;   Pricing and
the profitability of the product line 194;   The recovery of heavy
research and development expenditure 195;   Pricing to absorb
production capacity 197

16 Indicators for Action and Budget Revision   200

The basic indicators 200;   Indicators of profitability 201;
Sales and gross profit variances 203;   Production budget
variances 206;   Standard cost variances 207;   Operating and non-
trading expenses 211;   Other indicators 212;   Revision of budgets
and standards 213

17 Cost and Profit Control   215

Scope of the chapter 215;   Information for cost control 216;
Control action 218;   Reducing unit costs 219;   Increasing
turnover 221;   Reviewing the sales mix 222;   Loss leaders and
special offers 224;   Profit planning for joint products 225

18   Acquisitions, Buy-outs and Disposals   228

Introduction 228;   Public and private company transactions 228;
Acquisitions 228;   Valuations 230;   Disposals 231;
Management buy-outs 233;   Leveraged buy-outs 234;
Mergers 234

APPENDICES   237

1   **The Essence of Business Taxation**   237

2   **Franchising**   244

3   **Financial Terminology**   252

SELECTED BIBLIOGRAPHY   257

INDEX   259

PREFACE

This book is specially directed to marketing and sales executives. It sets out and explains the accounting and financial information which is relevant to the marketing and selling functions, and which the managers need to understand. In writing the book we have endeavoured to avoid jargon, and to be clear, precise and realistic. We believe that the book will also be of value to other non-accountant managers who seek to know how the accounting service can assist them in planning and controlling the business operations.

A book suitable for managers should, we feel, also be appropriate reading for would-be managers, in particular those studying for the examinations of the Chartered Institute of Marketing, and students on business courses with a strong marketing content. For this reason we have ensured that the following pages amply cover the revised syllabus of the institute's Certificate examination entitled The Financial Aspects of Marketing. The needs of both marketing managers and marketing students are implicit in this syllabus which emphasizes the importance of financial literacy, the application of financial concepts to marketing, and the ability to interpret accounting information. These requirements precisely represent the approach to the subject applied in this book.

This is not a textbook on book-keeping or, except incidentally, on the legal aspects of accounting. It does, however, provide a thoroughgoing exposition of accounting principles, conventions and techniques of which all business executives should be aware. Managers should be aware of the financial consequences of their plans and actions, particularly so far as their decisions affect profit, cash flow and the financial position of the business. In discussions of a financial nature, in which sales and marketing managers are frequently involved, it is important that they understand the terminology used, so that they can participate fully.

No attempt is made in this book to over-emphasize the importance of the accounting function. The essential purpose of a business is to produce and sell its goods and services. Nevertheless, managers should ensure that the income from sales exceeds the costs and expenses incurred by the business. For this purpose they need accounting information to inform them of how the surplus or deficiency arises. The accounting function should, however, provide more than a historical record of transactions. It should in addition be forward-looking and be an aid to managers in the preparation of plans for the future and in the control of the performance. It should evaluate the monetary effects of alternative courses of action and thus provide a service to assist the decision-making process.

We believe it important for managers to appreciate that accounting is not an exact science. The accounts do no more than show 'a true and fair view' of the profit and of the financial position of a business, with the implication that there could be variants of that view. Cost is said to be not a fact but a convention; it depends on fairly generally accepted methods of calculation, but these will vary according to the assumptions made and the purpose for which the figure is required. Budgets and standards are not immutable and need amendment when circumstances change. At the same time the application of recognized accounting principles and conventions gives the accounting statements consistency for comparative purposes, such as with past results. The inference to be drawn from these observations is that managers need to understand the bases on which accounting information is prepared.

With a view to presenting the subject matter in a progressive and orderly framework the book has been divided into four parts dealing, successively, with basic accounting, financial analysis for planning, market planning and controlling the performance. After a discussion on the relationship between marketing and accounting, Part One is concerned with the interpretation of the financial position, the trading results and the costing system. Part Two deals with budgeting, planning for economic/stockholding, finance and investments in capital projects. It also considers the recent trend towards the capitalization of brand names. Part Three covers planning from a marketing and sales viewpoint but with financial implications, including market measurement, forecasting, territorial planning, new and abandoned products and exporting, leading to the preparation of the sales plan.

Part Four is specifically devoted to controlling the performance, but it should be appreciated that the techniques of planning are, in general, equally applicable to control. Thus the price of the product, which is the subject of the first chapter of this part, needs to be pre-planned as well as subsequently adjusted to changing circumstances. The chapter on indicators for action includes a form of case study showing the conclusions which may be drawn from a specimen set of trading results, and emphasizes the need for the revision of budgets which have become ineffective. A further chapter sets out techniques for the control of costs and hence profit, and a final chapter on mergers and takeovers has been included because these activities have become a major influence on the business scene.

The scope of the subject is clearly wide, but we have endeavoured to provide full explanations of each topic, not ignoring the controversial nor the qualifications inherent in much accounting information. In our efforts to avoid superficial treatment of the subject matter we are likely to have included discussions which are not of immediate interest to particular readers. However, the organization of the book permits selective reading and all the topics may be useful for reference purposes when the need arises.

The authors would like to thank in particular John Murphy, Managing Director of Interbrand Group plc, without whom Chapter 11 could not have been written. Dorothy Mackenzie of Michael Peters Brand Development Ltd provided some very useful statistics on new product development for Chapter 12. Ernst & Young's booklet *Acquisitions and Disposals* was very helpful in preparing Chapter 18. Chapter 8 was produced with reference to *Capital Investment and Financial Decisions* by H. Levy and M. Sarnet. Finally, our appreciation to Caroline Ashton MA (Cantab), who word processed much of the manuscript, should be acknowledged.

A.H. TAYLOR
K.J. STEWARD

PART ONE

Basic Accounting for Control

1 OBJECTIVES, STRUCTURE AND PRINCIPLES OF ACCOUNTING

The Development of Accounting

Evidence survives of rudimentary accounts kept by traders many thousands of years ago, and these accounts recorded transactions with customers and suppliers as well as their goods for sale. Accounts in monetary terms derive from classical Greece where coinage first came into use, and it is reasonable to suppose that the traders found it necessary to carry out some form of forecasting. Developments naturally occurred with the growth of trade, and the two aspects of a transaction, the giving and receipt of a benefit, appear to have had widespread recognition in the thirteenth century. In 1494 a Franciscan friar, Luca Pacioli, published a book containing a system for double-entry accounting, which remains in essence the principle applied today. Later a distinction was made between transactions on capital account and on revenue account, thus also foreshadowing a fundamental feature of modern accounting. Whilst the keeping of accounts has no doubt been assigned to clerks and stewards for many hundred years, an organized profession of accountants was not established in the UK until the middle of the nineteenth century. One reason was the need for skilled accountants by the large-scale corporations which were appearing and which had to account to the providers of their capital in terms of profit and financial strength.

The form and contents of the accounts prepared for shareholders was regulated by a succession of UK Companies Acts (as well as statutes for other kinds of organizations) culminating in the Companies Act 1985. At the time of writing a further Companies Bill (Companies Act 1989) is before Parliament extending the legislation to provisions required by the European Community. At the same time the organized bodies of accountants in various countries compose their own standards of accounting practices (in the UK these are Statements of Standard Accounting Practice or SSAPs) and these supplement the statutory regulations. A recent development has been the formulation of international standards. As a consequence of these developments accountants now carry out the following functions:

1. As employees of undertakings in both the public and private sector they have responsibility for maintaining the necessary financial records, for providing information to aid managers in their functions of control and forward planning and for preparing annual accounts for shareholders and other interested parties.
2. As accountants in public practice they provide various financial services to clients, especially the audit of business accounts, as required by the Companies Act or other statutes. Practising accountants are also heavily engaged in preparing tax computations

for individual and business clients and in conducting receiverships and liquidations. They are skilled at providing financial advice on a wide range of matters, although their management consultancy services are usually conducted by separate partnerships or companies.

Objectives of Accounting

So far as accounting in business is concerned the subject has two basic objectives: to provide information for management, and to produce accounts for shareholders and external parties. These two aspects of business accounting are clearly associated since each depends on the same basic information. The accounts for shareholders are produced annually, or, exceptionally, more frequently, and are historical records of past progress and of the financial postion of a business at a more or less recent point of time.

Information for management is essentially forward-looking and is concerned with the efficiency of the various business activities. This book is mainly concerned with accounting information for managers – the so-called management accounting – especially marketing managers. However, marketing management cannot be divorced from the management of other business functions, such as the production of goods and services for sale, buying, administration, research and development, and finance.

What financial information do managers require? For present purposes the answer to this question can be put in only general terms. This is because of the enormous variety of undertakings for which accounts have to be kept, and also because of the complexity of the operations of each individual business. As a basis for planning future operations, managers require information about the recent past and the probable future.

Historical Information

Assets and Liabilities

A fundamental requirement, common to all aspects of business accounting, is to record in monetary terms the assets and liabilities, hence the capital employed of the undertakings. This involves maintaining an exact and detailed record of all transactions, showing the amounts owing to or from creditors, customers and others, the stocks available for sale, the cash transactions, the balance of cash in hand or at the bank, and the fixed assets.

Profit on Sales

Another basic requirement is to produce a statement of the profit made or loss suffered by the business over a period of time. For management purposes, especially marketing management, the overall profit or loss needs to be attributed to its sources, i.e the various categories of sales.

Costs

In interpreting the profit or loss it is necessary for costs and expenses also to be analysed to their sources, which are the various activities carried on in the business, and to be expressed in terms of units of output and activity. The costs, if related to standards, will indicate the efficiency with which the work has been carried out and thus point to areas where remedial action is required.

Solvency and Funds Flow

The inflow and outflow of funds will be a major factor in determining the solvency of a business, and a position of solvency is vital for survival. Coupled with the ability to acquire further funds, the net liquid assets, including cash balances, limit the scope of future activities, including the turnover which can be sustained. For this reason management will need historical statements analysing the cash flow over a recent period. It is relevant to note that such statements are now also prescribed by the accountancy bodies in the annual accounts for shareholders.

The only real benefits for managers in studying past operations are in helping them correct errors and inefficiencies and to make decisions for the future. For these purposes management accounting provides services under the following broad headings.

Services for Control and Forward Planning

These comprise recording the relative effects on profit and cash flow of using resources in different ways, resources which embrace funds, manpower, buildings and plant. Fundamentally all management decisions involve choices between alternative courses of action, but the following headings are of special importance.

Changes in the Sales Mix

Exercises to show the best mix of sales in relation to limited resources.

New Products

Calculating the viability of proposed new projects of investment, whether in research and development, fixed assets or new products. Conversely, the benefits of rationalizing the range of sales lines by eliminating those which limit overall profits and cash flow.

Changing Operating Methods

This heading refers in particular to methods of producing products, including make-or-buy decisions, and increasing mechanization. It could also apply to changes in selling methods, such as the use of direct mail marketing and the licensing of factors; to distribution, such as choices between land, rail or air transport; and to administrative and service functions, including the subcontracting of catering, computerization of remuneration and accounts, etc.

Budgetary Control and Standard Costing

Management accounting provides a service for recording the standards and budgets, and for comparing and investigating variances. These services involve forecasts of probabilities and are described in detail in later chapters.

The Balance Sheet, Financial Position and Capital Employed

The accounting service produces two fundamental statements: one is the so-called 'balance sheet' which illustrates the financial position of the business *at a point of time*, and the other is the profit and loss account which shows the profit made or the loss suffered *over a period of time* ending on the balance sheet date. In addition, of course, the accounting function produces a great variety of subsidiary information for line managers, such as on cash flow, sales and costs.

The expression 'financial position' needs interpretation. In the form of a balance sheet, it shows two aspects of the same figures. These two aspects are: (1) the net assets (values owned) consisting of assets less liabilities (values owed to external parties), and (2) the sources from which the net assets have arisen, i.e. the capital placed in the business by owners (shareholders), and the profits retained in the business (otherwise called 'reserves'), thus arriving at a preliminary subtotal of shareholders' or owners' interests; to this subtotal is added long-term loan capital. The two aspects obviously arrive at the same total, usually called 'capital employed'. A typical form of a balance sheet, shorn of inessential detail, is illustrated below.

X Company Limited

Balance sheet at 31 December 19–0

CAPITAL EMPLOYED

		£
Issued shares		700 000
Reserves		1 800 000
Shareholders' interests		2 500 000
Loan capital		2 000 000
Capital employed		£4 500 000
NET ASSETS		
Fixed assets		4 000 000
Current assets	1 300 000	
Less: Current liabilities	800 000	
Net current assets		500 000
Net assets		£4 500 000

Note:

Fixed assets are those which are held to earn income over a period of years and are not for selling in the normal course of business. Current assets consist of cash and assets such as stock and debtors which are due to be converted into cash in the short term of about a year. Likewise current liabilities are those payable in a year.

Unfortunately there is some variety in the form in which balance sheets are prepared. Some are in statement form, others are double-sided. Some show total assets as the one aspect and show capital, reserves, loan capital and external liabilities as the other aspect of the financial position. This lack of a standard form of presentation is understandably confusing to the non-accountant manager. An example of the double-sided form of presenting the figures is given below.

X Company Limited

Balance sheet at 31 December 19–0

	£		£	£
Issued shares	700 000	Fixed assets		4 000 000
Reserves	1 800 000	Current assets	1 300 000	
		Current liabilities	800 000	
Shareholders' interests	2 500 000			
Loan capital	2 000 000	Net current assets		500 000
	£4 500 000			£4 500 000

In many parts of the world the figures will be placed on opposite sides to the above. The following example shows total assets and total liabilities in statement form, but the double-sided form might be used.

X Company Limited

Balance sheet at 31 December 19–0

TOTAL ASSETS

	£
Fixed assets	4 000 000
Current assets	1 300 000
Total assets	£5 300 000

TOTAL LIABILITIES

	£
Issued shares	700 000
Reserves	1 800 000
Shareholders' interests	2 500 000
Loan capital	2 000 000
Current liabilities	800 000
	£5 300 000

The Profit and Loss Account

Once again this statement is sometimes shown as a double-sided account, but more usually is found in the following (simplified) form:

X Company Limited

Profit and loss account for the year ended 31 December 19–0

	£	£
INCOME/SALES		9 000 000
Less: Cost of sales		5 400 000
GROSS PROFIT		3 600 000
Less: Operating expenses		
Administration	1 200 000	
Distribution	2 150 000	
Total operating expenses		3 350 000
OPERATING PROFIT		250 000
Less: Net financial and exceptional expenses		200 000
PRE-TAX PROFIT		50 000
Provision for taxation		17 500
NET PROFIT for the year		32 500
Balance of profit brought forward from previous year		5 500
AVAILABLE PROFIT		38 000
Dividends		20 000
RETAINED PROFIT		£18 000

It will be noted that the above statement shows the stages involved in the ascertainment of profit and its appropriation to dividends, leaving the final balance of retained profit to be added to reserves. The retained profit represents the value by which the capital employed in the business has been increased as a result of the year's transactions. There may also be other additions to capital, i.e. to reserves, as a result, for instance, of the sale of fixed assets or the issue of shares at above their nominal value, that is at a premium. These capital profits are not normally available for the payment of dividends, and must therefore be added to what are called 'non-distributable reserves'.

It is important to note that profit is not necessarily reflected as an increase in cash; it is an increase in value, arrived at by applying a number of accounting principles and conventional practices as described below. These principles and conventions have been developed to give reasonable consistency to the ascertainment of profit, so that it is broadly comparable period by period and, even less precisely, between different businesses. Profit is not, therefore, an absolute and precise amount as, for example, is the height of a building. It is the result of applying accounting rules and practices, which often require the exercise of judgment and even opinion. There is, for example, scope for the adjustment of profit by means of depreciation rates and valuations of stock and work in progress. The essential principle is to be objective in the application of judgment; that is to say that there is no justification in what has been called 'creative accounting', which implies arriving at a desired profit by adjusting valuations of assets.

More Detailed Analysis

The foregoing has briefly examined the main objectives of presenting the overall financial position of a business, and the profit or loss. Marketing and other executives need, however, much more detailed information to help them manage their various operations, to solve problems concerning the best use of resources, to plan forward and control performance. Marketing and sales managers will, for example, expect to receive from the accounting function information on the past and probable future profitability of product lines and of sales by market segments. The analysis of profitability involves the analysis of cost. Questions of where effort and resources are best applied are largely dependent on the analysis of cash flows which emanate from particular projects.

The analysis of past events has only one essential purpose for marketing management, and that is to assist in forecasting the future. The past is dead and cannot be resurrected; management is concerned with the future, both short term, i.e. a matter of days or weeks, and the long term which may be many years ahead.

As an aid to forecasting, the management accounting function needs to subdivide the figures in the overall accounts according to the requirements of the managers. The income and expenditure as well as, where necessary, cash flow and capital items need analysis under the following main headings:

1. By divisions, e.g. more or less self-governing units (which may or may not be incorporated) dealing with distinct lines of products or services.
2. By the major groups of products or services within the divisions.
3. By segments of the market or marketing areas, especially distinguishing between home and export sales. Export sales need analysis by major countries or political groups and home sales may need analysis by appropriate areas of the UK.
4. Further detailed analysis which may be called for on an *ad hoc* basis might include information on the cost and profitability of specific orders, of small orders, of sales teams, of product launches, and of the measurable benefits of various forms of publicity. The analysis of costs is, of course, a well-established aspect of the accounting system.
5. In addition, the financial function of the business normally has the responsibility for evaluating proposals for capital expenditure, such as for additions to premises, plant and vehicles, and for projects of development.

Methods of making such evaluations are described later in this book.

Figures in isolation are meaningless. Thus it means nothing to say that the turnover of a certain company was, say, £10 m last year. For that figure to take on any meaning it needs relating to the turnover of the previous year or, better, a succession of prior years, alternatively it could be usefully related to the capital employed in achieving those sales. Thus, the accounting service should, in addition to purposeful analysis, express the results as:

1. *Trends* both short and long term; and
2. *Relationships*, which might be percentages of related figures, such as of costs to sales, the number of times capital is turned over in cost of sales, the profit per man hour, and so forth. The trend of these and other relationships is often illuminating.

The message conveyed by the figures can often be made more apparent to the busy manager by means of diagrams and charts.

Principles and Conventions

It is often difficult to distinguish a principle from a convention, at least as far as accounting is concerned. A convention might be described as a method which has evolved over many years and has become accepted as a standard practice. The following list might be more comprehensively referred to as the accepted rules of accounting. For example it has become an accepted rule that fixed assets must be distinguished from current assets. Many of the accepted rules have been formalized in Statements of Standard Accounting Practice (SSAP) issued by the UK joint accountancy bodies.

The Entity Concept

This means that the business, whether legally incorporated or not is treated as an entity separate from the owners or shareholders. Thus the balance sheet shows the capital employed in the business as an entity.

Measurement in Money

Accounting as an information service embraces not only monetary figures but also non-monetary statistics. However, in the basic accounts all transactions are primarily expressed in terms of money. The figures in the accounts, unless adjusted for inflation, represent what is known as 'historical cost', in other words the original money laid out to acquire an asset or service or the payment due on a liability.

Because money values change, a statement of the financial position and of profit in terms of historical cost needs careful interpretation. Various techniques have been proposed for the conversion of historical cost to current money values and, although some methods are applied by certain companies, the subject is fraught with controversy.

The Concept of Profit

In its fundamental sense the final net profit made by a business represents the amount by which its capital has been increased as a result of the transactions made over a certain period of time. That increase in capital may, of course, have been lessened by allowing for the payment of shares of profit, e.g. dividends, to the owners or shareholders. The profit which is distributable amongst the owners normally arises from the trading activities, but profit may also arise from transactions of a so-called capital nature, such as on the sale or increase in value of fixed assets or investments. Capital profits are not normally distributable to the shareholders. It follows from the foregoing that profit depends on valuations of assets and liabilities, and such valuations are susceptible to matters of judgment and even opinion. However, the accounting rules which follow are intended to limit the scope for variability in the ascertainment of profit.

The Conservative or Prudent Approach

It is a general rule that profit expected to arise in the future must not be anticipated in the accounts; that stock and work in progress should be valued at the lower of cost or net realizable value (essentially market value); that allowance should be made in the accounts for losses expected in the future; and that wasting assets, such as plant, should be depreciated over their useful lifetime.

The 'Going Concern' Rule

Unless a business is in the process of being wound up or completely reconstructed, the assumption is made that it will continue in being indefinitely. This assumption has an effect on valuations of assets, for if a business were wound up or 'liquidated' its assets would be sold at what they would fetch in the market, in many cases far less than their cost or their value to the business as a going concern.

Consistency

The methods, principles and conventions used in preparing accounting statements should be applied consistently period by period. The general rule of consistency may, however, be qualified where a change in circumstances demands a different treatment of the figures. Thus rates of depreciation should, for example, be standardized, unless it becomes evident that the existing rates will not write off the cost during the useful life of the assets. Likewise a change in the method of valuing stock, such as in the basis of the overhead rate applied, would only be justified where existing methods were likely to produce an over-valuation.

The Matching Principle

The general idea behind this oft-quoted principle is that costs should, so far as possible, be 'matched' or set off against the income which they produce. The obvious example is where the costs of buying goods or making products are set off against the sales of those goods or products. The application of this principle means that the cost of the goods is not charged in the profit and loss account until they have been sold, i.e. delivered to customers. Meanwhile, the cost is carried in the balance sheet as an asset, either work in progress or stock for sale.

It is difficult, if not impossible, to match against income much of the expenditure of a business, especially the administrative, distributive and selling overheads. These overheads are therefore, as a matter of prudency, charged in the profit and loss account of the period when they are incurred, and usually described as 'operating expenses'.

Special consideration needs to be given to expenditure of a capital nature when applying the matching principle. Depreciation of production plant is incorporated in the production overhead rate and in consequence adds to the value of stock and work in progress. Depreciation on buildings is normally included in general overheads, or 'operating expenses', and so is depreciation on fixed assets other than those in the production departments. Expenditure on development is initially treated as an asset (or more strictly a 'deferred charge') in the balance sheet, where there is a reasonable expectation that it will be recoverable out of income; more prudently it is written off in the profit and loss account of the period when the expense is incurred. To the extent that development costs are treated as assets, the amount must be written off against the income which it produces over a conservatively assessed period. Sometimes heavy launching costs of a new product are also treated as deferred charges and written off over a short period, but the practice is exceptional and rarely appropriate.

It may be concluded that the application of the matching principle allows considerable variability of treatment, and needs to be applied with caution and prudence. This conclusion is reinforced with the growth of automated processes where a large proportion of expenditure cannot be attributed with precision to sales.

Marketing Management and Accounting

Marketing and sales management basically need simple statements of past and probable future sales, costs and profit, analysed as necessary for their purposes. They are not interested in accounting technicalities but, nevertheless, need to be able to interpret the information with which they are provided, and for this reason they should understand the principles and conventions underlying the figures. For instance, a cost is produced to serve a particular purpose, expressed or assumed. If it is used for a different purpose then the calculation will change.

The information available from the computerized accounting service of a substantial company can be varied and voluminous, but then a large business is a complex entity. Managers rightly resent having to pore over masses of irrelevant data when they could be applying their time more productively to making and selling the product. In this context the principle to be applied is management by exception. There is no need for managers to study items of income and expenditure which are proceeding according to plan, such as sales or expenses which are on budget, or costs which are conforming to pre-assessed standards, particularly when special information is required. Managers should have a sound understanding of accounting essentials, its potential and limitations, in order to discuss their needs with the accountant.

2 INTERPRETING THE CORPORATE FINANCIAL POSITION

PART A CAPITAL EMPLOYED

The Importance of the Subject

Marketing executives need to have some skill in interpreting the financial position of a business. They should be able to assess the financial strengths and weaknesses of their own company when formulating the marketing plan. They should be aware, for example, whether the company has or can bring into being sufficient resources to sustain the long-term plan, the projected turnover and the marketing expenditure entailed; or whether the marketing effort must concentrate on achieving the utmost profit and cash flow in the short term. For this purpose there needs to be informed communication between marketing and financial management and the plans of each major business function must be co-ordinated and integrated.

Certain specific and detailed indicators should be appreciated by marketing and sales management. For instance, if the rate at which capital is turned over in sales is slow, corporate profits will benefit by increasing turnover, even at the expense of gross profit margins. Efforts should be made to reduce stocks which are high in relation to sales and are slow moving, if necessary by selling them at a book loss, for such stocks incur running expenses, restrict space and represent idle capital which could be used to earn income for the company. When customers are shown to be slow in paying their accounts, credit terms may need revision and so may the direction of the selling activity.

In addition to being able to appraise the financial position of their own company, marketing managers should be able to make sound judgments on the finances of existing and potential customers, particularly when large contracts are being negotiated. The major question in this respect is whether the customer has the financial resources to pay within the credit terms on offer – or, indeed, at all. Furthermore, the marketing function is inevitably involved in other managerial activities, such as the sourcing of materials for a contract, and hence must be able to assess the financial strength of suppliers and subcontractors.

Sales and marketing executives have an important role to play in the many management meetings which seem to be unavoidable in the conduct of a modern business. They are frequently involved in critical discussions with the managers of their customers and suppliers. In these meetings, especially when accountants are present, financial expressions are often used (sometimes incorrectly) and the marketing member of the meeting should have a precise understanding of accounting terminology and its implications to avoid being at a considerable disadvantage.

What Is a Balance Sheet?

The financial position of a business is basically shown by the balance sheet. This statement has been briefly discussed in the preceding chapter but it will now be explained in more detail how the financial position can be appraised.

The description 'balance sheet' is a commonly used but somewhat archaic and uninformative title, so-called because it shows two viewpoints of the same figures which agree in total, or 'balance'. This remarkable balancing feat is achieved by using the time-honoured 'double-entry' system of accounting. The basic principle behind double entry is that every transaction has two aspects: the giving and the receipt of a benefit. Thus, when a business sells goods it loses an asset (stock) and receives another asset (a debtor); when a business buys goods it obtains an asset and incurs a liability to the seller. A knowledge of the mechanics of double entry is a useful skill but by no means essential for the interpretation of the accounts.

The two viewpoints of the business capital shown by the balance sheet are: (1) the net assets or the assets less the liabilities to external parties, often called 'employment of the capital', and (2) the sources from which the capital has been obtained, frequently called 'capital employed'. This Part specifically considers capital employed and the following Part deals with net assets. The capital employed consists of the funds provided by the shareholders, essentially the 'issued share capital' (the nominal value of the shares issued), the profits retained in the business, that is the 'reserves', the long-term loan capital, such as debentures.

The word 'capital' used in the present context merits further definition. It is unfortunate, if not ironic, that whilst the terminology of accounting is intended to impart precision to the subject, some commonly used expressions have different shades of meaning. The wider meaning of the term 'capital', as used above, refers to the funds injected into a business by the owners or shareholders, or long-term lenders, plus the values accumulated in the business by way of net profits retained. The total capital is represented by the net assets. The word is, however, often applied in a more restrictive sense to the owners' capital or the issued shares, to loans obtained by a business, and to transactions involving so-called 'capital assets', more strictly fixed assets and investments.

It should be appreciated that when assets are bought or produced by a business they are entered in the accounts at their cost, and when liabilities are incurred the contractual amount payable is recorded. The cost of wasting assets is reduced periodically by depreciation, normally based on cost; in the case of stock and investments the cost may be reduced for anticipated losses. The values of the assets shown in the balance sheet basically represent costs and therefore the total capital employed is also normally expressed in terms of 'historical cost'. The assets are not shown at saleable values, except by coincidence, and it follows that the capital employed is not the amount obtainable by selling the assets piecemeal and paying the liabilities.

In some companies the so-called 'historical cost' of fixed assets, especially land and buildings, is adjusted to reflect increases in money values, due to inflation or other causes. When an asset's cost is increased in this manner exactly the same amount must be added to a reserve which cannot be used to pay a dividend, and is usually called a 'revaluation reserve'. A few companies make more extensive adjustments to the accounts to reflect changing money values, but methods of 'inflation accounting' are subject to considerable controversy.

Forms of Business Organization

The following brief outline of the major forms of business organization is provided as a necessary background for the analysis of capital employed.

Sole Traders

Many new businesses are started by sole traders, known in tax terminology as 'self-employed'. Even though they may operate under a trade name, sole traders make contracts as individuals, they can be sued in the courts and can be made bankrupt. Their capital consists of the cash and assets with which they set up the business, plus any profits retained. In many cases sole traders are largely financed by bank overdrafts and loans.

Partnerships

As his business develops the sole trader may find it necessary to take in one or more partners, who may bring in further capital; in some cases a business is begun as a partnership, often of husband and wife and other relatives. An incoming partner may be required to make a payment for the share he acquires of the goodwill created by the original trader. This payment, if retained in the business, is similar to the premium payable when further shares are issued by a prosperous limited company. It may be treated as increasing the capital of the original trader or the existing partners.

The shares of profit payable or credited to the partners, as well as various provisions for the management of the business, should be set out in Articles of Partnership. In the absence of such Articles, or appropriate provisions in them, the partnership is regulated by the Partnership Act 1890.

A partnership is called a 'firm' in legal language, although the term is popularly applied to other forms of enterprise. The partnership firm is not a legal entity (except in Scotland) as a limited company is, and the partners can be sued individually or collectively for its debts. Except in the rare case of a 'limited partner', there is no limitation on the liability of the partners.

A partnership is defined in the Partnership Act as 'the relation which subsists between persons carrying on business with a view of profit'. Thus to constitute a partnership there must be a business and there must be an intention to make profit. The word 'persons' embraces legal persons such as limited companies who often form partnerships for joint marketing and other ventures. The number of partners must not exceed twenty, except for professional firms.

Limited Companies

General

The next stage in the development of a business is its incorporation as a limited company, although in some cases a limited company is created at the inception of the business. The main inducement is for the owners of the business to obtain the advantage of limited liability. This means that the shareholders' liability for the company's debts (in a winding up, for instance) cannot exceed the amount they have paid or agreed to pay the company for their shares.

The company is a legal entity, or 'legal person', distinct from the shareholders, and it will sue in the courts or be sued under its corporate name. Its operations will be governed by the Companies Acts and, more particularly, by its own articles and memorandum of association. The articles deal with internal affairs, such as the rights of shareholders and the obligations of directors and officers. The memorandum is concerned with the company's relations with external parties. Every company must have a professionally qualified auditor and the annual accounts have to be submitted to the Registrar of Companies with an Annual Return, these documents being available for inspection by the public.

Every company must have at least two members or shareholders, so that the expression 'one man company' is a popular misnomer, although a shareholder may hold only one share.

Private Companies

The first type of company to be formed by a sole trader or partnership is usually a 'private company'. These are generally the smaller companies although some are quite large in terms of assets, especially where they are subsidiaries of major corporate bodies. Their 'private' nature is reflected in the fact that they cannot issue capital to the public at large, but only to a restricted group of persons, such as members of a family or business associates; they must impose a restriction on the right to transfer shares, usually the approval of the board of directors; their membership is limited to fifty, plus employees or ex-employees. Because of these restrictions they cannot obtain a quotation for their shares on a stock exchange. A private company may be recognized by the requirement that its name must end with the word 'limited', whereas the name of a public company ends with the words 'public limited company' or the abbreviation 'plc'. Welsh readers will note that the Welsh translation of these words may be used by a company registered in Wales.

Public Companies

These are the larger type of limited company and they must have an authorized capital of at least £50 000. They may invite the general public to subscribe for their shares and debentures by means of a prospectus, the shares are freely transferable, and the company may apply for a quotation on a stock exchange.

Other Kinds of Organization

Statutory companies are governed by special Acts of Parliament distinct from the Companies Acts. A *chartered company* is one regulated by a charter from the Crown, as were the trading companies of the sixteenth and seventeenth centuries. The grant of charters is now confined to professional associations and bodies of national importance. Professional associations are also incorporated as *companies limited by guarantee* under the Companies Acts; they do not issue shares but their liabilities under a winding up are guaranteed up to specified amounts by a limited group of members. Mutual associations, such as *friendly societies* and *building societies*, are governed by special statutes as well as by their own Rules.

Unincorporated bodies (other than partnerships) include clubs, charities, trusts and other forms of association, and their liabilities are the responsibility of the committee or trustees.

Obtaining the Capital

Issues by Private Companies

When a company is formed to take over an unincorporated business, or possibly to establish a new business, it is likely to be a private company. The company obtains its initial capital by inviting certain persons to become shareholders. Some of the shareholders will be allotted shares, by agreement, for 'a consideration other than cash', and that consideration might be for the transfer to the company of the assets and goodwill of the business taken over. Others will be required to pay cash, usually the nominal value of the shares allotted to them.

Payment by Instalments

If the total nominal value of the shares payable in cash is not required immediately, it may be payable in instalments when calls are made by the directors. Thus shares of a nominal value of £1 each may be payable by 50p on allotment, 25p at the end of a year and a further 25p six months later. If the company prospers and needs more capital for development, it may subsequently make a further issue of shares (within its authorized limit) and may then be in a position to require the payment of a premium for them.

Issues by Public Companies

Eventually, because of increasing size and capital needs, the private company may be converted into a public limited company. It will then be able to invite the public at large to subscribe for an issue of shares and debentures. To crystallize its reserves, and to give the existing shareholders a larger proportionate stake in the company, it may issue bonus shares to them before the public issue is made or at the same time. The existing shareholders may also be given preferential rights to subscribe for the new issue on various terms.

Quotations on the Stock Exchange

At the same time as the public company offers shares to the public at large, it will probably apply for a quotation on the Stock Exchange, which was established in 1773 in a London coffee house to provide a market for the purchase and sales of the shares in the trading companies of those times. The requirements of the Stock Exchange are stringent and demanding in relation to the provision of information about the company's affairs, and the cost of obtaining a quotation is high. If the company is comparatively small, its directors may prefer to obtain access to the Unlisted Securities Market (USM), which was formally established in 1979, although a similar market existed before that date. The price of shares is not exactly 'quoted' on the USM but the prices at which they have recently changed hands is made public. The cost and formalities of access to the USM are considerably less than those for obtaining a full 'listing' or quotation.

Placings and Offers for Sale

Instead of being offered to the public by the company issuing the shares, they may be 'placed' with a financial house which may then trade in the shares at whatever price they can obtain. In some cases the financial house may make a formal 'offer for sale' of the shares to the public. Shares on the USM are normally first subject to a placing (with a value of up to £3m) or an offer for sale (with a value of up to £15m).

Underwriting

When a company issues shares or debentures it will invariably arrange for underwriters to take up those shares for which investors do not apply, in other words in the case of an 'undersubscription'; the underwriters will naturally charge a fee or commission for this form of insurance. If a large volume of shares remains with the underwriters, the shares are likely to be quoted at a discount, i.e. below their nominal value, on the market. The company does not, as a result, suffer a monetary loss since it will receive the amounts payable on the issue either from the public or the underwriters, but an undersubscription may affect the credit standing of the company. Conversely, in the case of an oversubscription, the shares will probably be quoted at a premium on the market. The company does not gain, because in the case of this kind of premium, the quotation for the shares is simply the price at which they are transferred from one investor to another.

Premium on Shares

However, the fact that a company's shares are quoted at above their nominal value does enhance the company's standing in the eyes of investors and existing shareholders, and facilitates the issue of further capital when it is required. If the existing shares are quoted at, say £1.50 for shares of nominal value of £1, then the company should be confident that it could obtain a premium of up to 50p on a further issue. In this case the company actually receives the nominal value plus the premium for each share issued, the total premium being credited to an undistributable reserve. That reserve, nevertheless, forms part of the shareholders' interests in the company.

Published Information

Information about dealing in shares and loan stock is published daily in the finanical pages of many national newspapers. The following figures are shown for each share or nominal amount of stock:

1. The highest and lowest quotation for the year, normally expressed in pence or as the price of £100 nominal of loan stock.
2. The day's middle market price.
3. The rise or fall of the price on the previous day.
4. The net dividend per share.
5. The dividend cover, i.e. the number of times the dividend is covered by available profit, or 'earnings'. If the earnings per share are 25p and the dividend is 10p then the cover is 2.5.

6. The gross yield. This is the percentage which the last dividend bears to the current market price of the shares. Thus, if the current quotation was 200 (i.e. £2 a share) and the last dividend was 10p a share then the yield would be shown as 5, or 5 per cent.
7. The price earnings ratio, abbreviated to p/e. This is the price per share divided by the earnings per share, the earnings being the profit available to the shareholders concerned, irrespective of the amount paid out as dividend. With a price of 200p and earnings per share of 25p the p/e ratio is 8.

The calculations above have been simplified to eliminate tax complications.

An Analysis of Capital Employed

As a basis for the analysis of capital employed that section of the balance sheet presented in summary form in the previous chapter is now shown in more detail in Fig. 2.1.

Balance Sheet of X Company at 31 December 19–0

CAPITAL EMPLOYED

	£	£	£
Issued shares:			
5 000 000 ordinary shares of 10p each, fully paid			500 000
200 000 10% redeemable preference shares 1995/98 of £1 each, fully paid			200 000
Total issued shares			700 000
Reserves:			
Distributable:			
General reserve – profits retained		1 100 000	
Undistributable:			
Share premium account	100 000		
Revaluation reserve	600 000		
		700 000	
Total reserves			1 800 000
Total shareholders' interests			2 500 000
Loan capital:			
$12\frac{1}{2}$% debentures 2001, secured by a floating charge on the undertaking			2 000 000
Total capital employed			£4 500 000
Authorized share capital:			
10 000 000 ordinary shares of 10p each			1 000 000
200 000 redeemable preference shares of £1 each			200 000
Total authorized capital			£1 200 000

Figure 2.1

The Meaning of 'Shares'

When a person obtains shares in an incorporated body, such as a limited company, he becomes a 'member' of the body and part owner of the undertaking, in much the same way as a partner is part owner of the partnership business. A limited company is itself a legal 'person', or legal entity distinct from its shareholders, and can own shares in another company. In fact a large proportion of the shares of the major companies are owned by other companies, such as holding companies, unit and investment trusts and insurance companies, amongst others.

The shareholder's rights are set out in the Companies Acts, or other statute regulating the particular corporate body concerned, and further detailed in the company's articles of association which provide rules for the conduct of its internal affairs. The principal merit of the status of a shareholder in a limited company, compared with that of most partners in unincorporated businesses, is limited liability for the debts of the business. Limited liability means that if the company is liquidated (or 'wound up') a shareholder could lose the amount he has paid on his shares, but cannot be compelled to contribute more than he has agreed to pay on them. If, for example, a shareholder held 1000 shares of nominal value of £1 each, but had only paid 75p on each share, he would have a possible liability to contribute 1000 × £0.25 = £250 when the company was wound up. This would, of course, be the situation only when the company, having realized all its assets, did not have sufficient resources to pay its creditors and other dues in full.

Ordinary shareholders, with special exceptions, are entitled to vote at shareholders' meetings, for instance to appoint directors and to resolve certain fundamental issues. Otherwise the shareholders cannot intervene in the company's business for they delegate the management of the enterprise to the directors. The right of preference shareholders to vote is confined to situations where their interests are in jeopardy, such as on a resolution to wind up. The ordinary shareholders receive a proportionate share of the profits by way of dividend, which must be recommended by the directors and cannot be increased by the shareholders. The preference shareholders receive the stated rate of dividend on their capital in priority to any payment to the ordinary shareholders, assuming that sufficient profits are available and subject to the directors' recommendation. In some cases preference shareholders 'participate' with ordinary shareholders in the balance of profit.

In a liquidation of the company the ordinary shareholders will, as stated above, be liable to contribute to any deficiency but they will share in any surplus after all creditors have been paid. Preference shareholders are entitled to repayment of their capital before any return is made to ordinary shareholders.

The Nominal Value and Premiums on Shares

Shares have a 'nominal value' as stated in the company's memorandum and articles of association. In the above statement the ordinary shares have a nominal value of 10p each, the low amount being probably to encourage small shareholdings and to facilitate transfers, and the preference shares have a nominal value of £1 each. When the shares are issued by the company the nominal value of each share taken up is payable to the company plus, in certain circumstances, a premium, or addition to that value. Shares cannot be issued at a discount, otherwise than in exceptional circumstances and the approval of the shareholders and the court. Such circumstances might arise when the company has lost some of its capital but has prospects of future prosperity.

The nominal value plus any premium may be payable by instalments when the directors make 'calls'. This could be the situation when all the money payable on the shares was not required immediately. In some companies, especially with banks, the terms of an issue of shares provide that the final instalment of the nominal value is not payable until the company is wound up, and the balance uncalled would be described as 'reserve capital'. Such a provision gives greater security to depositors and creditors.

Assume that in the case of X Company, as illustrated above, the original issue of ordinary shares was of 2 500 000 at 10p each, payable as to 6p on allotment, and 4p six months later. The whole of the issue was for cash, although in many cases on the formation of a company some shares are issued 'for a consideration other than cash', such as where shares are issued to the previous owners of a business taken over in consideration of the transfer of assets and goodwill. In the case of X Company each of the calls was paid but in some cases applicants failed to pay their calls. Long delay in paying the calls would have been followed by forfeiture of those shares and their eventual reissue to other applicants.

Five years later the company needed further funds for development and a second issue of 2 500 000 shares was made. The company had prospered and had transferred substantial profits to reserve; furthermore, the quotation for the shares on the stock exchange had recently averaged around 16p a share. The directors therefore decided that the second issue should be at a premium of 4p a share, making a total payment required of 14p a share. The total money received by the company from the issue of ordinary shares was as follows:

	£	£
From first issue:		
On allotment: 2 500 000 shares at 6p		150 000
Six months later: call of 4p a share		100 000
Proceeds from first issue		250 000
From second issue:		
On allotment:		
Nominal value at 10p on 2 500 000 shares	250 000	
Premium of 4p	100 000	
Proceeds from second issue		350 000
Total proceeds from issues of ordinary shares		£600 000

As will be seen from the above 'capital employed' section of the balance sheet of X Company, the nominal value of the two issues appeared under the heading of 'issued shares', whilst the premium was credited to a reserve which could not be distributed as a dividend, i.e. it was part of the permanent capital of the business.

Authorized Capital

The authorized share capital is shown as a note to the balance sheet, these figures not being part of the double-entry accounts. The total share capital which a company is authorized to issue is stated in its memorandum and articles of association. In examining a balance sheet it is important to note whether a company can issue further shares, within the authorized limit, for the purpose, for instance, of launching a new marketing project, or for the acquisition of another business (of which the consideration may be in shares, in cash or partly in shares and partly in cash). The authorized capital can be increased by resolution at a shareholders' meeting.

Types of Shares

The holders of *ordinary shares*, whose rights have been outlined above, are the main risk-bearers. They will be the first to suffer loss if the company fails but share amongst themselves in exceptional profits. They look for profit in two ways: from their dividend and from a rise in the marketable value of their shares. The expectations of different groups of ordinary shareholders are further examined below under the section on dividend policy.

The *preference shareholders* are entitled to their contractual rate of dividend (assuming it is 'declared' by the directors and there are sufficient profits). Their fixed rate of dividend is payable in priority to the dividend to ordinary shareholders but, of course, after allowance for loan interest. In a liquidation the preference shareholders normally have priority over the ordinary shareholders of repayment of the nominal value of their shares, in some cases plus a premium. Whilst ordinary shares cannot be repaid otherwise than in exceptional circumstances and in a liquidation, preference shares are usually redeemable. That is to say they are repayable at stated dates shown in the balance sheet. They are usually 'cumulative', which means that the arrears of dividend unpaid can be carried forward for payment in a future year. They may be 'participating', meaning that they share with the ordinary shareholders in the balance of profit after their fixed dividend has been taken into account. Thus preference shares provide greater security than ordinary shares but their shares of profit and other rights are limited.

Various other classes of shares with varying rights may be issued. These include the following:

1. *pre-preferential shares*, otherwise called 'first preference shares', entitled to a dividend in priority to the other preference shares;
2. *preferred ordinary shares* taking a dividend in priority to the ordinary shareholders but after the preference shares;
3. *deferred shares*, often issued to the owners of a business taken over by the company, and with their dividend deferred until a stated rate has been paid on the ordinary shares;
4. *employee shares* issued to employees or to trusts for employees, usually with restricted rights of voting and transfer.

Loan Capital

Loan capital means loans obtained over the long term, at least five years, sometimes for considerably longer periods. Such loans bear interest at a fixed rate and this interest is payable whether the company makes a profit or not. A long-term loan forms part of the capital employed in the business, and should be distinguished from temporary finance, such as by bank overdraft, which is classed as a current liability.

However, it should be noted that in some cases, particularly with the smaller business, a bank overdraft remains for so many years that it effectively becomes part of the capital employed.

Loan capital, frequently called 'debentures', may be unsecured or, more often, it is secured on specific property or by means of a floating charge on the whole under-taking. When secured on land and buildings the loan is called a 'mortgage debenture'. If the company defaults in the payment of interest or the repayment of the capital of a mortgage debenture, the debentureholders have the right to take possession of the property and eventually to sell it to satisfy their debt. On default in the case of a floating charge, the debentureholders, or more likely a trustee appointed by them, can usually install a receiver and manager of the business to ensure that the debentureholders are paid their dues out of the company's income, and ultimately, if necessary, to put the company into liquidation.

Convertible debentures are those which, after a period of years, can be converted into shares. The issue of debentures on these terms can facilitate the finance of long-term development if a modest rate of interest is payable while the development is proceeding. The attraction to investors is that when the development bears fruit they will participate in the profit as shareholders.

When examining the accounts of a company it is important to consider the extent and manner in which it is financed by loan capital, and the comparative 'stake' in the company of the risk-bearers, the ordinary shareholders; the provisions, if any, made by the company to repay the loan at the due date, such as by setting up a sinking fund invested in readily realizable securities; and the 'gearing' of the capital, which is examined below. A successful company may be able to repay its loan capital out of a further issue of shares.

Shareholders' Interests in a Company

In considering the extent to which a company is financed by loans or shares, the total shareholders' interests are compared with the loan capital. The total shareholders' interests are the issued shares of all kinds plus the reserves. In the balance sheet of X Company shown above, the total shareholders' interests are £2 500 000 and the loan capital is £2 000 000 – a very high proportion of loan capital at 80 per cent of shareholders' interests. It should be appreciated in this connection that the value of the shareholders' interests is dependent on the values attributed to the assets. If, for instance, the fixed assets such as land, buildings and plant have not been revalued, the shareholders' interests will be below their current money values. Some intangible assets such as patents, trade marks and copyrights may be stated at cost, or are more usually written down to a nominal value as a measure of prudent accounting. The 'valuation' of brand names is a recent innovation and is discussed in Chapter 9.

Of perhaps greater significance is the interests of the ordinary shareholders, called the 'equity interests'. This consists of the issued ordinary share capital plus the reserves, preference shareholders being entitled to repayment of their nominal capital in a winding up. In X Company the equity interests are the issued ordinary shares of £500 000 plus the reserves of £1 800 000, making a total of £2 300 000. Thus the equity interests are 51 per cent of capital employed, an unusually low proportion.

Another use of the figure of equity interests is as a basis for calculating the 'earnings' the shareholder obtains on his capital. The term 'earnings' means the profit available to him, whether paid out as a dividend or retained in the business as part of the reserves. Earnings are alternatively calculated as an amount or rate per share.

An ordinary shareholder's proportion of the total equity interests, as shown in the balance sheet, will not correspond with the amount returnable to him on a winding up of the company, for that amount will depend on the net amount remaining after selling the assets, paying the liabilities, including the loan capital, and repaying the preference shares. Furthermore, the assets and liabilities are stated in the balance sheet on the assumption that the business is a going concern, unless liquidation is imminent.

The saleable value of a shareholder's holding is obtained by multiplying the number of his shares by the market price, e.g. the stock exchange quotation. When applied to all the shares this exercise results in what is known as the market capitalization of the company but, as in any market, the price will vary, possibly daily, as a result of supply and demand amongst many other influences.

Capital Gearing

The Meaning of 'Gearing'

A company's gearing is said to be high when it has a high proportion of fixed interest capital compared with equity capital. Fixed interest capital includes preference capital as well as long-term loan capital.

In the statement of capital employed of X Company on page 18 the relevant figures are as follows:

	£	£
Equity capital:		
Issued ordinary share capital	500 000	
Reserves	1 800 000	
Total equity capital		2 300 000
Fixed interest capital:		
10% preference capital	200 000	
$12\frac{1}{2}$% loan capital	2 000 000	
Total fixed interest capital		2 200 000
Capital employed		£4 500 000

In this example the gearing is very high, fixed interest capital being nearly 50 per cent of total capital employed.

The Effect of Gearing on Profit

A more positive view of capital gearing is to calculate the effect which it will have on the profits available to the ordinary shareholders, their 'earnings'. To illustrate this effect, and for the time being ignoring tax implications, two somewhat extreme situations are shown below.

Situation 1: earnings at £115 000

	£	£
Surplus before fixed interest		385 000
Deduct:		
Preference dividend	20 000	
Loan interest	250 000	
		270 000
Earnings of ordinary shareholders		£115 000

In this situation the loan interest represents the high proportion of 70.1 per cent of the surplus before charging that interest, and the resultant earnings of the ordinary shareholders are only 5 per cent of equity interests. The fixed interest is therefore a heavy burden and the company would have difficulty in paying it if profits and cash flow fell.

Situation 2: earnings at £460 000

	£	£
Surplus before fixed interest		730 000
Deduct:		
Preference dividend	20 000	
Loan interest	250 000	
		270 000
Earnings of ordinary shareholders		£460 000

In this situation the fixed interest, whilst still high, is only 34 per cent of the surplus and the earnings percentage has risen to 20 per cent of equity interests. The fixed interest is therefore comparatively cheap finance so far as the ordinary shareholders are concerned.

Taxation Aspects

The impact of capital gearing is affected by taxation. The following examples are necessarily simplified because taxation rates change and the amount payable depends on the tax computation applicable to a particular company. For these illustrations a corporation tax rate of 35 per cent is assumed to apply to the relevant profits. The critical point to note is that loan interest gives tax relief, but not dividends on ordinary or preference shares. The net cost of the loan interest is not the contractual rate of $12\frac{1}{2}$ per cent but that percentage less tax at 35 per cent giving a net rate of 8.125 per cent. It follows that if the earnings of the ordinary shareholders exceed this rate and the rate on the preference shares, they will obtain an advantage from the gearing; if the earnings rate is below the net fixed interest rate, the ordinary shareholders will bear the excess percentage.

Consider the following further illustration in which, to simplify the exposition, the complication of preference capital is eliminated. In column *A* the company is wholly financed by ordinary shares, the equity interests being £4 500 000. In column *B* the capital employed consists of £2 500 000 of equity interests and £2 000 000 of $12\frac{1}{2}$ per cent loan capital. In column *C* the loan carries interest at 20 per cent. 'Profit' before interest and tax is £700 000 in each case.

	A	B	C
	£	£	£
Profit before tax and interest	700 000	700 000	700 000
Less: Loan interest		250 000	400 000
Percentage of loan capital		$12\frac{1}{2}\%$	20%
Chargeable to tax	700 000	450 000	300 000
Tax at 35%	245 000	157 500	105 000
Earnings of ordinary shareholders	£455 000	£292 500	£195 000
Equity	4 500 000	2 500 000	2 500 000
Percentage earnings on equity	10.1%	11.7%	7.8%

In column *B* the ordinary shareholders obtain a greater percentage return on their capital than when they wholly finance the company as in column *A*. This is because the net rate of interest on the loan is effectively only 8.125 per cent after tax relief, a lower rate than on the equity in *A*. In column *C* the ordinary shareholders' return is reduced because the loan interest is at an effective rate of $0.65 \times 20\% = 13\%$, i.e. higher than the return on equity in column *A*.

General Conclusions

The conclusions which may be drawn from the foregoing are:

1. A company's capital gearing affects the ordinary shareholders' available profit, which is partly paid out as dividend and partly retained in the business. The ordinary shareholders are the risk-takers; the success of a company is basically measured by the earnings attributable to them.
2. If the company is stable, and consistently achieves a high level of profit, a substantial proportion of fixed interest capital can be an advantage to the ordinary shareholders, but only if the rate of interest after tax relief is below the return to the latter.
3. If profits fluctuate widely a high gearing can put the survival of the company in jeopardy. The company will also be in danger if it fails to make adequate provision for repaying the fixed capital at the due date.

Dividend Policy

The proportion of profits paid out as dividends varies widely from one company to another. At one extreme, the directors of some small companies aim to distribute to the shareholders as much of the profit as possible; at the other extreme, the dividend policy of a few large public companies is to retain most of the available profit, the shareholders relying on the consequent increase in the share price. In general many factors influence the amount of dividend to be paid and are examined below.

The Available Profit

Obviously the upper limit to the amount of dividend which can be paid is the profit available to the class of shareholders concerned. Net profit for the purpose is arrived at after charging the due interest on loan capital and tax on the 'adjusted profit' for the year. The net profit is then reduced by the fixed rate of dividend on preference shares. The balance represents the amount available to the ordinary shareholders, that is their 'earnings'. The distributable reserves, i.e. those arising from trading, are also available for the payment of dividends. They are rarely so used because they form part of the capital employed in the company, but might be drawn on in a year of temporarily low profits due, for instance, to heavy development expenditure.

The Available Cash

A further and sometimes more decisive limit to the amount of dividend is the cash available to pay it. In this connection it may be necessary to emphasize that profit is not necessarily represented by net cash inflow, for the incoming cash may have been spent in acquiring more assets and reducing liabilities. Cash inflow may be reduced by selling to slow payers and by a marketing policy of extended credit terms.

If cash is short it may be obtained from temporary borrowings, but finance obtained in that way is better applied to the trading operations of the business. It would be even more unwise, if not illegal, to pay dividends by raising long-term loans. In short the owners of the business – the shareholders – must be prepared to forgo their dividends when cash is not available to pay them. Furthermore, even if the company has a sufficient balance at the bank, those funds may be required to pay liabilities due in the near future, to acquire necessary assets and generally to develop the business.

Bonus Shares

A possible method of conserving funds where the profit, but not the available cash, can cover the normal dividend, is to issue bonus shares. The accounting entries involved are simply to transfer from distributable reserves to the share capital account the amount of the dividend. The value attributed to the shareholders' interests remains unaltered by the transfer. Each shareholder receives more paper, representing his additional bonus shares but his proportionate interest in the company remains the same, subject to the fact that it has been increased by the profit retained. If the bonus issue doubled the number of issued shares, the market value per share would theoretically be halved; but this is not necessarily the effect on the market and, with a prosperous company, the market capitalization is sometimes increased by a bonus issue.

Dividend Cover

Subject to the availability of cash the question remains as to what proportion of the available profit should be paid out to the ordinary shareholders by way of dividend. The dividend cover of quoted companies varies from about 1.5 to 4, sometimes very much higher, and in a few cases less than these multipliers. One basis for dividend policy is for the directors to maintain a satisfactory figure of cover, so that the company retains a substantial proportion of profit for development and contingencies.

Shareholders' Expectations

In many companies, especially where profits do not fluctuate widely, it seems that the directors seek to keep the rate of dividend steady, increasing the rate only where an increase in profit is assured in the long term. The question then arises as to what factors influenced the original decision as to the appropriate dividend. The answer to this question depends, it is suggested, on the expectations of the dominant group of shareholders, who have the voting power to appoint and can ultimately discharge the directors.

Individuals who rely on investment income, and probably pay only the basic rate of income tax, are likely to seek the highest dividend consistent with security of their capital. The more affluent shareholder may be less interested in the dividend than in the appreciation of his capital on the stock exchange, and will consequently favour a high cover. The dominant shareholders are frequently institutional investors, such as insurance companies, unit and investment trusts, pension funds, etc. With some exceptions the institutional investors seek capital appreciation because they are prepared to buy and sell shares and stock in relation to market opportunities.

Summary

Dividends are limited not only by the profits but also by the availability of cash. The maintenance of a satisfactory cover for the dividend is important but so is the need to retain substantial profits to aid the growth of a business, as well as to combat inflation. The expectations of the dominant shareholders must be considered, some seeking good current income, others capital appreciation.

In examining the accounts of businesses, their dividend policy over three to five years should be assessed. The following signs would suggest questionable financial management: a low cover for the dividends in terms of available profit; the payment of dividends out of borrowings; severe fluctuations in the dividend rate; drawings on reserves to pay dividends; an unexpected increase in the dividend, especially if this is a tactical device to stave off a takeover bid.

PART B   NET ASSETS

Introduction

The capital employed in a business, as analysed in the preceding Part, is invested in, or represented by, the net assets. These are the assets (values owned by the business) less the liabilities (values owed to external parties). For this purpose the liabilities do not include loan capital, such as debentures or loan stock, for long-term borrowings form part of the capital employed.

The total of the net assets is the same as the total of capital employed, and the terms are to this extent synonymous, but represent different viewpoints of the funds in the business. The capital employed section of the balance sheet shows the sources from which the funds have been obtained, i.e. the capital subscribed plus the retained profits (or reserves); the net assets section shows how these funds have been applied in acquiring assets and incurring liabilities.

Figure 2.2 is a statement of the net assets of Company X, of which the capital employed was shown in Fig. 2.1. The statement generally conforms to Format 1 in Schedule 4 of the Companies Act 1985. Format 2 of that Schedule contains the same detail but shows total assets separated from capital and liabilities. These formats are obligatory for the published accounts of limited companies although some modifications are permissible. Comparative figures for the preceding year must be shown.

The statutory accounts presented to the shareholders need to be accompanied by notes to the accounts providing, where necessary, further details of the figures and additional information. The notes to the accounts would include, for example: analysis of sales by major product groups and geographical areas; tax provisions; details of fixed assets and depreciation; details of borrowings, reserves, contingent liabilities and capital commitments; details of employee costs and average number of employees; and details of directors' remuneration.

The following paragraphs explain and enlarge upon the constituents of net assets.

Fixed Assets

Meaning

Fixed assets are those held for the purpose of carrying on the business operations, that is in earning income. They are not held for sale in the normal course, as stock is, nor for conversion into cash, as debtors are. Obviously, however, fixed assets are sold when they require replacement or become redundant to the current activities. For economic reasons they may be sold and leased back from the purchaser, and this operation is sometimes applied to land and buildings in particular.

In accordance with the Companies Acts fixed assets are subdivided into those which are (1) tangible, i.e. have a physical nature and susceptible to touch, such as buildings, machinery and equipment; (2) intangible, such as patents, trade marks and goodwill; and (3) investments intended to be held in the long term, certainly over a year, such as investments in associated companies.

Balance Sheet of X Company at 31 December 19–0

NET ASSETS

Fixed assets:	£	£	£
Intangibles			250 000
Tangible			2 350 000
Investments, long term			1 400 000
Total fixed assets			4 000 000
Current assets:			
Stocks and work in			
progress	1 575 000		
Debtors	1 875 000		
Investments	230 000		
Cash	100 000		
Total current assets		3 780 000	
Current liabilities:			
Creditors due in 1 year		3 600 000	
Net current assets			180 000
Liabilities due after 1 year			120 000
Provisions, accruals and deferred income			200 000
Net assets			£4 500 000

Notes:

(1) Contingent liabilities	250 000
(2) Capital commitments	700 000

(3) Tangible fixed assets:

	Cost of valuation	Accumulated depreciation	Net book value
	£	£	£
Land and buildings	2 100 000	600 000	1 500 000
Plant and machinery	700 000	200 000	500 000
Vehicles	500 000	300 000	200 000
Furniture and fittings	250 000	100 000	150 000
Totals	£3 550 000	£1 200 000	£2 350 000

Figure 2.2

Tangible Fixed Assets

The examples shown in Fig. 2.2 are common, particularly in manufacturing companies, but they would be included under current assets if they were held for sale in the course of the normal trading operations, such as where a business traded in plant, machinery, vehicles, etc.

In interpreting the financial position of a business an informative statistic is the proportion of total assets which is represented by the fixed and tangible category. In what are sometimes called 'capital intensive' industries such as heavy engineering, that proportion can be high, possibly 50 per cent or more. On the other hand, a high proportion of fixed tangible assets in a business providing professional services, such as an advertising agency, would be questionable. It may be noted, however, that some companies and associations invest heavily in land and buildings partly, at least, for the purpose of capital appreciation.

Except for land, tangible fixed assets have a useful life extending over a number of years. For this reason it would give an irrational view of profits, period by period, if their whole cost was charged against income in the year or month when they were acquired. The cost is therefore apportioned over each asset's useful life by means of a depreciation charge. Depreciation is sometimes defined as the loss of an asset's value due to use and age, but this loss is difficult if not impossible to quantify with precision. Depreciation in accounts does not therefore basically represent an attempt to assess loss of value but is the result of apportioning a past cost over a period of years.

A simple method of calculating the annual charge is shown by the following example. A machine is bought for £5000 and its estimated useful life is five years, at the end of which it is not expected to have any residual value. The annual charge against income for depreciation is calculated as £5000/5 = £1000 per annum. The depreciation so charged each year is accumulated and the total provision at the end of a particular year is deducted from the cost of the machine to show what is called a 'book value' in the balance sheet. Thus at the end of three years the net book value of the machine would appear in the balance sheet as:

	£
Cost	5000
Less: Accumulated depreciation	3000
Net book value	£2000

Some companies show fixed assets in their balance sheets at the cost of replacement and charge depreciation on the basis of that cost.

The nature of depreciation, and methods of calculating the charge, are more fully examined in the next chapter.

Intangible Fixed Assets

These include development costs not yet written off in the profit and loss account, the cost of patents, trade marks, licences and similar rights, goodwill, and payments made on account. Their value is uncertain and variable, so that on the grounds of prudent accounting they are frequently written down to a nominal amount. A recent innovation is to value brand names in the balance sheet – see Chapter 9.

Goodwill needs particular consideration. It is commonly referred to as the value inherent in a business above the value of the other net assets; that value depends on matters not subject to precise assessment, such as the reputation of the business and its future sales potential. Where a value needs to be assessed, such as on the sale of a business, a reasonably scientific method is to calculate the present value of the expected super profits, i.e. those above a minimum return on capital. For this purpose the expected super profits are discounted over a term of, say, 5 to 20 years. Whilst ostensibly precise the calculation contains a number of variables and uncertainties, such as the rates of interest and the period and the amounts of the super profits. Even with such a calculation as a basis the total price paid for a business taken over is likely to be the result of a bargain, as influenced by supply and demand.

In the accounts of the acquiring company, goodwill is the excess of the consideration paid over the value of the net assets acquired, after those assets have been revalued if necessary. The consideration may consist of cash or the shares of the acquiring company (at an agreed value) or a combination of both. The goodwill at cost may be included in the balance sheet as an intangible asset, or, more prudently, may be deducted from reserves in the year of acquisition or over a short term of years.

Long-term Investments

Investments in shares and securities may be acquired for long-term purposes such as for the redemption of capital due to be repaid many years hence. In many cases, however, this heading includes investments in subsidiaries and associated companies. Substantial holdings may be obtained in other companies for the purpose, for instance, of ensuring sources of supply or widening distribution outlets.

Valuations of Fixed Assets

Assets are initially entered in the accounts at their cost, that is the money paid for them. Unless the cost is adjusted it does not reflect saleable value, value to the business, replacement value of any other concept of value; nor does it reflect changes in the purchasing power of money. Where an asset's value has risen substantially and permanently above cost it may be shown in the balance sheet at its current value, the increase over cost, or over a previous valuation, being transferred to a revaluation reserve. An increase in a reserve produces a similar increase in the total of capital employed. As a result an unchanged profit will represent a lower percentage on capital employed, and the fact needs to be recognized when that percentage is used as a performance indicator.

Land and buildings, in particular, are frequently revalued, either by a professional valuation or by the application of an index of property values. Investments are normally shown in the balance sheet at cost, but the current value of those quoted on a stock exchange must be shown as a note to the accounts. As a means of accounting for inflation a few large companies show fixed assets in terms of current money values, or at replacement cost, by the application of appropriate indices.

Where a permanent and substantial reduction has occurred in the value of an investment its value as shown in the balance sheet should be reduced to the new value, as a measure of prudent accounting. This will involve a reduction in reserves or a charge to the profit and loss account. Because many assets, such as plant and machinery, are subject to depreciation and have a terminal life, it is necessary to reduce their value regularly by charging the estimated depreciation to the profit and loss account (or, in the case of production equipment, to the manufacturing account).

The depreciation so charged is accumulated in a depreciation provision account for each class of asset, and the accumulated depreciation is set off against the assets' cost or valuation in the balance sheet. In addition to plant and machinery, depreciation applies to vehicles, leases, mines, quarries, patents and copyrights.

Some assets of which the value is uncertain (in any sense of the term) are often written off on acquisition, and in any event should be depreciated (or 'amortized') over a short term of years. Examples include goodwill and development expenditure.

Net Current Assets/Liabilities

Meaning

Current assets consist of cash in hand and at the bank plus assets expected to be realized in cash within a year. They include stocks and work in progress, debtors, temporary investments and bills of exchange receivable in a year. These assets are further examined below.

Current liabilities are payments due within a year and include: trade creditors, taxation liabilities, bills of exchange payable, bank overdrafts, short-term loans and dividends payable or recommended by the directors.

A surplus of current assets over current liabilities is a primary indication that the business is solvent, at least that it will be able to pay its debts within a year. Where, on the other hand, current liabilities exceed current assets a question arises as to the solvency of the business, unless it is assured of further incoming funds (e.g. by bank overdraft) to finance the trading operations. An important financial indicator is the ratio of current assets to current liabilities, and the trend of that ratio. The figure of net current assets is sometimes referred to as 'working capital', but that term can be ambiguous; it may be used, for example, simply to apply to available cash.

A more immediate indication of the ability of a business to pay its debts is net liquid capital. Liquid capital consists of those current assets which are cash or likely to be realized in cash within the short term, normally about three months. In assessing liquid capital stocks are normally excluded unless the stock turnover is very swift, such as in many retail stores. The items embraced by liquid capital are thus cash in hand and at bank, debtors (which even on long credit terms can normally be factored (i.e. transferred to a finance house for collection), bills of exchange receivable (which can be discounted or 'negotiated') and saleable investments. Net liquid capital is arrived at by deducting current liabilities from liquid assets. The existence of a negative figure of net liquid assets is the first sign that further funds are required, for creditors will not usually wait more than three months before they take action to recover their dues.

Although net current assets and net liquid assets are primary indicators of liquidity, much depends on future cash inflow and outflow. Cash management is best effected by means of a cash forecast against which actual receipts and payments are compared and which is revised monthly.

It is undesirable that a positive balance of net current assets should exceed more than is required to meet contingencies and the unexpected. Furthermore, unforeseen calls for funds can usually be covered by arranging a bank overdraft facility which exceeds estimated requirements. The existence of a very high total of net current assets shows that some of the capital is idle, and could be applied to earning income by investment in the business or externally. Such idle capital may be represented by redundant or slow-moving stocks or by debtors taking excessive credit.

The net current assets of £180 000 in Fig. 2.2 indicate that the business is able to pay its creditors within a year, and that there is, ostensibly, no idle capital. Nevertheless, creditors are over 95 per cent of current assets and liquidity appears to be tight, with little scope for contingencies. Net liquid assets are:

	£
Current assets	3 780 000
Less: Stocks	1 575 000
Liquid assets	2 205 000
Creditors	3 600 000
Negative balance	£(1 395 000)

The position is now shown to be dangerously illiquid in the short term and the detailed figures require further analysis on the lines indicated below.

Stocks and Work in Progress

Stocks include raw materials, parts and components, work in progress, finished products and goods bought for resale. They are valued at cost or at net realizable value if this is below cost. Raw materials are normally valued at cost, except for items which are redundant or very slow moving. Work in progress should be valued at net realizable value (that is the expected sale proceeds of the finished product) where that value is less than existing costs plus costs to come for completion of the products. For finished products and bought-out goods for resale the net realizable value would be the expected proceeds on sale. The principles for valuation of stock are set out in a Statement of Standard Accounting Practice (SSAP) issued by the joint UK accountancy bodies.

A useful indicator of whether stocks are high or low is the number of months or days which are likely to elapse before they are sold using, where available, the forecasted cost of sales for the purpose. In Fig. 2.2 the value of stocks is £1 575 000. Assuming sales continue at last year's level, their cost per month is £4 500 000/12 = £375 000 or per day £4 500 000/365 = £12 329. The stocks therefore represent £1 575 000/375 000 = 4.2 months' sales or £1 575 000/12 329 = 128 days' sales. These indicators would not appear to be too high for a manufacturing business, depending on the length of the production cycle, but may be considered excessive for a retail store.

Redundant and very slow moving stock should be disposed of at the best available price so as to save space and administrative costs. Such stock should therefore be written down to its disposable value. Marketing and sales management have the responsibility of ensuring that stock does not become too old, even if this means selling the goods at a low margin. For this purpose an 'ageing' statement of stock held should be produced at monthly intervals on the lines shown in Fig. 2.3.

AGEING STOCK

	Months					
	Under				Over	
Category	1	2	3	4	4	Total
	£	£	£	£	£	£
A						
B						
C						
etc.						
Totals						

Figure 2.3

Debtors

In order that debtors be kept to a minimum, and thus save capital, it is important that a credit policy should be established for different classes of customers and not exceeded except with special authority. It is necessary for marketing and sales departments to be involved in credit control in order to achieve the right balance between customer goodwill and the need to obtain speedy payment of accounts. Likewise there is a need for an efficient system of collection, involving the prompt dispatch of invoices and the follow-up of late payers.

The overall indicator of whether debtors are excessive is the number of months', or days', past sales they represent. If in Fig. 2.2 sales had been at the rate of £750 000 a month for, say, the last three months the debtors of £1 875 000 represent $2\frac{1}{2}$ months' sales. This would be high where payments were due by the end of the month following receipt of invoices, but probably about normal where up to 2 months' credit terms were offered.

A further useful device for monitoring debtors under various customer groups is a monthly statement showing their ages, in the form shown in Fig. 2.4.

Bills of Exchange

A bill of exchange is a negotiable instrument, i.e. transferable from one holder to another. It is drawn by a creditor on a debtor requiring the latter to pay a stated sum, with or without interest, at a specified date. Cheques are bills of exchange which are drawn on a banker and payable on demand. Bills of exchange, payable at a future date and drawn on the buyer, are frequently used for export sales. They may be associated with a letter of credit arranged by the buyer with a UK or overseas bank, the amount stated in the credit being payable to the seller when title to the goods has passed to the buyer. They are also used to obtain loans, the lender drawing the bill on the borrower.

AGEING OF DEBTORS

Customer group	Under 1	Months 2	3	4	Over 4
	£	£	£	£	£
A					
B					
C					
etc.					
Total					
Previous month					

Figure 2.4

The advantages of transactions by means of bills of exchange are (1) that the debtor thereby obtains a period of credit for his purchases or loan, and (2) the creditor can obtain immediate payment (less charges and discount) by discounting or negotiating the bill, i.e. transferring it to a third party for value. Normally bills receivable by a seller are discounted with a bank. They require acceptance by the debtor but, subject to the bank having a right of repayment from the creditor if the bill is unpaid on maturity, they can normally be discounted (more strictly, negotiated) before acceptance.

Investments

The investments included under current assets are those held for the short term of about a year. Investments may be made to earn a return on cash surpluses not likely to be required for the operations in the near future but would be available for realization when the need arose. For these reasons the investments are likely to be those not subject to appreciable risk of depreciation in value, and would be valued at cost, unless their value did in fact fall considerably.

Current Liabilities

These consist of liabilities due to be paid in about a year and would include trade creditors, taxation, loans and overdrafts, payments received on account, bills of exchange payable, amounts owing to subsidiaries and associated companies, accruals, deferred income and dividends due and recommended by the directors.

Trade creditors should, for management purposes and to aid cash forecasting, be analysed by a subsidiary ageing statement, similar to that shown in Fig. 2.4 for debtors. The current liability for taxation is the amount payable, or estimated to be payable within a year, not 'deferred taxation' as described below. Accruals and deferred income are also explained below.

Miscellaneous Items

Liabilities Due after 1 Year

This is a separate heading in the statutory balance sheet. It covers the same items as are listed above in the section on current liabilities, but only the amounts which are payable after a year, such as creditors given long terms of credit. In Fig. 2.2 the amount shown of £120 000 is not particularly large but, in view of the questionable liquid position of the company, suggests that additional funds may be required eventually for payment of these liabilities. They will in due course be transferred to the current liabilities heading.

Provisions

These are estimates of expenses and losses known to have been incurred but of which the precise amount cannot be ascertained with substantial accuracy. They might include, for example, estimated costs and damages under legal actions, possible payments for delays under contracts, and claims under guarantees and warranties. Provisions for depreciation of fixed assets, for estimated losses on stocks and for doubtful debts are deducted from the assets concerned.

The terms 'provisions' and 'reserves' are often used as though they are synonymous, but they have quite different meanings so far as accounting terminology is concerned. A provision is an expense which must be charged against current income in the profit and loss account; a reserve is an appropriation of profit.

The Companies Act 1985 requires that provisions shall be shown under a separate heading in the statutory balance sheet, and details provided of those which are substantial. It would, however, seem reasonable to include certain provisions under 'current liabilities', such as where the estimated amount was shortly payable.

Reserves

When the net profit has been ascertained, the directors allocate or 'appropriate' certain amounts for the payment of dividends and to reserves, leaving a balance to be carried forward to the next year. This balance is in itself of the nature of a reserve. The amount allocated to reserves is otherwise known as 'retained profit'. Reserves derived from trading profits are distributable, that is they can be used for the payment of dividends, although this practice is unusual and only occurs in years when profits are exceptionally low. Reserves arising from profits of a capital nature, such as premiums on shares, or revaluations of assets, are not distributable except, of course, in a liquidation of the company.

Accruals and Deferred Income

Expenditure is said to be accrued where an ongoing expense is not due for payment at the date of the accounts. A simple example is rent payable in arrear. The amount accrued is included in the profit and loss account as part of the relevant charge and as a liability in the balance sheet. The converse is accrued income which is ongoing income not yet due to be received, such as rent receivable in arrear. The income so arising is included in the profit and loss account and as an asset in the balance sheet. The distinction between accrued income and deferred income can be fine, but the latter expression more particularly refers, for example, to the future amount receivable on a hire-purchase contract.

Prepayments

A prepaid expense is a payment made in advance of the period to which the outgoing refers. Typical examples are rates and insurance premiums. The amount is shown in the balance sheet as an asset, often combined with accrued income. Prepaid income arises where money is received in advance and represents a liability, normally combined with accruals and deferred income.

Deferred Taxation

This is essentially a provision and usually represents the additional net profit gained when capital allowances for taxation purposes (see Appendix 1) are in excess of the depreciation charged in the accounts. This provision would be reduced when, in due course, the saving in tax was offset by reduced capital allowances.

Contingent Liabilities

These are possible liabilities which may become payable on the occurrence of some future event. A typical example is the potential liability under a guarantee, such as for another company's or person's debt. Contingent liabilities are not included in balance sheet totals but are shown as a note to the accounts. It would, however, be prudent to make a provision for the likely liability.

Capital Commitments

These would again be shown as a note to the balance sheet. The amount would cover 'capital expenditure', i.e. on fixed assets, which the company had agreed to make where delivery of the equipment, and payment for it, would not occur until some time in the future.

Conclusions for Marketing and Sales Management

Amongst their many other preoccupations marketing and sales managers cannot be expected to be expert in the interpretation of accounts. Nevertheless, there are many occasions where a sound general understanding of a balance sheet should be of value to them in carrying out their responsibilities. At least they should, as members of the management team, understand the terminology used in discussions with their accounting colleagues.

The viability of the marketing plan will be affected by the financial resources available for its fulfilment. In particular, plans for increased turnover need financing, so that marketing managers are concerned with the liquidity of their own company, and should be able to ask the relevant questions about the possibilities of obtaining any further finance required. This is of special importance where stocks of goods for sale are limited by financial considerations. Sales management is directly concerned when stocks become slow moving.

The negotiation of contracts is facilitated where the selling party is aware of the financial position of the purchaser. In this context the essential question is whether the purchaser has the capacity to pay in accordance with the terms offered. This question may be quickly resolved by an examination of the customer's accounts and, where doubts as to the latter's financial status arise, the negotiating manager should know when to initiate investigation by his accounts department.

Sales management are also likely to be involved when an ageing statement of the company's debtors reveals that a high proportion of customers are slow payers.

3 ANALYSING THE TRADING RESULTS

The Stages of Profit

As indicated briefly in Chapter 1, the final profit made by a business over an accounting period is arrived at in stages. These stages are, successively, gross profit, operating profit, pre-tax profit and net profit. In using past results for forward planning it is necessary to consider the nature of the expenditure applied at each stage. The results are presented in the form of a trading and profit and loss account as shown on page 7 of Chapter 1. (The word 'trading' is now usually omitted.) The essentials of this account are as follows:

Pro forma profit and loss account

	£
SALES	
Less: Cost of sales	———
GROSS PROFIT	
Less: Operating expenses	———
OPERATING PROFIT	
Add/deduct: financial, exceptional and extraordinary income and expenses	———
PRE-TAX PROFIT	
Less: Provision for taxation	———
NET PROFIT for the year	£ ———

The remaining part of the statement shows how the profit available has been appropriated and is sometimes called the 'appropriation account'. The total available profit is divided between allocations to reserves and dividends on shares, leaving an amount of retained profit which is added to the existing balance on the profit and loss account. The total retained profit constitutes a reserve of a general nature, and is carried forward on the balance sheet as part of the shareholders' interests in the company. It may be reduced by adjustments to intangible assets such as by the write-off of goodwill.

NET PROFIT FOR THE YEAR

		£
Less: Dividends paid and recommended		_____
Less: Transferred to specific reserves		_____
PROFIT RETAINED for the year	£	_____

The Companies Act 1985 requires that the annual published accounts show comparative figures for the previous year. For internal management the results should be compared with the budgets. Since the budgets will be based at least partly on the past, there seems little point in an additional comparison with the results for the previous period. Management needs monthly accounts, presented as soon as possible after the end of each month. Since one month's results may contain seasonal and exceptional influences, the accounts should also show the results for the preceding 12 months. Appropriate headings might be as follows:

Current month		12 months	
Actual	*Budget*	*Actual*	*Budget*

The major variances between the actual and budgeted results should be analysed, at least by their price and volume elements (see Chapter 5 on responsibility accounting).

Gross Profit and Cost of Sales

The gross profit, sometimes called the 'gross margin', is of particular interest to marketing executives, for it represents the surplus of the sales over their direct costs. It should be appreciated that the cost of sales is not the total costs incurred by the business over the period, but only the cost of those goods or services which are sold in the period. There will remain in the balance sheet, as current assets, the stock unsold, including raw materials, bought-out goods and work in progress.

Where the business manufactures goods for sale the cost of the sales is the cost incurred in the workshops, including material, components and labour, plus a production overhead rate. The cost is derived from the manufacturing account, which is examined below. Where the cost of sales includes the resale of purchased items (such as in wholesaling and retailing) the cost is that paid for the goods.

The adequacy of the gross profit is usually indicated as a percentage of sales, and it is useful to show the trend of this percentage over the past months or years. Obviously this percentage will be affected by changes, not only in cost, but also of price.

For certain planning purposes it will be informative to show the percentage gross margin on cost. Using the example of X Company on page 7 of Chapter 1, the figures are as follows:

	£m	%	%
Sales	9.0	100	$166\frac{1}{3}$
Cost of sale	5.4	60	100
Gross profit	£3.6	40%	$66\frac{1}{3}\%$

The percentage gross profit on cost indicates, for example, that if volume of turnover could be increased, the additional cost would yield $66\frac{1}{3}\%$ profit. (The above figures, however, are simplified and do not account for the almost inevitable changes in cost, and possibly price, which would follow from a change in turnover.)

More extensive analysis of the effect of changes in cost, price and volume is contained in the next chapter. Such analysis is normally made on the basis of marginal cost, and it should be noted that the conventional cost of manufactured goods includes production overheads, much of them being of a fixed nature and not therefore marginal in the short term, if at all. Most businesses sell a variety of products or services, so that for management purposes it is necessary to analyse the turnover by the major selling lines, and to show the comparative contribution to overall profit made by each line. The Companies Act 1985 requires that the published accounts should show comparative figures for the previous year and should analyse turnover and profit by the main classes of business and the main markets.

Where standard costing is used the management accounts should show first the gross profit after deducting standard costs from sales – 'gross profit at standard' – then deductions or additions are made for standard cost variances, leaving a 'gross profit, actual'.

Operating Profit and Operating Expenses

This is the profit after operating expenses have been deducted from gross profit. The operating expenses (often loosely described as 'overheads') are those which cannot be attributed with precision to the units sold, as can the cost of sales. The distinction in terminology is between 'cost' and 'expense'. The operating expenses include expenditure for selling, distribution, publicity, administration and research and development.

For all these expenses it is desirable to set up detailed budgets, against which the actual outgoings are compared. Some of the expenses will be, at least in the short term, of a fixed nature, and therefore unrelated to the current level of sales. The fixed operating expenses would include, for instance, depreciation on sales and distribution vehicles and on office equipment, and a substantial proportion of the expenses, especially for administration, would be for control and recording purposes, again independent of turnover in the short term. Some expenses, particularly research and development and much of the publicity, would be aimed at producing future sales.

A substantial proportion of the operating expenses could, however, be expected to be variable, that is to vary in relation to turnover. The variable expenses would, for instance, include carriage not charged to customers, travelling expenses, commission and stationery.

In the long term all expenditure must be paid for out of sales income. For this reason it should be related to sales by a percentage. The trend of this percentage over each succeeding period of 12 months should be carefully monitored. Marketing management is directly concerned with controlling expenditure on selling, distribution, advertising and other methods of promotion.

Pre-tax Profit and Non-trading Items

The next stage in the ascertainment of profit is to deduct from or add to operating profit what may be called 'non-trading' expenses or income, thus arriving at the profit before taxation. For this purpose 'non-trading' includes financial, extraordinary and exceptional items. Financial items include interest payable on loans and overdrafts, interest receivable, and income and payments for licences and royalties. The distinction between what is extraordinary or exceptional tends to be fine. Both terms refer to events outside the normal operations of the business and include profits and losses on the sale of assets, especially land, or of businesses which have been taken over.

Net Profit and Tax

The final exercise in the ascertainment of profit for a period is to deduct a provision for tax. The essence of business taxation is set out in Appendix 1 but the following brief notes are relevant at this stage.

The tax liabilities of the business will not be settled for a considerable time after the accounts have been prepared, and in any event the computation is likely to be complex. At the end of an accounting year, however, it is necessary that a provision shall be made for the estimated tax liability so that a reasonable indication may be given of the profit available for the shareholders by way of dividend and allocation to reserve. These are basically end-of-the-year decisions. Although tax provisions are frequently made in the monthly management accounts, they are of little interest to functional managers, for the tax payable is largely outside their control. A further point which is relevant in the present context is that the tax provision is not simply the result of applying the corporation tax rate (or, in the case of unincorporated businesses, the basic income tax rate) to the accounting profit. Many adjustments may be required to the latter in taxation computations, including those for disallowable expenses, and for depreciation for which capital allowances are substituted.

The Appropriation Account

The net profit for the year is the amount available for appropriation by the directors. The directors decide the amount which can be allocated to dividends, having regard to any interim dividends already paid, and the amount to be transferred to reserves. These deductions from available profit will leave an amount to be added to the existing balance on the profit and loss account reserve. It is possible, but unusual, for this 'distributable reserve' to be drawn on for the purpose of paying a dividend in a year of low profits. It may also be used to write down or write off intangible assets, such as goodwill.

The Manufacturing Account

A manufacturing account is prepared by a business producing goods. The prime objective of the account is to arrive at the direct cost of the completed production which is transferred to the finished goods store. A typical form of manufacturing account is shown in Fig. 3.1. This account does not have to be included in the published accounts and is prepared for internal management.

A similar kind of statement is an operating account. This applies where a business provides services such as transport, construction, maintenance and repair work. The purpose of the operating account is to show the direct cost of the operations and the services provided.

The account will be subdivided as required to show the costs arising in cost centres such as, in a manufacturing business, the foundry, press shop, machine shop, and fitting and assembly shops. Further analysis of the costs by jobs, production runs and eventually by products will be made by the costing system.

Manufacturing account for the year ended 31 December 19–0

	£	£
Total production costs:		
Direct costs:		
Labour		
Materials consumed		
Bought-out parts consumed		
Other direct charges	————	
Total direct costs		
Indirect costs:		
Indirect wages and salaries		
Employee benefits		
Indirect materials		
Services		
Other indirect costs	————	
Total indirect costs		
Recovered by overhead rate	————	
Under-/over-recovery	£————	————
Total production costs for the year:		
Add/Deduct: Change in work in progress:		
At beginning of year		
At end of year	————	
		————
Cost of completed production		£————

Figure 3.1

The essential elements of this account are examined in the following notes.

Direct Costs

These are the costs which can be charged with reasonable precision and convenience to the units of output. These units may be jobs, production runs, products, contracts, etc., according to the nature of the operations and the information required. The direct costs are analysed by the costing system. Direct labour represents the time charged to jobs etc. valued at the hourly rate of the operatives concerned, or at a standard rate (see under standard costs). Direct material and bought-out parts and components are those incorporated in the product, except for items of no great value and difficult to cost, such as paint and small pieces of hardware. Direct material is charged to jobs etc. by means of requisitions on stores, valued by various methods including standard prices. Bought-out parts may be charged at invoiced cost.

Other direct costs might include subcontractors' charges and various expenses directly chargeable such as those recoverable in contract prices.

Indirect Costs

These are the production (or operating) costs which cannot be attributed precisely to units of output. They constitute the 'overheads' of the production or operating function and are applied for costing purposes to the jobs etc. by means of an overhead rate. In a sophisticated system of costing, differential overhead rates may be established for the major operations, e.g. the foundry, machine shop, paint shop and assembly shop.

The overhead rate or rates must be established before the beginning of an accounting period, normally a year, so that they can be applied to the units of output as the production proceeds. An overhead rate is therefore necessarily an estimate which is based on forecasts of the indirect costs and of the output. For the purpose of calculating the rate, the output needs to be expressed by the factor which best represents the volume of work carried out. This factor is often direct labour hours or machine hours or may be a quantitative measure where output is homogeneous. (Costing methods are examined in detail in a later chapter.)

For present purposes assume that a single overhead rate is to be established and is based on labour hours. The forecasts for the coming year are: direct labour hours 800 000; production overheads £1 600 000. If it is the intention that the overheads shall be fully 'recovered', i.e. completely absorbed by the units of output, the appropriate overhead rate would be £2 per direct labour hour. Assume, however, that the forecast of 800 000 hours was below the normal capacity of the workshop, which was capable of producing 1 000 000 hours of work in a year, at which rate overheads would rise to £1 800 000. These figures give an overhead rate of £1.80 an hour, and would be more realistic on the grounds that the former method would produce an excessive cost per job and hence per product. The former rate included the cost of under-utilized facilities.

The use of an excessive overhead rate in ascertaining the cost of products can have a seriously adverse effect on marketing policy and planning. The resulting high recorded cost of the products could indicate that some of them were uneconomic at the prices obtainable, or could influence the price at which they are marketed, causing them to be uncompetitive.

It should be appreciated that, because the overhead rate is necessarily based on estimates, there will always be, at the end of an accounting year, a balance of production overheads 'under-' or 'over-recovered', i.e. more or less of the actual indirect cost incurred is absorbed by units of output. (The term 'recovered' is used because it is customary, but it should be noted that no costs are actually 'recovered' until the product is sold.)

Assume that an overhead rate of £1.80 an hour was established on the basis of the second calculation above. However, the actual output for the year represented only 750 000 direct labour hours (owing to a recession in trade, a strike or some other cause). The actual indirect or overhead costs incurred totalled £1 550 000. The under-recovery, compared with the estimates, would then be as follows:

	Actual	*Estimate*
Direct labour hours	750 000	800 000
Overheads	1 550 000	1 600 000
Overhead rate per hour	1.8	1.8
Overheads 'recovered'	1 350 000	1 440 000
Under-recovery	£200 000	£160 000

When the overhead rate was originally assessed it was expected that there would be an under-recovery of £160 000, due to estimated output being below normal capacity. In fact actual output was 50 000 hours below the estimate and, although economies had been made on the overheads, the actual under-recovery had risen to £200 000. This amount, being essentially the cost of under-utilized resources (*not* the cost of making product), would be written off against income for the year in the profit and loss account as a costing variance.

The following further notes on indirect production costs or overheads are relevant. The indirect wages include the proportion of direct operators' time not applied to output, e.g. waiting time, paid holidays, maintenance and attendance at meetings, etc.; much of the cost would arise from supervision, works offices, maintenance, etc. The employee benefits include employer's national insurance and pension scheme contributions. Indirect materials include machine oils and small pieces of hardware. Services would cover light, power, heating and possibly external fees.

Completed Output and Cost of Sales

The cost of the completed production, as shown by the manufacturing account, will be transferred to a finished goods account. From this account deductions, representing the cost of goods sold, will be made as product is delivered to customers.

The essentials of the finished goods account are as follows:

Finished Goods Account

	£
Stock at beginning of period	
Add: Completed output for the period	_____
Stock available	
Less: Deliveries transferred to cost of sales	_____
Stock at end of period	£ _____

The finished stock at the end of the period will appear under current assets in the balance sheet and will probably be amalgamated with stocks of raw materials, parts, bought-out goods and work in progress.

Depreciation in the Accounts

Nature and Effect

Depreciation is usually defined as the loss in value which occurs on fixed assets due to age and use. The subject is considered in this chapter because depreciation may have a significant effect on the trading results, especially in an undertaking with a large investment in plant, vehicles and other equipment. Moreover, the charge for depreciation is distinct in many ways from such current outgoings as payments for materials, remuneration and various services. It arises from past expenditure on the purchase of fixed assets, and is the apportionment of this expenditure to the future years in which the asset will be used in the business operations. It is essentially an estimate, subject to many different methods of calculation. It does not affect cash flow.

Depreciation on production or operating machinery and equipment is an indirect cost and therefore is an element in the overhead rate. In this way depreciation has an effect on unit costs and increases the cost of production, work in progress, finished goods and, consequently, cost of sales. Thus gross profit is reduced by depreciation on production plant, and the amount of the charge must be of interest to marketing management in particular.

Operating expenses are also increased by depreciation. Distribution expenses, for example, include depreciation on vehicles and equipment; selling expenses include depreciation on the sales force's cars; and administration expenses are increased by depreciation of executives' cars, premises and office equipment.

Methods

The methods and rates used in depreciating fixed assets can vary widely from one business to another, thus impairing the validity of inter-firm cost comparisons. The methods most frequently used are called (1) fixed instalment or straight line; and (2) reducing balance or reducing instalment. Other more sophisticated methods (for which reference should be made to specialist accounting literature) include sinking funds, annuities, present values and sum of digits. Particular methods and rates of writing down allowances apply to tax computations, but these are not necessarily appropriate for the business accounts.

The essential principle is to write off the cost (or value) of an asset over its useful life. Because the useful life must be estimated on the acquisition of the asset, the calculation is never exact, and a balance of undercharged or overcharged depreciation has to be accounted for when the asset is disposed of.

Fixed Instalment Method

Assume a machine is bought for £12 000; its estimated useful life is five years and its residual value estimated at £2000. The annual depreciation charge is, therefore:

$$\frac{£12\ 000 - 2000}{5} = £2000 \text{ p.a.}$$

For reasons of prudent accounting the life is usually estimated conservatively and residual value is frequently ignored.

Reducing Instalment

This method involves calculating the percentage which, applied to the reducing value of the asset, will arrive at the residual value at the end of the asset's useful life. The formula is $B = 100\ (1 - RV/C)^{1/n}$, where B is the percentage rate of depreciation, RV is the residual value, C is the cost, and n is the years of useful life. For this calculation some residual value must be assumed but it can be a nominal amount. In the above example for the fixed instalment method, the percentage, rounded off, is 30 per cent.

The Two Methods Compared

Year		*Fixed instalment*	*Reducing instalment (30%)*
		£	£
1	Cost	12 000	12 000
	Depreciation	2 000	3 600
2	W/d balance	10 000	8 400
	Depreciation	2 000	2 520
3	W/d balance	8 000	5 880
	Depreciation	2 000	1 764
4	W/d balance	6 000	4 116
	Depreciation	2 000	1 235
5	W/d balance	4 000	2 881
	Depreciation	2 000	864
6	W/d balance	£2 000	£2 017

It is apparent that in the early years the reducing instalment method gives a higher charge against profit than the fixed instalment method, and likewise makes a greater reduction in total assets and hence capital employed. The converse arises in the later years. The advantage usually claimed for the reducing instalment method is that it offsets rising maintenance costs in later years.

Disposal and Replacement of Assets

Consider now the accounting entries if at the beginning of year 4 it was decided to replace the asset by one costing £15 000, the amount obtained by selling the old asset being £5000. The comparative figures are as follows:

	Fixed instalment method	*Reducing instalment method*
	£	£
Cost	12 000	12,000
Accumulated depreciation	6 000	7 884
Net book value	6 000	4 116
Sale proceeds	5 000	5 000
Book profit/(loss)	£(1 000)	£884

These 'book' profits or losses do not represent a cash inflow or outflow but are simply deficiencies or excesses of the depreciation charged in prior years. Past years' accounts cannot be altered, so the 'book' profits or losses have to be carried either to the profit and loss account (as exceptional items) or to the general depreciation provision account for the class of asset concerned.

The depreciation charge on the higher-costing replacement asset will tend to be above that for the old asset, especially if the reducing instalment method is used. The increase will be subject to any revised estimates of life and residual value. Assuming, however, that the new asset is more efficient than the old one, the increase in the cost of depreciation should be more than offset by operating savings. In a few companies the 'jumps' in the depreciation charge on replacing fixed assets are smoothed by calculating the annual charge on replacement values.

4 THE COSTING SYSTEM

The Meaning of Cost

A cost is the figure obtained by analysing the expenditure of an organization for a particular purpose. The first analysis is by category of expenditure, such as wages and salaries, materials, various expenses and fees. This kind of basic analysis is shown as a matter of course in a detailed manufacturing or profit and loss account. It will also be useful for appraising past expenditure of a business and for forecasting future expenditure.

For planning and control purposes, in particular for budgeting, the categories of expenditure are then analysed by the divisions and departments in which the outgoings arise, e.g. Production, Buying, Research and Development, Selling, Accounting, etc. Within these departments there will be distinct functions or operations, usually described as 'cost centres' (e.g. machining, assembly, paint-spraying, etc.) to which the costs may be allocated. For a simple form of costing a department may be treated as a cost centre, e.g. the production department as a whole.

It is the costs allocated to the production or operating cost centres which form the basis for calculating what may be broadly called 'unit costs'. A wide variety of 'units' are used for the purpose, e.g. jobs, production runs, contracts, sales orders, man hours, machine hours, operating hours, measures of product produced and so forth. Unit costs may, for example, be calculated per tonne mile or passenger mile in a transport undertaking, per area of counter space in a retail store, and per bed in a hospital. The unit used in a particular case will depend on the nature of the undertaking or function and the objectives of the costing exercise.

It is a mistake to consider costing as confined to the direct operations of producing goods or providing services. Costing for the control of expenditure can also be applied with benefit to selling, accounting and administrative departments. Thus it could be useful to ascertain the cost of obtaining a sales order, the canteen cost per employee, the cost per letter typed, etc.

The Objectives of Costing

A costing system can involve considerable expense in clerical time and in processing the figures, e.g. by a computer. Of equal importance is the time which managers are expected to spend in considering the information. All this time and effort will be wasted unless the costs fulfil their purposes. The objectives of a costing system fall under the general headings of (1) accounting, and (2) planning and control, which embraces pricing policy.

In a manufacturing business costing is an essential part of the accounting process for the valuation of stocks, including materials, work in progress and finished goods. When the finished goods are delivered to customers, the cost of those goods must be ascertained to arrive at the gross profit. In a contracting business, the costs charged to contracts must be calculated for similar reasons. Likewise it is necessary to arrive at the cost of items of stock in a wholesaling or retailing business.

Planning and control covers an immensely wide variety of managerial decisions and actions. Essentially planning is directed at the use of the resources of an undertaking in the most effective manner, and then at the control of the execution of those plans. Both aspects of the managerial function involve analysis and consideration of past and current costs; in addition, an important aspect of the cost accounting service is to forecast future costs.

It is necessary to emphasize at this point that the costs derived from the routine costing system are rarely appropriate, without considerable adaptation, for forward planning and control purposes. The cost attributed to goods and services sold is arrived at by applying various conventional practices designed to give a fair and consistent view of profit or loss. For instance, the loading of unit costs by an overhead rate is simply a device for spreading indirect costs over the output; the resulting total cost does not represent the cash spent by making a particular product. A cost, it has been said, is 'a convention'. It is not an absolute quantity and it will vary according to the purpose for which it is required. That purpose may not be fulfilled by using the figures of cost applied to the valuation of stocks.

The Mechanics of Costing

The costs produced by the routine costing system ostensibly show the direct cost of the sales and hence the gross profits from the various products and services. It will be necessary to adapt these figures for marketing decision-making, for example when considering the elimination of one product or the exploitation of another. The necessary adaptations to costing information for various purposes are considered below. In interpreting the figures produced, and in calling for costs designed for particular purposes, it is necessary that the manager should be aware of the methods typically used in the costing system.

That system applies direct costs to units of output plus an overhead rate. Direct costs are those which can be applied to the units of output with precision and convenience. They normally consist of labour, materials, bought-out parts and various directly chargeable expenses. Athough the direct cost of a job or product is apparently an exact figure, that statement needs qualification, as indicated in the following notes.

Direct Labour

The time booked by operatives against job numbers are valued by the cost department at the appropriate hourly rate. The time for which an operative is paid will not be wholly applied to making products or providing services for sale. A proportion of the pay will be inevitably charged to production overheads, such as idle time (e.g. waiting for work), time on maintenance, holiday pay, etc. Clearly, a responsibility of production management is to minimize idle time.

The common practice of charging jobs and ultimately products with the actual time taken multiplied by the actual rate paid can produce anomalies. In, for instance, a recession, when available work is short, a natural human tendency will be to spend more time than normal on a job. A similar effect will appear on new jobs involving a learning period known as 'the learning curve'. In some circumstances it may be necessary to occupy the time of higher-paid employees on low-grade work. If in these circumstances the actual time taken at the actual rate paid is costed to the job, stock in the balance sheet will be at an inflated value, and so will the cost of sales. This could lead to incorrect decisions of the potential profitability of the product.

The answer to this problem is, it is suggested, to record the cost of the job on the basis of the normal time and the normal rate of pay – in short, to use *standard costing*, which is examined in more detail later. The actual money paid for the work must, of course, be recorded in the accounts. This will be achieved by including the difference between the actual cost and the standard cost in 'costing variances' to be deducted from gross profit at standard.

Direct Material

The material drawn from stores by the workshops is recorded on a 'requisition' which is valued by the costing department. Where excess material is drawn due to spoilage or unsatisfactory quality, the cost of the excess should be charged to production overheads, or if a standard costing system is used, to costing variances. The major problem lies in valuing the requisitions where the material in stock was bought at different prices.

The bases for valuing material are usually first in first out (FIFO), average cost and standard cost. Exceptionally, the material is valued at so called actual cost (applicable to bought-out parts and material which can be segregated by purchase prices), next in first out (NIFO), last in first out (LIFO), and replacement cost. Each method will give a different cost of jobs, of stock and of sales. Compare the effect of the two commonly used methods, FIFO and average cost in the following example of a material stock account.

1. First in first out method – prices rising

Week	Unit price	Additions Quantity	Value	Unit price	Withdrawals Quantity	Value	Stock Quantity	Value
	£		£	£		£		£
1	5	120	600				120	600
2	6	180	1080				300	1680
3				5	80	400	220	1280
4				5	40	200	180	1080
				6	60	360	120	720
		300	1680		180	960		

2. Average cost method

| Week | Additions | | | Withdrawals | | | Stock | |
	Unit price	Quantity	Value	Unit price	Quantity	Value	Quantity	Value
	£		£	£		£		£
1	5	120	600				120	600
2	6	180	1080				300	1680
3				5.6	80	448	220	1232
4				5.6	100	560	120	672
		300	1680		180	1008		

Note: The average unit price at week 2 is $\dfrac{£1680}{300}$ = £5.60 and would be recalculated after every further purchase.

It will be observed that when prices are rising the FIFO method tends to show a lower total material cost and a lower stock value than does the average cost method. The reverse tendency would obviously occur when prices are falling. If the last in first out, next in first out or replacement cost methods were used, costs would approximate to current prices, but the resulting stock values would need adjustment, for they would otherwise tend to diminish to nil value.

Once again, it is suggested, the problems of material costing would be largely simplified and rationalized by using standard costs. Assume that a standard price of £5.50 a unit had been established for the material, having regard to economical buying but no doubt reflecting any likely and unavoidable price rises in the year concerned. The price applied to each addition or withdrawal would then be £5.50, and the total figures would be:

Additions	£5.50 × 300	=	£1650
Less: Withdrawals	£5.50 × 180	=	990
Final stock			£660

The differences between the prices actually paid and the standard prices would have been extracted on receipt of suppliers' invoices. The differences (or 'variances') would be transferred to a costing variance account, as shown below:

Purchase price variances

| Week | Quantity | Actual | | Standard | | Variance | |
		Unit price	Amount	Unit price	Amount	Unit price	Amount
		£	£	£		£	£
1	120	5.0	600	5.5	660	0.5	60
2	180	6.0	1080	5.5	990	(0.5)	(90)
	300		1680		1650		(30)

Two general conclusions can be drawn: (1) that in a period when prices change, the material cost attributed to a job or product must be a convention – there is no such thing as the actual material cost of a job; and (2) managers need to understand the particular convention used in their business if they are to interpret the cost.

Other Direct Costs

Other costs directly chargeable to the jobs include bought-out parts and components, subcontractors' charges and various expenses.

The Overhead Rate

To the foregoing direct costs an overhead rate is added and this represents an apportionment of production or operating indirect costs. Methods of calculating this rate are discussed below. It should be appreciated that the overhead rate does not normally cover selling, marketing distribution, administrative or financial expenses. The possible exception is where goods or services are produced under contract to a customer's specification and the remuneration is based on total cost. When, therefore, considering whether the marketing of a product is a viable proposition at the price obtainable, an addition needs to be made to the manufacturing cost for applicable selling and any other expenses likely to be incurred.

Costs for Different Purposes

The foregoing sections of this chapter have been largely concerned with the routine costing system, which aims to produce what may be called a 'normal' cost of the products and valuation of stock. If sales of all the products exceed this cost, then a gross profit will be made by the business, but, as explained below, in certain circumstances sales at below this 'normal' cost could produce more profit. Many different ways of calculating cost are appropriate for particular purposes, e.g. for comparing the relative contribution made to overall profit by different lines of sales; for meeting competition; to aid pricing policy; and for make-or-buy-out decisions. It is essential to use what has been called the 'relevant cost' for the purposes in mind. In deciding what is the relevant cost to use it is first necessary to consider the various viewpoints or concepts of cost, as described below.

Direct and Indirect Costs

As explained earlier, direct costs are those which can be applied with reasonable precision and convenience to the output. The remaining costs in a factory or operating centre are indirect and charged to units of output by an overhead rate. These classifications apply specifically to the routine costing system.

Fixed and Variable Expenditure

Fixed expenditure is that which does not vary with activity (e.g. output or turnover) *in the short term*. Conversely, variable expenditure *does* so vary. Variable expenditure may be subdivided into (1) directly variable, and (2) semi-variable expenditure. This analysis applies not only to production or operating *costs*, but also to operating *expenses*, e.g. selling and administration. The purpose of dividing business expenditure in this way is to aid planning (especially forecasting), budgeting, decision-making, and control of performance.

Fixed costs or fixed operating expenses include depreciation, rent and rates of premises, and remuneration of supervisors, permanent staff and managers. Direct costs of labour and material are variable. This is, however, subject to the qualification that modern employment legislation and many agreements with trade unions are tending to make the remuneration of the workforce more of the nature of a commitment unrelated to temporary fluctuations in output. A proportion of indirect costs is usually considered variable, including indirect labour, indirect materials and power. Operating expenses also include many variable items, such as the commission and expenses of the salesforce, carriage, remuneration of temporary staff, stationery and telephone calls. The overall measure of activity which determines whether an expense is fixed or variable is usually turnover. For detailed control purposes, however, the activity might be represented, as appropriate, by numbers of personnel, sales calls, numbers of transactions, etc.

Fixed expenditure is not literally 'fixed'. It will increase with rises in costs and prices, and it will change as new facilities are installed or economies are made in existing facilities. In the long run all business expenditure must be limited by the sales income. What is the long or short run depends on the nature of the cost or expense. Thus depreciation will increase when a machine needs replacement at a higher cost; rent and rates will rise when further accommodation is obtained; the salary bill will become larger when it is necessary to employ more staff.

In spite of these qualifications, the division of expenditure into fixed and variable headings is an essential prerequisite to forecasting, followed by the setting up of budgets, as illustrated by the following very simplified example.

Assume that the present activity and the indirect costs of a production department were as in column A below. For next year activity was expected to increase by 20 per cent; directly variable costs would rise at the same rate; semi-variable costs are estimated to rise by 10 per cent; fixed costs would remain unaltered. Column B shows the forecasted costs for the following year.

	A *Current annual costs*	B *Forecast next year*
Activity (in man hours)	200 000	240 000
	£	£
Fixed costs	300 000	300 000
Semi-variable costs	200 000	220 000
Directly variable costs	500 000	600 000
	£1 000 000	£1 120 000

It will be observed that the overhead costs have risen by 11.2 per cent and the overheads per man hour have fallen from £5 to approximately £4.70. Column B could form the basis for next year's budgets, subject to such amendments of detail as may be necessary.

Marginal Costs

The marginal cost is theoretically the additional cost of producing one more unit. However, the additional cost of producing another unit is in practice impossible to ascertain; furthermore, marginal savings on reduced output are also important for management purposes. Therefore, it is more useful to consider marginal costs as the change in total outgoings which will result from a change in output. The latter definition is also known as 'differential cost' or, for additional outgoings, the 'incremental cost'.

Further confusion in terminology arises from the fact that the expressions 'marginal cost' and 'variable cost' are often used as though they are synonymous, but this is not really so. Suppose, for example, management is considering a substantial increase in the sales of a product. Then the additional turnover will be justified if marginal income exceeds marginal cost, even though the additional sales value is below routine costs (perhaps due to a reduction in price). In such a case the variable costs and expenses are largely marginal for most practical purposes. However, further assume that the increase in turnover involves the renting of additional stores premises, another sales car is purchased and another clerk engaged on the permanent staff. These expenses would not be treated as variable but they are marginal because they represent further outgoings due to the higher turnover. A proportion of the variable costs may not be marginal, such as when output could be raised without incurring additional labour cost or more indirect material.

It follows that the viability of the proposed increase in turnover depends on detailed assessment of the additional outgoings involved. This exercise may entail adjustments to existing variable costs and the inclusion of extra 'capital' expenditure and fixed costs.

The inclusion of capital expenditure raises a problem. If the salesman's car is assumed to have a life of five years and the assessment was made over that period, then the cost of the car less its estimated residual value would be a marginal cost and included in the calculation. If the project were considered to be short term, lasting for, say, a year, it would obviously be misleading to include the whole net cost of the car. Depreciation, it should be noted, is neither a variable nor a marginal cost. The solution is to treat the cost of the fixed asset as the original cost less its saleable value (whether it is to be sold or not) at the end of the period used for the assessment. An alternative, specially applicable where additional land and buildings are bought, is to substitute a fair rent for the premises in the form of an 'imputed' or 'opportunity cost' (see below).

In the ensuing pages it will be found that considerable emphasis is given to marginal costs in connection with forward planning and decision-making, particularly with regard to decisions on alternative courses of action. For these purposes the marginal or 'incremental' cost will be the relevant cost to use, and it will need separate assessment in relation to each management problem. It is therefore necessary to appreciate the real nature of the marginal cost, as the expression is used in this book.

In the first place it is essential to distinguish the marginal cost from the cost figures produced by the routine costing system. The prime objective of the routine costing system is to value work in progress and finished stock as part of the process of ascertaining the profit made or loss suffered by a business as a whole. The routine costing system produces a unit cost which is historical in nature and includes allocations and apportionments of 'sunk' costs and of expenditure which does not move in relation to turnover, at least in the short term. Routine costs are not, therefore, marginal in the sense of future outgoings.

The marginal or incremental cost, on the other hand, is an estimate of the future outgoings which are relevant to the problem under consideration. Future variable costs are accordingly marginal since, by definition, they move in relation to activity; so, as mentioned above, is the cost of additional resources acquired for the activity concerned. There is, moreover, a further type of cost which may be called 'quasi-marginal' and which needs to be brought into account in decision-making. This is the cost of existing resources which are to be applied to the project being considered, and which were hitherto idle or, possibly, will be diverted from other uses. These resources may include, for example, vacant space and under-utilized equipment or administrative facilities. The basis for treating existing resources as marginal is where their continuing cost would be otherwise eliminated, e.g. by letting vacant space, selling redundant equipment and reducing administrative expenditure.

Opportunity Cost and Imputed Cost

These are notional costs which are not reflected in any business costing system. Both terms refer to income which is forgone by taking one course of action in preference to another. Imputed cost is the interest forgone such as money lying idle in a bank current account, or the interest which could be earned if the business premises were sold. Opportunity cost refers more particularly to profit foregone, such as the selling of a quality product perhaps for policy reasons rather than a more profitable 'popular' version.

The assessment of imputed/opportunity costs is often of vital importance to general management and to marketing management. Many businesses have moved from premises in London for cheaper accommodation elsewhere, either obtaining interest on the surplus, i.e. the imputed cost of the London premises, or using it for profitable purposes. An opportunity cost is often involved in continuing to market traditional materials (e.g. natural fibres) whereas conversion to a more modern product (such as artificial fibre) would be more profitable.

Standard Costs

In the preceding pages frequent reference has been made to standard costs, and the nature and objectives of this approach to costing will now be more fully examined. The standard cost is what the cost should be for efficient operations and a reasonable utilization of capacity. Standard costs are applied to direct operations, i.e. in the manufacturing processes or where services are provided, but can with benefit also be applied to administrative functions.

The purposes of standard costing are to obtain a rational view of the cost of stock hence of cost of sales, to assist in the control of costs by comparing actual cost with the standards, to aid pricing policy, and to forecast and plan forward. It should be appreciated that standard costing represents a philosophy of costing and accounting quite different from the attempt to ascertain so-called 'actual costs', and to use the latter for valuations of stocks or for control and planning purposes.

Standards are initially established for each of the operations in the workshops, e.g. machinery, fitting, assembly, etc., and for this purpose work studies and time and motion studies can be used with advantage. The standards usually consist of efficient times and rates for each of the jobs. Standard material costs are also formulated, having regard to efficient buying, and are in terms of price and quantity required for each job.

The overhead rate applied to unit costs is also at standard and is derived from an assessment of the economic overheads required to service the direct operations, and a volume of output (or measure of activity) at reasonable utilization of capacity. Standard costs may take the form of labour costs per unit, machine hour rates, operating or production hour rates, as well as material costs per unit.

As a result the finished product, goods for sale and units of services provided will be valued at standard. With a standard costing system it is unnecessary also to collect 'actual costs' by units of output or product, thus saving considerable administrative expenses. For cost control the expenditure incurred is collected by sizeable production runs, or their equivalent where services (such as transport) are provided, and that expenditure is compared with the total standard costs for the output.

The differences between the standard costs of production and the actual money expended on the operations must, of course, be recorded in the accounts. These differences are called 'variances', and are basically in terms of price (or rate) differences and quantity (or volume) differences. For special control purposes these basic variances may be further analysed by such headings as waiting for work, material rejects, calendar variances (differences in calendar times), revision variances (where the standards are due for revision), and so forth. A report on variances for a particular manager should also indicate the extent to which they are controllable or uncontrollable by him.

Standard Cost Variance Analysis

The analysis of variances is specifically designed to assist managers in controlling performance and planning forward. It is therefore important that managers should understand the rules and conventions applied to the calculation of standard cost variances, and this particular section is devoted to that purpose. Whilst the methods outlined below are believed to be logical and realistic, it needs to be appreciated that some variants exist in practice, so that managers should make themselves aware of the methods applied in a particular business and, indeed, be prepared to question those methods, if necessary.

Accounting for the Variances

Because only the standard costs are applied to the output the differences between the standard and the actual costs must be charged or credited in the profit and loss account. These differences, or 'variances', should be written off monthly, and certainly in each accounting year. In the profit and loss account the gross profit is first shown at standard and then the variances are added or deducted, as in the following example:

Profit and Loss Account for the month . . .

	Current month £	Cumulative year to date £
SALES	50 000	300 000
Less: Cost of sales at standard	30 000	180 000
Gross PROFIT AT STANDARD	£20 000	£120 000
Less: Production variances:		
Labour	(1 000)	(5 000)
Material	50	(200)
Overheads	(5 000)	(20 000)
Total variances	£(5 950)	£(25 200)
GROSS PROFIT actual	£14 050	£94 800

So far as marketing planning is concerned the profitability of the sales is basically shown by the gross profit at standard. Nevertheless, it would be wise also to take into account those variances which are uncontrollable and due for revision, such as changes in material costs and wage rates which cannot be remedied by improving efficiency. The standards which are due for revision should be segregated in the more detailed variance analyses which are examined below. It is usually unwise to amend standards for uncontrollable variances except at yearly intervals, so that the accounts record a consistent valuation of stocks and cost of sales during each accounting year. Standards may also require revision for changes in (1) working methods, (2) make-or-buy-out policy, and (3) in available capacity, but they should not be revised merely because controllable variances occur. One of the great merits of standard costing is that it informs management of the inefficiencies which can be remedied.

At this point it may be desirable to mention that standard costing should not be confused with budgeting, although the two systems are associated. Budgets are forecasts of the total income and expenditure of a company, division, department or cost centre; standard costs refer to the costs per unit of output. At the same time the expense budgets should be based on the standard costs arising in each centre of operations.

Variance Calculations – Labour and Material

For labour and material costs there are always two major variances, the price and the quantity. In the case of labour costs the difference between the actual rate of pay and the assessed rate (i.e. the 'price' of labour) is conventionally multiplied by the actual hours worked, and is called a 'rate' variance. The difference between the actual hours worked and the standard hours is multiplied by the standard rate and is called an 'efficiency' variance. For materials the price variance is the difference between the actual and the standard price multiplied by the actual quantity, and this is best calculated when the invoice is received. The quantity of material used in the processes less the assessed standard quantity is called a 'usage' variance and is multiplied by the standard rate, being accounted for when the material is drawn from stores. Somewhat different considerations apply to overhead variances, as explained below. Specimen calculations are shown in the following example.

Example

Actual and standard cost comparison

Batch No. . . .

	Actual £	Standard £	Variances £
Labour:			
Hours	520	500	(20)
Rate	4.50	4.00	(0.50)
Values	2 340	2 000	(340)
Material:			
Quantity in kilos	110	100	(10)
Price	1.80	2.00	0.20
Values	198	200	2

Analysis of variances:		
Labour:		£
Rate:	£0.50 × 520	(260)
Efficiency:	£4.00 × 20	(80)
Total		£(340)
Material:		£
Price: £0.20 × 110		22
Usage: £2.00 × 10		(20)
Total		£2

Variance Calculation – Overheads

General Considerations

As mentioned earlier, the term 'overheads' tends to be ambiguous. It is variously applied to the indirect costs of manufacturing (or other centre providing goods or services) and to the expenses which are charged below gross profit in the profit and loss account, such as the distribution, selling and administrative expenses. In the present context the term is confined to the indirect costs of production.

A basic, but unsatisfactory, method of showing a production overhead variance is simply to deduct the total budgeted overheads from the actual expenditure, or vice versa, showing an overspending or underspending compared with the budget, as in the following example:

	£
Actual production overheads	1 225 000
Budget	1 000 000
Overspending	£225 000

The next exercise is to ascertain the extent to which the overheads have been 'recovered', as it is termed, by being applied to unit costs through the overhead rate. With a budgeted output of, say, 200 000 hours, the overhead rate on a budgeted expenditure of £1 000 000 would be £5 an hour. Assume actual *standard* hours generated were 250 000, the over-recovery would be:

	£
Charged to unit costs:	
250 000 hours at £5	1 250 000
Actual overheads	1 225 000
Over-recovery	£25 000

These simplistic calculations conceal, however, a number of facts of significance to management. The production overheads will include those which can be expected to move in more or less direct relation to the output, that is the variable element such as indirect labour and indirect material, power, etc., and those which are 'fixed', e.g. depreciation, premises expense, rentals and supervision, and do not change with the volume of output, except in the long term. The division of the overheads into the two categories of fixed and variable is bound to involve some arbitrary decisions, but the outcome can, as shown below, produce some useful indicators for planning and control.

Assume that the total actual and budgeted overheads are divided into their fixed and variable elements, as follows:

	Budget	*Actual*	*Variance*
	£	£	£
Fixed	300 000	325 000	(25 000)
Variable	700 000	900 000	(200 000)
Totals	£1 000 000	£1 225 000	£(225 000)
Output in standard man hours	200 000	250 000	

Since the fixed overheads should not have changed in relation to the increased output, the variance of £25 000 represents excess expenditure – an 'expenditure variance' – which needs to be traced to the items of expense which have caused the increase. Some increases in cost are bound to be found uncontrollable and should be shown as such in the further analysis.

The budget variance of £200 000 for the variable overheads is composed of two elements: one, the excess over the budget which could naturally be expected from the 25 per cent rise in output above the budgeted level, and, secondly, excess spending. The budget variances are:

	£
Volume variance: 25% of £700 000	175 000
Expenditure variance, the balance of	25 000
Total	£200 000

The fact of a volume variance occurring is not an adverse sign, except that it will affect requirements of finance. The expenditure variance again needs tracing to its sources but for this purpose the individual items will need grossing up by 25 per cent. Where a flexible budgeting system is operated the variable overhead budget would be amended in relation to the increased level of output to 1.25 × £700 000 = £875 000.

Costing Implications

The effect of the above figures on the costing system is now considered, because the overhead rate applied to units of stock, and hence to cost of sales, affects the profit shown in the accounts. A more comprehensive statement of the under-recovery of £25 000 (see page 60) is obtained by calculating separate overhead rates for fixed and variable overheads, thus:

Fixed overhead rate: $\dfrac{£300\ 000}{200\ 000}$ hours = £1.50 an hour

Variable overhead rate: $\dfrac{£700\ 000}{200\ 000}$ hours = £3.50 an hour

The application of these rates to the output produces the following accounting entries:

	Charged to stock £	Actual expenditure £	Costing variances Expenditure £	Volume £
Fixed overheads:				
250 000 × £1.50	375 000	325 000	(25 000)	75 000
Variable overheads:				
250 000 × £3.50	875 000	900 000	(25 000)	—
Totals	£1 250 000	£1 225 000	£(50 000)	£75 000

The variances which appear in the accounts, as distinct from the budget variances, represent the differences between the amounts charged to unit costs and hence stock through the overhead rate, and the actual expenditure. For the fixed overheads there is now a volume variance which consists of the increase in the actual output over the budgeted output multiplied by the overhead rate, i.e. 250 000 hours – 200 000 hours × £1.50 = £75 000. It should be observed that this error in estimating the output has inflated unit costs and as a consequence stock and cost of sales, and thus reduced profit. As events turned out the true fixed overhead rate was £300 000/250 000 hours = £1.20 an hour, and this rate applied to the output would have charged stock with only £300 000.

This irrational result is likely to confuse marketing management as regards unit costs and the profitability of sales. Although the error of 25 per cent in estimating output may appear large, it could happen where, for instance, an unexpected surge in demand occurred. There are two ways by which the situation could have been avoided. The first and most acceptable approach is to base the overhead rate, not on the estimated output, but on the capacity of the plant, the latter being a more or less fixed quantity. Another alternative, rarely applied and generally frowned on by the accounting profession, is to charge to unit costs only variable overheads. By the latter method the profit and loss account first shows a surplus (usually called the 'contribution') after deducting variable expenditure from sales, and the fixed overheads are then written off in their entirety together with operating expenses. This method is particularly useful for short-term purposes and for comparing the relative profitability of the different sales lines. It may, however, impair the validity of the unit costs for long-term purposes, especially where production involves heavy fixed costs, such as in an automated plant.

It will be observed that no volume variance is shown in the accounts for variable overheads because they were expected to increase in relation to output. The charge to unit costs is accurate because if it had been possible to predict the output of 250 000 hours the overhead rate, after eliminating the expenditure variance, would have been the same as that applied, i.e. £875 000/250 000 hours = £3.50.

Efficiency Variances

In companies which do not operate a standard costing system the overhead rate is charged on the actual man hours worked (or other measure of output) thus inflating unit costs by the overhead cost of inefficiency. Where standard costing applies the overhead rate is charged on the standard hours and the cost in overheads of the excessive time can be segregated as an 'efficiency' variance. Assuming in the above example the actual time taken was 260 000 hours compared with a standard time of 250 000 for the output produced, then a variable overhead efficiency variance of 10 000 hours at £3.50 = £35 000 would arise.

The variable overhead variances derived from the costing system may now be explained as follows:

	£
For the 260 000 hours actually worked the expected spending on variable overheads would be: 260 000 × £3.50 =	910 000

	£
This amount was, however, inflated by the cost of inefficient working of 10 000 hours at £3.50 =	35 000
Leaving allowable overheads based on standard hours of: 250 000 hours × £3.50 =	875 000
Actual expenditure was:	900 000
Giving an expenditure variance of:	£25 000

No efficiency variance arises for the fixed overheads because they are not affected by the time spent on the work.

Capacity Variance

The volume variance and the capacity variance for fixed overheads are synonymous terms where the volume on which the overhead rate is based represents a practical attainable level of capacity working, as it should be in normal circumstances. In some situations, however, a severe and long-term recession in sales turnover may be expected, and there is no hope of the plant working at the level of capacity for which it was set up. At the same time the major part of the fixed overheads represent the cost of facilities, particularly the expense of premises and depreciation of machinery designed for capacity working. This situation has occurred in shipbuilding and armament manufacture.

In these situations the fixed overhead rate is often based on the output expected rather than the output at capacity. That method has practical justification where the plant is working on government contracts for which the remuneration is based essentially on actual costs. For commercial contracts in a competitive environment, however, the practice would inflate unit costs and tend to result in excessive price quotations.

If the capacity of the plant in the above example were 300 000 hours, the fixed overhead rate based on that output would have been £300 000/300 000 hours = £1.00 an hour instead of the rate applied of £1.50 an hour.

	£
The amount in fact charged to the unit costs, using an overhead rate of £1.50 an hour, was:	375 000
The amount which should have been charged to the output of 250 000 hours at £1 an hour was:	250 000
Giving an excess charge of:	125 000
The amount already accounted for as a volume variance was:	75 000
So that the true capacity variance was £1(300 000 − 250 000) =	£50 000

Conclusions for Marketing Management

Variance calculations have been examined above at some length because it is important that marketing managers be able to interpret – and maybe to question – the information presented to them by the accounting service. In particular, the manner in which unit costs and hence profit are calculated is of obvious significance in the formulation of marketing policy and strategy.

Because considerable variations in the treatment of the figures are applied in different businesses, it is essential that managers understand the methods used in their own companies and, where possible, in those companies with which they negotiate.

What are the main reasons why marketing managers should be concerned with costs and standard cost variances?

1. *To assess the profitability of existing and potential sales.* For this purpose the standard costs should be used, for they are presumed to have eliminated variances due to some form of inefficiency or inadequate output. Nevertheless, uncontrollable variances should be taken into account as they will eventually be incorporated into the standards at the revision periods. The validity of the overhead rate needs special consideration because it would inflate unit costs where as it could be reduced by improving efficiency or increasing turnover.

2. *To establish or amend pricing policy.* Although product costs are unlikely to decide prices which are necessarily market based, they are relevant in deciding whether new products should be launched and whether existing lines are worth further exploitation or, perhaps, discontinuing. In this context the standard marginal cost is usually appropriate, especially for short-term purposes.

3. *To consider the comparative profitability of the sales mix.* This exercise, which is considered in more detail in Chapter 17, involves studies of the likely related movements in price, turnover and cost, the relevant costs again usually being standard marginal costs. But where, in the long term, fixed overheads can be precisely attributed to a class of sales, then the volume of turnover will affect the 'spread' of these costs and thus the profit. For this purpose the existence of a capacity or volume variance will be significant.

PART TWO

Financial Analysis for Planning

5 BUDGETING AND RESPONSIBILITY ACCOUNTING

Objectives and Scope of This Chapter

The purpose of this chapter is to provide a general overview of budgeting control and responsibility accounting. It is desirable to consider the broad objectives and scope of the subject before proceeding to the more detailed aspects as analysed in subsequent chapters.

The previous chapters have been mainly concerned with the historical recording and analysis of business transactions. But accounting as a management tool is also forward-looking – as it must be, for an important function of management is to plan for the future. Thus the forward plans of each division and department, when resolved and co-ordinated, are expressed as financial budgets by the accounting service, and the actual performance is compared with the budgets at frequent intervals, usually monthly. The historical records will inevitably have an influence on the preparation of the budgets, if only to indicate the past inefficiencies and planning errors which need to be remedied.

The divisional and departmental budgets are ultimately consolidated into a master budget, which represents the overall company or group plan for the future period. The master budget essentially corresponds with the four main historical accounting statements, i.e. manufacturing or operating account, trading and profit and loss account, balance sheet and cash forecast. These projections should be prepared (1) for the short term, normally for the next twelve months, and (2) for the long term, which may extend for five or even twenty years ahead. The long-term plans should be formulated first, since they will influence the nature of the short-term budgets. Nevertheless, the long-term projections, even though they will be on broad lines, will need amendment year by year in the light of changing circumstances, including new marketing opportunities, changes in technology, government intervention and management intentions.

The preparation of the budgets should follow logical stages:

1. The first step should be a general review of the current marketing opportunities in the field in which the business operates. A detailed investigation of these markets should be initiated but the eventual sales forecast cannot be drawn up without knowledge of the resources available for its implementation.
2. The resources available for exploiting the market should then be appraised. The resources include premises and plant, management and personnel capability, and the finance which is or can be made available. A statement of the existing marketing and selling resources will be of special significance.

3. From the statement of resources various limiting factors or constraints will become evident and should be noted. Limitations on turnover will be imposed by selling and production or buying capacity. In particular, the level of activity will be limited by the available space, the potential of the plant, the key materials which are obtainable, and the manpower which can be engaged or retained. The overall constraint will be the finance which can be raised.

4. A private enterprise must satisfy the shareholders, for the sale of their shares can cause financial difficulties, and ultimately they have the power to bring the business to an end. There is, moreover, increasing pressure for a profit motive to be applied to public bodies and organizations. Thus the next stage is the assessment of the minimum profit target as a return on capital. The profit target should be sufficient to provide, after allowance for taxation, adequate dividends and allocations to reserves.

5. The directors should now be in a position to state their specific objectives (obviously the main objectives of the business will have been set out when it was set up, but they may have been amended subsequently). The objectives will depend on such factors as the comparative situation of the company in the market and the prevailing economic circumstances – even, perhaps, on the ambitions of the dominant personality. Objectives may include, for instance, plans for expanding outlets at home or abroad, developing new brands, expanding sources of supply and for diversification. A programme of takeover bids may be contemplated for these purposes. On the other hand, the objectives may be to rationalize turnover, reduce costs and improve efficiency.

6. The next logical step is the preparation of a preliminary sales forecast. This will be based on an appraisal of the potential market, and the likely share of the market obtainable by the organization in the products or the services to be sold. The sales forecast will necessarily have regard to the existing resources and those which can be made available, to the constraints, the profit required and the company objectives. No doubt many amendments will have to be made to the original forecast before it is finalized into a definite budget for both long and short terms. Once the sales budget is finalized it will determine the budgets of the other activities of the business, e.g. production, purchasing, administration and finance.

7. The final exercise will be to draw up the overall company budgets, showing projections of the profit and loss, financial position and cash flow. The preliminary projections may indicate that the departmental plans are not viable and have to be reassessed. This situation may, in particular, emerge from a cash forecast which shows that the existing plans cannot be financed.

The Profit Target

As mentioned above, at an early stage in the forward planning process the directors should establish a profit target. This will provide an overriding incentive for the managers to apply the resources of the business most effectively. For the purpose of establishing the profit target the logical first step is to calculate the minimum profit which a company must achieve simply for survival in the long term. The profit target finally established must be higher than the minimum, since every business is subject to risk. The final profit target will depend, not only on the risks inherent in the business, but also on more-or-less subjective factors, such as the directors' appraisal of future trading conditions, the need to retain shareholders' goodwill and the support of the stock market, a desire to present a demanding target to the managers, and so forth.

The minimum profit is a basic return on the capital employed. This is theoretically the rate of interest which could be obtained on that capital if it were invested elsewhere with equal risk. For practical purposes it is convenient to use the yield obtainable on a virtually riskless security, such as a long-dated government stock. It is therefore, in effect, a 'cost of doing business', although not recognized as such in the accounts.

Assume the capital employed is £4 500 000 (as in the balance sheet of X Company shown in Chapter 3) and a riskless rate of interest is 10 per cent, then the minimum profit required is £450 000 a year. Where, because of variable trading conditions, the profits of a company tend to fluctuate, the minimum profit might have to be considered as a long-term requirement, i.e. 5 × £450 000 = £2 250 000 over five years. For the purposes of the calculation 'profit' is pre-tax profit, and 'capital employed' is shareholders' interest (issued share capital and reserves) plus loan capital. The pre-tax profit is after accounting for interest payable on loan capital.

Simplified statements, as in the preceding paragraph, usually need qualification, especially when dealing with accounting data. For instance, the capital employed derived from most company balance sheets is stated at original cost, and needs to be converted to current money values, as far as it is possible to do so. This particularly applies to land and buildings and the cost of investments in items such as brand names and associated companies, the revaluation of other assets being subject to many complexities. In the balance sheet of X Company land and buildings appeared at a depreciated cost of £1 500 000. Assume these assets were acquired many years ago and their current value was assessed at £2 500 000. Then the capital employed in the company, as a basis for calculating the minimum profit, becomes £4 500 000 + £1 000 000 = £5 500 000; the minimum profit becomes 10 per cent × £5 500 000 = £550 000.

In determining the final profit target the actual rate of interest payable on fixed interest capital needs to be taken into account. Consider the following specimen figures:

	£
Capital employed:	
Shareholders' interests	3 500 000
Addition for revaluations	1 000 000
	4 500 000
Loan capital	1 000 000
	£5 500 000
Minimum profit at 10%	£550 000
Actual interest on loan capital at 15%	150 000
Included in minimum profit at 10%	100 000
Additional profit required above the minimum	£50 000

If the actual rate of interest payable on loan capital was below the minimum profit rate the difference in rates should be ignored – the company is borrowing cheaply.

The 'Contribution' Approach to Profit Planning

As a broad guide to the profit attainable by a company it is helpful to calculate the contribution to profit likely to arise at different levels of sales turnover. For this purpose all costs and expenses have to be segregated into their fixed and variable elements, the latter being those generally variable in relation to sales.

The 'contribution' is the likely amount obtained by deducting variable expenditure from sales, and is the balance available for meeting fixed costs and profit. The simple formula for the purpose is: $S - VC = FC + P$, where S is sales, VC is variable cost, FC is fixed cost, and P is profit.

Assume that the present trading results of a business are represented by the following figures:

Sales in units	1m
Price per unit	£5
	£000
Sales value	5000
Variable cost at £2 per unit	2000
Contribution	3000
Fixed costs	2500
Profit	£500

The assumptions are that price and variable costs will remain at the same rate per unit, and that fixed costs will remain the same in amount whatever the volume of turnover.

Given these assumptions (which will need qualification in practice) the formula can be used to estimate the profit from an expected increase in turnover. Assume the forecast turnover is, say, 1 400 000 units. In thousands of £s:

$$£7000 - 2 \times 1400 = 2500 + P$$
$$P = 4200 - 2500 = £1700$$

Or:

Sales in units	1 400 000
Price per unit	£5
	£000
Sales value	7000
Variable cost at £2 per unit	2800
Contribution	4200
Fixed costs	2500
	£1700

If the company is approaching a recession in its trade, it will be useful to assess the level of sales required to break even. The breakeven level of sales is usually taken to indicate the turnover at which there will be neither profit nor loss.

Following the argument in the preceding section it is more realistic to accept a breakeven level as the achievement of the minimum profit (i.e. basic interest on capital employed). Assume the minimum profit is £200 000. Using the above formula, where x represents the volume of turnover:

$$5x - 2x = 2500 + 200$$
$$3x = 2700$$
$$x = 900$$

Or sales at breakeven point are therefore 900 000 units:

Sales in units	900 000
Price per unit	£5
	£000
Sales value	4500
Variable costs at £2 per unit	1800
Contribution	2700
Fixed costs	2500
Profit	£200

Qualifications to these basic calculations could include a situation where an increase in turnover was only achievable by a reduction in price, or where the rate of variable cost also falls but the further facilities required involve an increase in fixed costs. Assume these changes apply to the additional, i.e. the marginal, sales. The profit issuing from those sales, added to the profit from the existing turnover, is as follows:

	Existing situation	*Additional sales*	*Total*
Sales in units	1 000 000	400 000	1 400 000
Price per unit	£5	£4	
	£000	*£000*	*£000*
Sales value	5000	1600	6600
Variable cost:			
Rate	2	1.80	
Amount	2000	720	2720
Contribution	3000	880	3880
Fixed costs	2500	50	2550
Profit	£500	£830	£1330

Charting the Figures

This method of depicting the existing and forecast future trading situation may have more impact if presented in the form of a breakeven chart or a profit graph. A

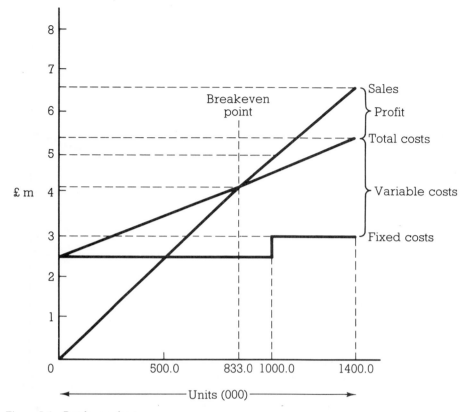

Figure 5.1 Breakeven chart.

breakeven chart based on the previous figures is shown in Fig. 5.1. The profit graph Fig. 5.2 depicts the same figures in a different format.

Figure 5.1 is drawn up on the basis of the figures in the preceding section, showing the effect on profit when sales are increased from £5m to £6.6m. It will be seen that when sales were £5m the business was perilously near the breakeven point. The increased sales had to be made at a reduced price and caused a rise in fixed costs, although the rate of variable costs showed a small reduction. As a result profit rose dramatically from £500 000 to £1 330 000. It would be dangerous to assume, without detailed calculations, that profit would continue to rise in proportion to any further increase in turnover, i.e. by extending the lines of sales and total costs. A business tends to reach an optimum size when diseconomies of scale appear. These diseconomies might include overtime working and substantial increases in fixed costs. The need for more plant and new premises would entail further capital with a consequent rise in the minimum profit required.

The profit graphs depict the same situation in a somewhat different form and highlights the profit or loss from different levels of turnover. In Fig. 5.1 the turnover is in terms of sales value and in Fig. 5.2 by units of sales. It will be appreciated that in a business selling a variety of dissimilar products it will be impossible to express turnover in units except, possibly, in production hours, where applicable.

The breakeven point of sales in Figs 5.1 and 5.2 may be obtained by measurement

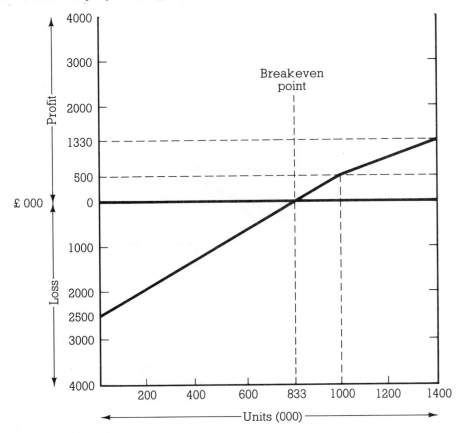

Figure 5.2   Profit graph.

or, more precisely, by the calculations shown below (note that the contribution is sales minus variable costs and at breakeven level is equal to the fixed costs).

1. *By Units*

The rates per unit are: sales £5 and variable costs £2, giving a contribution of £3 a unit. With an amount of contribution equal to the fixed costs, i.e. £2 500 000 the units sold at breakeven point are therefore 2 500 000/3 = 833 000 approximately.

2. *By Value*

The contribution is $\frac{3}{5}$ of sales and at breakeven point this equals the fixed costs of £2 500 000. Therefore:

$$\frac{3}{5} \text{ of sales } = £2\ 500\ 000$$

$$\text{Sales } = \frac{5}{3} \times £2\ 500\ 000$$

$$= £4\ 167\ 000 \text{ approximately.}$$

Note: £4 167 000 = £5 × 833 000 approximately.

These charts are necessarily simplistic, but they do show how profit can rise dramatically with additional sales, that is after fixed costs of the undertaking have been covered. It would, however, be unrealistic to extend the lines (exponentially) for, as indicated above, marginal sales usually cause changes in price, variable costs and fixed costs. The charts provide generalized pictures of the past, which can be a *guide* to the future. Nevertheless, forward planning for all but the simplest of organizations necessitates detailed appraisal of potential markets, resources required and likely movements in cost and expense.

The Allowable Cost Approach

In a situation where little can be done about increasing sales, or redirecting the marketing to more profitable outlets, effort has to be directed to cost reduction. Given that the fixed costs of the organization are largely uncontrollable, at least in the short term, then it becomes a question of establishing the level of variable costs which the business can afford. In elemental form the calculation is indicated by the following illustration:

	£000	£000
Forecast sales		5000
Less: Profit target	500	
Fixed costs	2500	
		3000
Allowable variable costs		£2000

With this approach it is necessary to ensure as far as possible that the sum of the variable costs of each division and department does not exceed the allowable costs calculated as above. Clearly this can be only an approximate guide, but could form the basis for the cost budgets to be approved for each section of the business. Where standards have been established for the direct costs of the goods or services for sale, these will in effect represent allowable costs. The total standard costs for the output required to sustain the budgeted sales can therefore be deducted from the total of allowable variable costs. The resulting figure will then represent the total allowable overheads of all departments. Following the above hypothetical figures:

	£000
Allowable variable costs	2000
Less: Direct costs at standard	1200
Allowable total overheads	£800

The final problem of allocating the allowable company overheads to each section will obviously involve detailed consideration of departmental requirements and, no doubt, considerable argument.

Formulating Departmental Budgets

The foregoing sections have dealt with the guidelines to setting up targets for a company or division as a whole. The fulfilment of the overall forward plan will, however, depend on the actions of the managers of the various departments. To provide them with incentives, and standards against which their performance can be compared, departmental budgets are prepared.

Budgets for the principal activities of the business will be first formulated in relation to the objectives and policies of the board of directors and the overall company targets as indicated above.

In this sense the principal activities mean, as a generalization, sales, production or operations and procurement of direct materials. Obvious modifications to this generalization occur in service industries such as extractive industries, transport, construction, repair and maintenance, financial and professional services. Usually the sales forecast dictates the scope of the other activities, but the need to sell the capacity will dominate the budgets where it is under-utilized.

Once the main budgets have been co-ordinated, the departmental cost and expense budgets can be formulated in relation to the relevant activity. Thus the selling expenses will be related to the volume of sales, the production costs and overheads to the output, the buying department's expense to the volume of orders to be placed. The budgets of the administrative departments should also be related to the main activities or some derivative of them; for example, the canteen cost, wages and salaries, and personnel department expenses logically depend on the numbers of employees; the costing expense should in many cases vary with some measure of output, such as man hours or machine hours. General services, including, for instance, accounting, the typing pool and security, are probably best related to sales or output.

It is usually considered psychologically most effective if the original forecasts of departmental expenses are formulated from below; that is, by the departmental managers themselves. Their budgets should consist only of expenditure within their control, generally variable expenditure. Arbitrary apportionments of expenditure from one department to another are useless and confusing for budgetary purposes: the machine shop supervisor cannot, for example, control the costs incurred by the tool room in supplying him with tools. It may well be necessary, however, for the managers to be required to review their forecasts where the total of the departmental expenses exceeds the allowable total for the company, as described on p. 73 above, or where they do not relate to the appropriate measure of activity. Indeed the whole of the preliminary forecasts may need adjustment when they have been amalgamated and a resulting cash forecast indicates that the proposed activities cannot be financed.

Capital Expenditure Budgets

In addition to budgeting for what may be called 'controllable revenue expenses', departmental managers should also be required to forecast the cost of the additional or replacement fixed assets they require. These would include vehicles for the sales-force and distribution services, machinery for production and equipment in other areas. Methods of appraising capital expenditure are examined in Chapter 8 and these appraisals should be made before the expenditure is included in departmental budgets.

The departmental budgets will be consolidated into a company or divisional capital budget. The company capital budget will include expenditure outside departmental control, but authorized and initiated directly by the board, such as new premises and thoroughgoing modernization of plant. The overall capital expenditure budget will affect the projected balance sheet, the depreciation provision and the cash forecast. The need to provide funds for capital expenditure demands careful consideration of the proposals by top management, and stringent control of the actual expenditure.

Responsibility Accounting

The preparation of budgets is in itself a healthy exercise for departmental and divisional managers. It requires that they analyse the efficiency of their separate functions and that they make the necessary arrangements to implement company plans and policies. However, much of the effectiveness of the budgetary control system depends upon comparisons of actual results with the budgets at regular intervals, usually monthly. In order that these comparisons are made it is necessary that the income and expenditure of the business is attributed to the managers responsible, essentially to departments and, where desirable, cost centres within departments. This involves an analysis of the accounting entries additional to the traditional analyses by expense headings and the further analysis by unit costs. A computer program can cope with this analysis without much difficulty on the basis of departmental references inserted on original documents.

In organizing a system of responsibility accounting it is essential that managers are not charged with expenditure outside their control. For this reason apportionments of expenditure from one department to another are quite inapplicable for budgeting purposes. For other purposes it may be desirable to ascertain the total cost of, say, operating a sales department, and this cost may well include apportionments of outgoings on distribution, payroll preparation, security and the canteen, but this is a different exercise from recording the expenditure under the sales manager's control.

A manager is responsible not only for preparing budgets of his or her controllable income and expenditure, but also for ensuring that the actual results conform to the budgets, so far as it is possible to do so. He or she is responsible for explaining differences between the actual and budgeted results, and can expect to receive analyses of these differences (or 'variances') from the financial department, as described later. Variances can – and often do – arise from circumstances outside a manager's control. For instance, an unexpected surge in turnover may cause unbudgeted increases in the cost of buying, production and administrative services. It then becomes a question of justifying the budget variance and, in due course, revising the budget. In many situations the ultimate responsibility for a budget variance lies with the management team.

Accounting for Divisions

This section refers to more or less self-operating divisions of a company or company group, controlled by a divisional manager who is responsible to the headquarters or group board of directors. A division may be itself a limited company, or may be unincorporated, but it will operate as a separate trading unit, subject to head-quarters' direction and control.

Two forms of divisionalization exist. One may be described as 'functional divisionalization', where divisions are created to carry out the major functions of production, research and development, selling and, in some cases, purchasing. In this situation the production division sells product to the sales division and may be authorized also to make sales outside the group. Likewise, the sales division may be given the right to buy product from outside suppliers. The other, and probably more popular form of divisionalization is where separate divisions are set up to deal with distinct brands or lines of sales or services. The latter form of division, in particular, will normally have its own production, buying and administrative departments. However, it may be expedient and economic to concentrate certain services, such as data processing, accounting and possibly buying, in headquarters, charging the divisions with an appropriate share of these facilities.

The merits of divisionalization include the segregation of responsibilities and the rationalization of the organization, especially in a large and diverse undertaking. Much of these advantages could, however, be achieved without setting up more or less independent divisions. The main benefit derived from the divisionalization of a company or company group is that it provides a profit motive for the divisional managers.

The divisional profit or loss arises from the sales made to other divisions of the company or outside the group. For this purpose it is necessary to determine prices for interdivisional transactions. The price may be based on a percentage mark-up on costs. The costs are, in this case, preferably standard costs, so that the variances due to inefficiency are borne by the division providing the products or services; normally no mark-up is charged on services from headquarters. Alternatively, the price may be negotiated between the two divisions concerned, but this method frequently gives rise to conflict, and may result in the buying division deciding to obtain the goods or services outside the group, with consequent loss of capacity utilization for the supplying division. Ideally the price is that current in the market, but where this is not possible to ascertain one of the other methods may have to be used. The element of profit included in the transfer price has to be eliminated for the purpose of the overall group accounts, which must record only sales and costs arising from transactions with external parties.

With a view to providing incentives to divisional managers, a profit target should be established for each division. Basically the profit target for a division should be calculated as a required percentage on its capital employed, in the manner outlined on page 68 above. First, a calculation should be made of the minimum profit, representing basic interest on the capital, or the higher cost of capital, to the controlling company. The amount (not the percentage) of profit achieved above this minimum, called 'residual income', will be a measure of the division's success. It is said to be a mistake to impose on a division a profit target exceeding the cost of capital to the parent company, in case the division rejects sales which yield less than the rate of profit required.

The percentage profit on capital employed depends on the turnover rate and the profitability of the sales. If capital employed is £5m and the turnover is £12.5m the turnover rate, i.e. the number of times capital is turned over in sales, is $12.5/5 = 2.5$.

A profit of £0.5m would represent 4 per cent on sales but $4 \times 2.5 = 10$ per cent on capital employed. Limits may be imposed on divisional management as to the price which can be charged for the division's products or services, but they can increase the amount of profit by improving the turnover rate.

Considerable academic argument has arisen from the idea of residual income. In practical terms, however, it is suggested that a divisional profit target will act as an incentive if it arises from the division's forward plans, which are subject to approval by top management of the group.

The division will prepare budgets of its income and expenditure as though it were an entirely separate organization. In the periodical comparison between actual and budgeted results it will be necessary to segregate expenditure controllable by the divisional manager from that over which he or she has no control (generally the headquarters charge for services to the division). In this way a figure of 'controllable profit' is shown, as in the following simplified form of account:

ABC DIVISION

Actual and budget comparison for month . . .

	Current month		Cumulative financial year to date	
	Actual	*Budget*	*Actual*	*Budget*
	£000	*£000*	*£000*	*£000*
SALES				
Less: Cost of sales	___	___	___	___
GROSS PROFIT				
Less: Controllable expenses	___	___	___	___
CONTROLLABLE PROFIT				
Less: Non-controllable expenses	___	___	___	___
FINAL PROFIT	£	£	£	£

For budgetary control purposes the profit target for the divisional manager will be the controllable profit. The final profit target should therefore include an allowance for non-controllable expenses. It is desirable, furthermore, that the headquarters charge (which is a non-controllable expense) should be fixed for each financial year in advance, any difference in fact being borne by headquarters.

The Master Budgets

When budgets have been finalized and approved for all the activities of the business, preliminary master budgets for the company as a whole are constructed. The master budgets consist of a projected manufacturing (or operating) account, profit and loss account, cash forecast and balance sheet, normally prepared in that sequence. It is possible that the position shown by the preliminary projections may be considered unsatisfactory by top management and revisions to departmental budgets may be required. Thus, the projected profit and loss account might arrive at an inadequate profit; the balance sheet might show an unsatisfactory financial position, e.g. lack of liquidity, too high gearing, etc.; or the cash forecast might predict an unacceptable cash deficiency.

In preparing these 'forward accounts' the double-entry principle must be followed as for historical accounts. The following examples show how the main forecasts are entered in the statements:

Sales	To profit and loss account
Add: debtors at beginning	From balance sheet at beginning
Less: Debtors at end	To balance sheet
Equals: Cash received	To cash forecast
Direct material purchases	To manufacturing account
Add: Creditors at beginning	From opening balance sheet
Less: Creditors at end	To balance sheet
Equals: Cash paid	To cash forecast
Closing stock	Deduct in manufacturing account and enter in balance sheet
Wages and salaries	To manufacturing or profit and loss account and cash forecast
Overheads and operating expenses	To manufacturing or profit and loss account and (subject to creditors) to cash forecast
Capital expenditure	To balance sheet and cash forecast

The projected manufacturing (or operating) account; profit and loss account and balance sheet take the same form as shown previously for the historical accounts (see Chapters 2 and 3).

The cash forecast should be drawn up showing monthly projections for 3–6 months, thereafter quarterly to the year's end, and thence for annual intervals. The principal elements of the forecast are as shown below:

CASH FORECAST

Period . . .

£000

Receipts:
  From trade debtors
  Additional capital
  Other receipts, including
    interest, royalties,
    sale of assets, etc.

Total receipts

£000

Less: Payments:
   To trade creditors
   Other creditors
   Wages and salaries
   Overheads and expenses
   Taxation
   Fixed assets
   Repayment of capital
   Dividends
                         —————

Total payments
                         —————

Change in cash at bank and in hand
   At beginning of period
   Addition/reduction
                         —————

At end of period   £ ———

The actual cash receipts, payments and balance is compared with the forecast each month, major differences being investigated and explained. Because forecasting of business transactions is an inexact science, particularly so far as cash flow is concerned, the forecast will need revising monthly and extending for a further 12 months. Longer-term projections need revising at least annually and extending for a further year.

The cash forecast is a vital document in forward planning because if it shows that a cash deficiency is likely to occur, arrangements have to be made well in advance to provide the funds required, or perhaps the forward plans will have to be revised. If the cash forecast predicts a substantial surplus, then plans should be considered for investing the available funds so as to gain interest. Methods of controlling liquidity and obtaining further finance are described in Chapter 7.

6 ECONOMIC STOCKHOLDING

The Importance of Stock Control

In many businesses a large proportion of the capital is invested in stock or 'inventories', and interest or profit is foregone on the investment until it is converted into cash through sales. In this chapter the word 'stock' is a general term used to cover raw materials, bought-out components, work in progress, finished product and goods for resale. In addition to interest foregone, stock holding incurs costs of clerical labour, insurance, storekeeping and deterioration; also, the space occupied by stock could be otherwise used for profit-making purposes.

Nevertheless, a trading concern must maintain a certain level of stock. In a manufacturing business stocks of materials and parts are essential for maintaining the production flow. Stocks of finished product and goods for resale have to be available for immediate or, at least, prompt delivery to customers; this is obviously of vital importance in retailing. The problem is therefore to calculate the optimum level of stocks which will balance the cost of stockholding against the loss of sales income arising from inadequate stocks.

Main Indicators from the Accounts

A broad indicator as to whether total stocks are high or low may be obtained by calculating the number of days or months which will elapse before the stocks are sold. Thus if the overall value of the stocks is, say, £200 000 at the end of a period, and the budgeted *cost* of sales is £40 000 a month, the stocks represent five months' sales. Whether the figure of five months' sales is high or low depends on the nature of the business, particularly the normal time involved in the production runs (because total stocks include materials and work in progress). Five months' stocks of goods would certainly be high for a retail store. This overall indicator should be monitored month by month and a rising trend should give rise to more detailed investigations.

The investigators need to consider separately the different categories of stock. A general measure of the production stocks of raw materials and work in progress could be their relationship to the planned output for future periods. The planned output could be expressed for the purpose as cost, or some key factor such as man hours or production hours. Once again, the trend of the relationship would be significant.

Monitoring Work in Progress

The value of the work in progress will be a consequence of the resources applied in the workshop to implementing the production plan. This plan should be to produce no more and no less than the required stock of finished products. It follows that the work in progress on the shop floor will be unduly high in value if it is likely to produce, in the future, product above the required level; or too low in value and need the application of further resources if it will produce less product than is required. The effect of the value of work in progress will, therefore, appear in the eventual cost of finished goods. The measurement of work in progress is, accordingly, a question of estimating when the various jobs will be completed and assessing the outcome in terms of completed production. The process may be illustrated as follows, assuming one product for simplicity:

		Estimated completion of work in progress					
Product	*Job*			*Nos of product per month*			
		Jan.	*Feb.*	*Mar.*	*Apr.*	*May*	*June*
A	A1	10					
	A2		50				
	A3			60			
		10	50	60			
Stock at start		40	10	15			
Total available		50	60	75			
Forecast sales		40	45	50	—	—	—
Stock at end		10	15	25			

If, in this case, the economic stock level was assessed at 15 units, then in January output is insufficient and might lead to loss of sales. In February output is on target, but in March it is likely to be excessive.

These forecasts, if they conformed to the actual results, would be reflected in the value of work in progress. The chart would need revision monthly and extended as further jobs were initiated.

Goods for Sale

The sales department is particularly concerned with stocks of manufactured product and bought-out goods to ensure that these stocks are adequate to maintain budgeted sales. At the same time general management has the responsibility for ensuring that these stocks are at an economic level so as to conserve funds and reduce stockholding costs.

The value of these stocks should, therefore, be segregated from the total inventory and a calculation made of the number of days' or months' future sales which they represent. Thus, if the cost of goods for sale was shown in the accounts at the end of a month as £60 000 out of the total inventory of £120 000, and the budgeted cost of sales was at an average of £24 000 (for, say, the next three months) then the stock would represent 2½ months' sales. Even if the sales department were happy with this level of stock it might be economically unjustified, as explained below. Where, as is frequently the situation, a large variety of goods are marketed, it would be necessary to apply the indicator to each major line of sales, in the manner shown below:

Months' sales in stocks of goods

	Total	Product groups		
		A	B	C
Stocks at cost	£60 000	10 000	20 000	30 000
Forecast monthly cost				
of sales	£24 000	8 000	10 000	6 000
Months' sales	2.5	1.25	2.0	5.0

This analysis of the total stock of goods for sale shows a wide disparity between the indicators for the three product groups. Stock of C is ostensibly excessive and merits further analysis for slow moving items. Stock of B may be considered to be necessary to cope with inevitable fluctuations in sales, but stock of A appears to be minimal.

A further meaningful analysis is to show the time periods over which the stocks have been held. Such an 'ageing' analysis would certainly be necessary for the main items included in product group C, but might also with advantage be carried out for the other product groups because the overall figures shown above might contain slow moving items. A form of analysis, in this example limited to product group C, is shown below:

Stock ageing analysis – product group C

Items	Months held						Over	Total
	1	2	3	4	5	6	6	
	£	£	£	£	£	£	£	£
X		5 000						5 000
Y							10 000	10 000
Z				15 000				15 000
		5 000		15 000			10 000	30 000

It is now apparent that item X is selling reasonably well. Further production or purchase of item Y should cease, and consideration should be given to disposing of this stock for whatever price it would fetch, possibly only scrap value, for its existence is incurring undue cost. Assuming some sales are being made of item Z, production or buying of further amounts of this stock should be suspended. (It should be noted in this context that as a matter of policy some businesses are prepared to hold for long periods service parts for old equipment which they have sold in the past.)

Economic Order Quantities

The economic order quantity (EOQ) will determine the economic stock level for a particular material or for a bought-out product. The calculation of the EOQ is based on assessments of the annual cost of buying and the annual storage cost as shown below. The assessments should exclude 'fixed' costs, i.e. those which will continue irrespective of the buying quantities or stock levels (unless abnormal changes occur in the turnover or activity).

In the assessment of buying costs, the amounts of discount obtainable for different quantities should be taken into account. Storage costs should include interest foregone on the capital invested in the stock as well as any rent which could be obtained for letting the space occupied by the stores. The assessments are bound to contain a considerable degree of estimation but a reasonable tolerance in the figures will have only a marginal effect on the EOQ resulting from the calculations.

When the buying and storage costs have been assessed the next step is to set them against a range of likely order quantities so as to ascertain which quantity will produce the minimum annual cost. For this purpose the buying and storage costs can be expressed as £s per unit, as they are likely to be variable with the quantities. The method is illustrated below:

1. Possible order quantities	100	200	300	400	500
2. Average stock (being half the above)	50	100	150	200	250
3. Total orders (annual requirements in units, 1200, divided by order quantities)	12	6	4	3	2.40
	£	£	£	£	£
4. Storage cost at £0.75 per unit × (2) above	37.50	75	112.50	150	187.50
5. Buying costs at £15 per order × (3) above	180	90	60	45	36
Total costs	£217.50	£165	£172.50	£195	£223.50

From the above illustration the economic order quantity lies at around 200 units and, with an estimated demand of 1200 units a year, would mean that 6 orders should be placed each year, i.e. one every two calendar months or every 8–9 weeks.

Alternatively, the approximate ordering quantity may be obtained from the following formula:

$$EOQ = \frac{2 \times AQ \times BC}{SC}$$

where

EOQ = the economic order quantity;
AQ = the annual quantity;
BC = the buying cost per unit;
SC = the storage cost per unit.

Substituting the figures in the above example:

$$\text{EOQ} = \frac{2 \times 1200 \times 15}{0.75} = 219.08$$

With an order quantity of 220 (after rounding off) the costs become:

		£
Storage: £0.75 × $\dfrac{220}{2}$		82.5
Buying: £15 × $\dfrac{1200}{220}$		81.8
		£164.3

This is very little different from the cost of £165 shown for an order quantity of 200 calculated above and it is probable that for simplicity the amount of 200 would be adopted.

The foregoing figures represent standards and guides for stock control. They need to be adapted to the realities of delay in deliveries and fluctuating demand.

Lead Time and Safety Stock

The lead time is the period which elapses between the date an order is placed and the date when the goods are due to be delivered. If the lead time was four weeks then the stock accounts, also in periods of four weeks, would be as follows, assuming sales of a product or usage of a material began in period 2:

Period	Order placed	Delivery	Usage	Stock
− 1	200			
1		200		200
2	200		100	100
3		200	100	200
4			100	100

However, it is common knowledge that in business events rarely, if ever, conform to expectations. Deliveries may be delayed and sales or production requirements may exceed the budgeted quantities. For these reasons it is desirable to arrange that a 'safety stock' is held. In addition to provision for possible delivery delays, the safety stock should consist, basically, of the excess of the maximum likely demand in a period over the standard demand. This maximum demand can normally be ascertained from past experience. If it is, for instance, 160 units in a period then the initial order in the above situation would need increasing by 60 units.

Seasonal Trade and Fluctuating Sales

In some trades a high demand occurs in seasonal periods, e.g. summer, winter, or around Christmas. Where the season of high demand occupies several months it will be desirable to calculate economic ordering and stock levels for each of such seasons.

Where demand fluctuates widely, and is virtually unpredictable for each period, practical and *ad hoc* methods have to be adopted for order quantities which will avoid stockouts. The economic order quantity will remain a standard and a guide, calculated on budgeted annual turnover, but will not dictate the amount or timing of individual orders which will be made when a 'reorder level' of stock is reached. The reorder level is essentially the planned minimum stock and, at the beginning of each period, is 200 units in the above example. If, because of high demand in the period, the stock has fallen to, say, 170 units, then the next order should cover 200 + 30 = 230 units, increased by any further expected usage.

In a situation of widely fluctuating demand, stock will need reviewing at weekly if not shorter intervals. When an unexpected and large surge in demand occurs, crisis measures may be necessary such as ordering before the prescribed date and expediting deliveries, to ensure that adequate stock is available. In this situation practical measures must replace the formal rules indicated in the previous sections above. Nevertheless, these rules of procedure should be reinstated when demand reverts to normal, and a reduction in the standard order quantity may be required to prevent the build-up of excess stocks.

Minimizing Storage Cost

A comparatively low unit cost of holding stock was used for the calculations shown in the preceding section. It may be assumed that the units of this stock were small in size thus incurring minor costs in space and services, and low in value thus economizing in interest on capital. Where, however, the stock consists of large and expensive items of plant and equipment, the storage costs can be very high and may well exceed buying costs. In all cases it is desirable to minimize storage costs, so far as is compatible with maintaining sales turnover. Various methods of achieving economies in these costs are set out below, each depending on the circumstances of the business and the nature of the stock.

Timing of Deliveries

As a generality it may be said that, where possible, arrangements should be made with suppliers for deliveries to be made at the time and in the quantities required to maintain the minimum stock levels. This is the practice, for example, with many large retail stores who have strong buying power. Especially where demand tends to fluctuate, these arrangements have the effect of transferring much of the storage cost to the suppliers. The latter will, no doubt, take account of this practice in their pricing policies; nevertheless, considerable economies can result for the buyer. Where the sales demand fluctuates, it may be necessary to ignore economic ordering quantities, and simply maintain minimum stock levels.

Deliveries from Suppliers Direct to Buyers' Customers

This procedure would virtually eliminate the buyer's storage cost but is likely to be confined to the sale of specialized equipment and that which conforms to a customer's specification.

Stocking of Sample Goods, Plant, etc.

Where a range of specifications for a product is available, and the customer accepts a short delay before delivery, it is usually sufficient for a stockist to hold samples only, and not the whole range. This might be the case with, for example, high-priced clothing which needs adaptation to fit the customer. (On the other hand, the need for a rapid rate of turnover justifies a stock of all normal sizes in the more popular clothing.) Motor car dealers normally need only display one or two variants of a particular model with the knowledge that they can soon obtain other types by, for instance, telex communications with associated stockists or from the manufacturer.

Centralization of Stores

Where a company owns a chain of outlets, such as supermarkets, overall stockholding costs for fast-moving goods can be reduced by establishing central stores. A number of central stores may be established where they have easy access to the retail outlets in the adjacent area and can replenish stock by weekly if not more frequent deliveries. Such a system in particular saves expensive space in the stores, hence interest on capital, and can reduce deterioration of perishable goods and pilferage. The advantages, however, need to be balanced against the high costs of operating a transport fleet.

7 THE AVAILABILITY OF FUNDS

The Meaning of 'Funds'

The funds in a business mean the resources available to pay the outgoings. The resources comprise (1) those which exist at a given point of time, and (2) potential resources for raising cash. Existing resources include not only cash in the bank account but also other current assets which are due to be converted into cash within about a year. For more immediate purposes funds are obtainable from liquid assets, which in general are current assets less stock. The funds available from the current assets should be held for the payment of current liabilities, so that only the excess should be used for development, such as the purchase of fixed assets. If there is a deficiency then funds must be obtained from other sources.

The potential resources consist of the ability of the business to raise money other than from the current assets. Potential resources include, for instance, the availability of loans and the other devices described below. Funds may be raised quickly by overdraft for short-term purposes, by term loans from banks or other sources for the medium term, and for the long term by issues of debentures or shares.

This describes the position at a specific point of time. In controlling the finances of a business it is also necessary to forecast the continuing inflow of funds, principally from sales, and the continuing outflow of funds of both a capital and a revenue nature. The final outcome of all the funds flows is the balance of cash at the bank.

The Need for Controlling the Funds Flow

The ultimate constraint on the forward plans of a business, and hence its development, is the cash which can be made available. Furthermore, lack of funds to pay creditors will eventually result in the liquidation of the business. The survival of an enterprise depends more immediately on control of its cash flow than on profit planning. A business can survive for many years with inadequate profits, or even suffering a loss, provided it can pay for current expenditure, although lack of profit will, in the end, cause a cash shortage.

Marketing management needs to be closely concerned with cash control and the availability of funds. The exploitation of potential markets depends on adequate supplies of finance to obtain the goods for sale and to pay the expenses involved. More particularly the sales function can have a direct and adverse influence on cash inflow by offering unduly extended credit terms or selling to financially unsound customers.

The business finances should be planned and controlled for the short term normally up to a year ahead, the medium term, say, for five years, and for the long term beyond five years or so. Short-term control is necessary to avoid financial stringency and to keep the business in existence by paying for ongoing expenditure. Medium-term control is designed to ensure that the business plans for that period can be fulfilled, and in modern business of any size a five-year plan is almost a *sine qua non*. The planning and control of finance for the longer term will reflect the major objectives of the management. The inflow and outflow of cash from current operations tends to be volatile as a result of changing market and economic conditions of the present age and, as a result, the cash forecast needs frequent and regular revision.

The Funds Flow Statement

Before dealing with the forecasting and control of cash flows it is desirable to consider the historical records. Since 1975 a Statement of Standard Accounting Practice (SSAP 10) issued by the UK joint accountancy bodies provides that annual accounts of large companies shall include a statement of the sources and application of funds. This statement shows 'the sources from which funds have flowed into the business and the way in which they have been used'; in other words, how the profit and changes in capital, assets and liabilities have affected the funds flow. The statement is primarily directed to shareholders and other interested parties, but it should also be of value to management in reviewing the movement of funds which has occurred in their own company and in those of customers and suppliers. Figure 7.1 shows a specimen statement. There is no prescriptive form for the statement and the illustration is reasonably straightforward. It can be adapted to show how the incoming and outgoing funds have changed the 'working capital' (the net current assets) or the bank balance.

	This year £	Last year £
Sources of funds:		
From operations:		
Profit before tax	220 000	160 000
Add: Depreciation	60 000	50 000
	£280 000	£210 000
From other sources:		
Loan received	–	160 000
Reduction in debtors	20 000	–
Reduction in cash	20 000	20 000
Increase in creditors	–	60 000
	£40 000	£240 000
Total sources of funds	£320 000	£450 000

Figure 7.1   (continued opposite)

	This year	Last year
Application of funds:	£	£
Fixed assets purchased	100 000	280 000
Dividends paid	80 000	60 000
Tax paid	40 000	30 000
Reduction in creditors	50 000	–
Increase in stocks	10 000	30 000
Increase in debtors	–	50 000
Loan repayment	40 000	–
Total application of funds	£320 000	£450 000

Figure 7.1   Sources and application of funds.

Comments on the Statement

1. It appears that last year the business had initiated a programme of development having acquired additional fixed assets costing £280 000. The increase in stocks and debtors could have been due to rising turnover, but the figures against these items in this year suggest that improvements needed to be made in stock control and collections from debtors.
2. The development was financed last year by a loan of £160 000, also by obtaining further credit from suppliers amounting to £60 000 and depleting cash by £20 000.
3. This year the development bore fruit in a substantial increase in profit. The consequent rise in the inflow of funds enabled a further addition to be made to fixed assets of £100 000, £40 000 to be paid off the loan, and the dividend to be raised.
4. At the same time a dramatic improvement was made in the efficiency of collections from debtors and the increase in stocks was limited. However, these movements caused a further fall in cash of £20 000, but this may have represented deliberate action to reduce idle funds.

How the Statement Is Compiled

Whilst there is no need for sales and marketing managers to become expert in accounting techniques, the significance of the statement will be clarified by an understanding of the principles on which it is prepared. The general principles are that the sources of the funds comprise increases in liabilities and decreases in assets, and the application of the funds comprise decreases in liabilities and increases in assets. In this context the capital, reserves and profit are treated as liabilities of the business to the shareholders. Certain specific payments, such as for dividends, tax and loan repayments, are highlighted.

The figures in the statement are thus the differences in the assets and liabilities shown in two successive balance sheets. These differences need adjustment, however, for changes which do not represent movements of funds, that is for accounting transfers between accounts. Accordingly, depreciation is added back to profit, because this represents a reduction in value, not a payment of cash; for the same reason the profit may need adjustment for such transfers between accounts as bad debts and provisions for stock losses. At the same time adjustments are required for the differences in fixed assets (for depreciation), in debtors (for bad debts written off), and in stock (for stock losses).

Subject to these adjustments, the rationale for compiling the statement is summarized as follows:

Sources of Funds

Reductions in assets mean that money has been received from the sale of the assets, or the settlement of debts to an amount above the income accounted for in the profit and loss account.

Increases in liabilities are either the amounts actually received, e.g. from a loan or share issue, or the payments delayed by allowing creditors to rise.

Application of Funds

Increases in assets are either payments for additional assets or the amounts payable by debtors that have yet to be received.

Reductions in liabilities include repayments of loans and capital and the amount by which creditors are reduced beyond the costs charged in the profit and loss account.

For those interested in the mechanics, the following calculations show how the statement in Fig. 7.1 was compiled.

	(1)	(2)	(3)		(4)	(5)
	Balance sheets				Transfers	Funds flow
	This year	Last year	(1) – (2)	Note		
Capital and Liabilities	£000	£000	£000		£000	£000
Capital employed:						
Shares	375	375	–		–	–
Reserves	400	350	50	(1)	(50)	–
Profit and loss account	45	25	20	(1)	50	
				(2)	60	280
				(3)	50	
				(4)	100	
Loan capital	120	160	(40)			(40)
Total	940	910	30		210	240
Current liabilities:						
Creditors	674	724	(50)		–	(50)
Taxation	46	36	10	(3)	(50)	(40)
Dividend	60	40	20	(4)	(100)	(80)
Total	780	800	(20)		(150)	(170)
Total capital and liabilities	£1720	£1710	£10		£60	£70
Assets:			(2) – (1)			
Fixed assets	640	600	(40)	(2)	(60)	(100)

	(1)	(2)	(3)		(4)	(5)
	Balance sheets				*Transfers*	*Funds flow*
	This year	*Last year*	*(1) – (2)*	*Note*		
Capital and Liabilities	£000	£000	£000		£000	£000
Current assets:						
Stocks	450	440	(10)		–	(10)
Debtors	610	630	20		–	20
Cash	20	40	20		–	20
	1080	1110	30		–	30
Total assets	£1720	£1710	£(10)		£(60)	£(70)

Notes:

1. Allocation to reserves from profit and loss account.
2. Depreciation added back to profit and deducted from fixed assets.
3. Provision for taxation added back to profit and transferred to taxation account.
4. Dividend recommended, transferred from profit and loss account to dividend account.

Appraising the Financial Resources of a Business

The Need for and Form of the Appraisal

A detailed appraisal of the financial resources of a business is a necessary preliminary to the preparation of the forward operating plans, because the funds which can be made available will determine the scope of the future activity.

The forward plans will be divided into short-term, medium-term and long-term projections, and it follows that the arrangements which can be made to provide funds should have reference to these periods. However, the finance appraisal falls logically under the headings of (1) existing resources, and (2) potential resources. Funds can be made available from existing resources immediately or at short notice, so that they would be available to finance short-term plans. Some of the potential resources, such as short-term loans, can produce funds within a month or so and, after that period, should also be available for short-term purposes. Other potential resources, such as the ability to raise further capital, will take much longer to arrange and would therefore apply to medium- and long-term operations.

Existing Resources

Existing resources capable of producing cash in the short term of about a year consist largely of the current assets. But sufficient of the current assets must be available to pay the current liabilities so that only the surplus, e.g. the net current assets, is free for developing the business, for instance by increasing stocks and fixed assets, and meeting payments to be made in advance of income such as advertising.

Even though current assets exceed current liabilities the incidence of cash receipts and payments could result in a cash deficiency within a year. For this reason it is desirable that the financial appraisal shall indicate the cash which can be raised from the current assets at short notice.

The existing resources will include the following:

1. *Cash in the bank accounts.*
2. *Temporary investments.* Realization at short notice may involve taking a loss.
3. *Bills of exchange (or 'notes') receivable.* Their face value, less charges and discount depending on their term, can be obtained almost immediately from a bank. See Chapter 2 for a fuller explanation.
4. *Debtors*, which may be assigned to a factor for collection. The factoring charge can be high and one consequence could be a loss of customer goodwill. The arrangement normally also applies to future invoices issued.
5. *Revolving credit.* Another method by which existing debtors and future invoices issued can be turned into ready cash is to arrange a revolving credit with a banking house. The method is for the bank to discount in the money market a bill of exchange for, say, a monthly or quarterly parcel of invoices, and to pay the proceeds, less charges, over to the company. The latter undertakes to pay the bill out of the next month's or quarter's receipts from debtors, when a further bill is drawn. Depending largely on current interest rates and charges, the cost can be substantial.
6. *Overdraft.* The unused balance of a bank overdraft facility may be considered as an existing resource available immediately, as could assured prospects of increasing that facility.
7. *Partly paid capital.* The balance payable on existing partly paid-up shares is a further financial resource which can normally be realized in a matter of months, and which does not involve undue expense or any addition to current liabilities. See also Chapter 2.

In addition to the above a company may hold redundant assets which can be sold. Future cash outgoings are sometimes reduced, for a time, by delaying payment to creditors. but this method may involve substantial loss of cash discount, delay supplies and cause loss of goodwill.

Potential Resources

Potential resources for raising funds are divisible into those which are available in a short time, say a month or so, and those which involve lengthy preparation.

Available in a Short Time

Bank Accommodation

For a sound company this can usually be arranged quickly, whether by way of overdraft or loan, especially if security is offered. The overdraft limit may be as low as £100 000 but bank loans, probably secured by a debenture, may in appropriate cases be for several million pounds, with terms up to 15 years, and subject to periodic drawings on the total facility. The amount of the potential loan may be difficult to quantify in the financial appraisal but it is unlikely to be less than three-quarters of the value of land and buildings which could be offered as security.

A substantial overdraft or loan is usually secured by a debenture which carries a fixed charge on land and buildings and a floating charge on the whole undertaking. On default by the borrower the lender is entitled to appoint a receiver and manager who takes charge of the business to ensure that the interest and agreed repayments are made. On continued default the receiver may sell the property charged, or the business as a whole, and ultimately enforce a liquidation.

Loans and mortgages from other sources

These may be obtainable from a variety of financial institutions, in addition to banks and, in appropriate cases, do not take more than a few months to arrange. In addition, debentures or bonds may be offered to the public on the terms that they are repayable in a comparatively short period of years.

Leasing plant and vehicles

The leasing instead of the purchase of additional plant or vehicles, such as when existing assets are due for replacement, will create a saving in outgoing funds, but the saving may take some time to become effective. In some cases it may be possible to obtain a current cash inflow by selling the existing assets to a finance house and leasing them back. Even large companies find it convenient to obtain their fleets of vehicles under contract hire arrangements, the benefits including the following: earlier tax reliefs, avoidance of risk in respect of resale values and replacement costs, responsibility for maintenance and replacement of vehicles in the hands of the lessors, greater precision in budgeting, saving in administration. The relative merits of leasing compared with purchase, however, need careful evaluation.

The sale and lease-back of land and buildings

Where a company has a large investment in landed property this arrangement can produce a considerable, one-off addition to available funds. Much depends, however, on whether the company can obtain a greater return on the money so realized than the cost of the rent. Other disadvantages are that the company forgoes the potential rise in the value of the property and may be subject to restrictive covenants in the lease. Any capital gain on the sale of the land must also be taken into account.

Government assistance

A wide range of financial assistance is obtainable from governmental sources for capital expenditure to assist employment in development areas, investment projects in the national interest, and research and development in advanced technology. Clearly it will not be possible to refer in the financial appraisal to this potential source of funds unless plans for the relevant developments have been formulated. The assistance available include grants for capital expenditure and tax reliefs for businesses established in enterprise zones. Various forms of financial assistance for selected projects are also obtainable from a number of European Boards. In addition the European Investment Bank provides loans at attractive rates of interest to assist regional developments.

Long-term Resources

For long-term purposes a company will need additional loan or share capital. Arrangements for the issue of further capital will involve considerable time and preparation except, possibly, in the case of a private company which is able to obtain capital from private sources. The amount of additional capital required will depend on the long-term objectives of the company and will be limited by the financial market's assessment of the company's standing and future prosperity. The best timing of the issue will be influenced by market conditions and therefore cannot usually be determined precisely far in advance. The financial appraisal may, accordingly, have to be limited to a review of these factors. The following notes discuss the considerations which need to be borne in mind in choosing between loan and share capital.

Loan Capital

Long-term loan capital is usually, but not invariably, evidenced by a debenture, secured in the same way as referred to under bank accommodation above. In addition, a trust deed is likely to be drawn up in favour of the debentureholders and a trustee appointed on their behalf. In a few cases the debentures are unsecured and in a liquidation the debentureholders then rank equally with the unsecured creditors.

The loan capital may not be due for repayment until many years, maybe twenty, have elapsed; in rare cases perpetual debentures are issued and these are not repayable except when the company is wound up. Provision needs to be made for the repayment of the debentures, possibly by means of a sinking fund or, more likely, by a fresh issue of capital. The debentures are described as convertible when they give the holders the right of conversion into shares at a specified date and at a specified conversion value. Where a company requires to finance a programme of long-term development which promises to produce high profits, convertible debentures can be attractive to investors and, at the same time, can enable the issuing company to benefit by issuing them at rate of interest below the market rate.

The effect of an issue of loan capital on the gearing of the company (see Chapter 2) needs careful consideration. The principal advantage is that the interest payable reduces the profits for corporation tax, whereas dividends on shares do not. However, for a company which operates in a volatile market, so that profits and cash flow tend to vary widely from year to year, a high interest charge may cause cash flow problems in a lean year. The interest is payable whatever the profit or loss of the company whereas a dividend can only be paid out of profit and the amount is at the discretion of the directors.

Share Capital

The different classes of share capital were described in Chapter 2. So far as the provision of funds is concerned, the two major categories of (1) preference shares and (2) ordinary shares are examined below, with additional notes on bonus shares and share values.

Preference shares

The main distinctions between preference shares and ordinary shares are that the former are redeemable, that is they are due for repayment at a stated date or within a stated period; their dividend is basically at a fixed rate; they have restricted voting rights at shareholders' meetings; and in a winding up of the company may or may not have preferential rights over the ordinary shareholders for repayment. Their basic rate of dividend is normally cumulative, meaning that arrears from one year are carried forward to the next year and so on. They may also carry rights to participate with the ordinary shareholders in profits remaining after their basic dividend has been accounted for.

The dividend represents a share of profit and does not, therefore, provide relief for corporation tax.

Thus, like debentures, an issue of preference shares is suitable for financing a period of development, but it has implications for the gearing of the company (see Chapter 2). From the point of view of the investor a preference share is less secure than a debenture and may, as a consequence, merit a higher rate of return. From the company's viewpoint it has the advantage that the dividend may be suspended in a year of loss or insufficient profit. Provision must be made for the redemption of preference shares out of profits (e.g. reserves) or out of a fresh issue of shares.

Ordinary shares

The principal feature of such capital in the present context is that it is permanent and cannot be repaid except in a winding up or other special circumstances.* An issue of ordinary shares is therefore appropriate only where a permanent enlargement of the company's scope and activities are contemplated, such as would occur when another business is to be taken over. The ordinary shareholders are the effective owners of the company, they appoint directors to act on their behalf, and they have wide-ranging powers of voting at shareholders' meetings on fundamental issues. The dividends, which are recommended by the directors, are adjustable to profits, and may even be paid in the form of additional shares, thus conserving cash. The ordinary shareholders are the ultimate risk-bearers and would only be induced to invest in a company with good prospects of profitability and capital growth.

Thus, where a permanent addition to the company's capital is proposed, the financial appraisal should consider the factors involved in issuing further shares to the public, or arranging to place them with a financial institution. Enquiries need to be made as to the price and amount of a new issue of shares acceptable to the market. The price could not be above the current or expected quotation for the shares on the stock exchange, for if it were potential investors would find it cheaper to buy shares in the market. On the other hand too low a price would be to the detriment of existing shareholders. Shares cannot be issued at a discount, that is below their nominal value save in exceptional circumstances. The excess of the price over the nominal value would be credited to a share premium account, which cannot be distributed as a dividend but forms part of the interests of the shareholders, both existing and new.

The success of a new issue of shares will depend on market sentiment towards the

---

* Under modern company legislation a company can buy back from shareholders its own shares, but this must be done in the market and the current market price paid.

company, in particular as to its plans for using the additional capital. Given an acceptable price, a safeguard against failure is to have a substantial proportion of the issue
underwritten, which means that underwriters agree to subscribe for those shares
which are not taken up by the public. With the underwriters' commission, professional fees and the publication of the prospectus, the costs of making a new issue of
shares can be heavy.

A simpler and usually more effective way for a company to obtain additional share
capital is to offer a 'rights issue' to existing shareholders. The latter are encouraged to
subscribe for the new shares by being offered advantages over outside investors in the
form of bonus shares and/or a more favourable price. It may be expedient to issue
bonus shares independently of any rights issue. The subject is considered below.

Bonus shares

An issue of bonus shares does not in itself produce additional funds; it may, however,
be a necessary preliminary to a further issue of ordinary shares so that the subject is
relevant to an appraisal of financial resources. Furthermore, a bonus issue widens the
market for the company's securities and, as a result, may improve the market capitalization, i.e. the total shares multiplied by the quotation.

All that happens when bonus shares are issued to existing shareholders is that
reserves are converted into share capital. The shareholders receive a number of additional shares in proportion to their existing holdings without further payment (except
in the case of an accompanying rights issue).

Example

	£000
A company has 2 000 000 issued ordinary shares of nominal value £1 each:	2 000
And available reserves of:	8 000
So that the interests of ordinary shareholders are:	£10 000

The directors decide, probably as a preliminary to a further issue of shares to the
public, that each existing shareholder shall receive three bonus shares for every share
presently held. The capital structure then becomes:

Issued ordinary shares of £1:		£000
Original	2m	
Bonus shares	6m	
Total	8m	8 000

Reserves	£000	
Original	8000	
Less: Bonus shares	6000	
		2 000
		£10 000

The proportionate interest of a shareholder originally owning, say, 100 000 shares was $\frac{1}{20}$th of £10m = £500 000. After he receives 300 000 bonus shares his proportionate interest in the company is unchanged, i.e. 400 000 divided by 8 000 000 times £10m = £500 000. In practice he may, nevertheless, receive a benefit from an increased amount of dividend and a consequent increase in the market value of his holding.

Example

Before the bonus issue:

1. Assume the total dividend paid was £600 000. This represents, on issued
   shares of £2m a rate of: 30%
2. Assume a quotation of £6 a share. The market capitalization is therefore
   £6 × 2m: £12m
3. The yield on the quoted price is therefore 0.3/6 or, using total figures,
   £600 × 100/£12 000:   5%

After the bonus issue:

1. Assume the expected total dividend on the increased share capital of £8m is
   unchanged at £600 000, this represents a rate of £600 × 100/£8000:   7.5%
2. The quotation per share will *tend* to fall to £1.50, if the market capitalization
   remains unchanged, i.e. £8000 × £1.50:   £12m
3. If the dividend is raised to, say, £640 000 the rate becomes £640 × 100/£8000: 8%
4. With a yield remaining at 5% the quotation will *tend* to be 8/5 or, using total
   figures, £640/£8000 × 0.05:   £1.60
5. The market capitalization then becomes £1.60 × £8m: £12.8m

Note: The above arithmetic is intended to indicate the calculations involved. The actual quotation will depend not only on the dividend expected but also on the market's view of the future prosperity of the company. The importance of the quotation in the present context is that it will have a decisive influence on the price at which further shares are issued.

The value of a share

Marketing managers are very familiar with the many factors which influence the price of a product in a market. One of these is the customer's intuitive or calculated assessment of the value of the product to him or her. Likewise the real value of a share to an investor is basically the income which it is likely to produce, not only by way of dividends but also capital appreciation. In theory this value can be ascertained precisely by calculating the present value of the discounted cash flow from the share, including any capital appreciation or depreciation on ultimate sale of the holding. (For an explanation of discounted cash flow see Chapter 8.) The calculation is, however, beset by imponderables, such as the discount rate to be used, the period to be assumed, and the prospects of capital appreciation. Even so, such a calculation could be of value in the appraisal of financial resources as a bearing on the price at which further share capital could be issued.

Public and Private Companies

At this point it may be informative to examine the relative positions of public and private companies with regard to the availability and sources of funds.

Only public companies can issue shares and debentures to the public, so that only this type of company can apply to the stock exchange for a listing. A great deal of information must, under the rules of the stock exchange, be published, and many formalities are involved before a listed quotation is obtained. For the smaller company a simpler procedure is to apply for a quotation on the Unlisted Securities Market. An offer of shares or debentures is made by a prospectus, which includes the recent accounts of the company, the last five years' results, a forecast of future results, and much information on the company's present and proposed activities.

Instead of inviting the public at large to subscribe for the securities, it may be expedient to place the issue with a financial institution, which subscribes for all the shares or part of them at an agreed price. The financial institution offers some for sale on the market in the normal way, or makes a formal offer for sale of the shares to the public at a stated price by means of a prospectus.

It should be borne in mind in this connection that 'the public' includes other companies and financial bodies, such as assurance companies, pension funds, banks and unit trusts, etc., as well as individuals. A holding of over 50 per cent will enable the shareholder to make a takeover bid for the company.

Private companies are prohibited from issuing shares or debentures to the public at large. Their original capital, and any further capital they require, must therefore be obtained privately, either from a restricted group of individuals or by agreement with other companies or finance houses. Private companies must also impose a restriction on the shareholder's right to transfer shares, and this may mean that a would-be vendor must first offer the shares to the directors or other shareholders.

For these reasons a private company cannot obtain a quotation for its shares on a stock exchange. The price at which any of its shares or debentures are issued or transferred is a matter of negotiation. Although many sources of finance are available for private companies, a potential subscriber of a large amount of additional capital would in most cases require security and in many cases a seat on the board. This will mean a certain loss of control by the directors and existing shareholders. At a certain stage in its development it will be desirable for a private company to be converted into a public company and to obtain a stock exchange quotation.

Planning Cash Requirements

General Considerations

The appraisal of financial resources will indicate to management the funds which are available and which can be raised to implement the operational plans. On the basis of the provisional plans it will be necessary for a cash forecast to be prepared, and this will show the amounts of funds required and the points in time at which they will need to be raised. If the necessary funds cannot be made available, then the operating plans must be appropriately curtailed or deferred, and a revised cash forecast prepared.

It is usually necessary to prepare a cash forecast for each of the first six months of the planning period, thereafter quarterly until the end of the first year, whilst for the longer-term annual forecasts will normally suffice. The long-term forecasts will include estimates of additional capital in pursuance of board policy for major development of the business. These developments could include, for instance, the acquisition of other businesses, development overseas and the establishment of further factories, branches and retail premises. Each project of this magnitude will require detailed financial analysis of the projected benefits and the capital involved.

The Preparation of the Cash Forecast

The following notes refer to certain important points to be observed in preparing the cash forecast.

Receipts

These will be largely derived from the sales budget, but will also include receipts of interest, dividends, royalties, licence fees, rents receivable, cash from sales of assets, and funds obtained from loans or by the issue of capital. The budgeted sales first need conversion into deliveries, and then into the cash likely to be received from the customers. The following illustration for a forecasting period of a year indicates the calculations involved:

	£	£
Debtors at beginning of period		300 000
Deliveries from sales of previous period	50 000	
This period sales	1 200 000	
	1 250 000	
Less: Current period's sales undelivered	150 000	
Deliveries this period		1 100 000
		1 400 000
Deduct: Debtors at end of period		
estimated at 2½ months' sales		250 000
Forecast receipts from sales		£1 150 000

Payments

Materials

Payments for materials should be calculated on the following lines:

	£
Creditors at beginning of period	120 000
Add: Purchases during period	600 000
	720 000
Less: Creditors at end of period, estimated at 2 months' purchases	100 000
Payments to creditors	£620 000

Other operational payments

The budgeted amounts for wages and salaries can normally be assumed to equal the payments to be made, but adjustments may have to be made for outstanding fees at the beginning and at end of the period. The budgeted overheads and operating expenses may also be treated as payments, except that deductions from them must be made for non-cash items such as depreciation, deferred charges and prepaid expenses.

Dividends and taxation

These payments, and their due dates, will need to be estimated.

Capital items

Estimates will need to be made for capital expenditure on fixed assets and much of the information for this purpose will be obtainable from the departmental capital budgets. The long-term forecast should reflect proposed expenditure on major projects authorized by the board. This heading must also include provisions for the repayment of loans and the redemption of capital, e.g. of preference shares.

Provision for Contingencies

Optimism is a typical characteristic of many managers, especially sales and marketing managers, so that expected sales are frequently overestimated and expenditure is underestimated. Unforeseen expenses almost inevitably arise and changes in external circumstances may make income budgets impossible to realize. A business with substantial financial resources may be able to cope with the unpredictable, but in any event it is desirable that the cash forecast shall be prepared on a conservative basis or that a contingency allowance be included in the forecast.

A Practical Example of Cash Forecasting

Short term

The following cash forecast for the ensuing year is prepared from the operating budgets. To simplify the illustration only quarterly forecasts are shown, although in practice the first six months would probably have been set out in monthly periods.

Cash forecast for first year

		End of quarters			
	1	*2*	*3*	*4*	*year*
	£000	*£000*	*£000*	*£000*	*£000*
Receipts:					
From operations	2 600	2 800	2 000	3 500	10 900

	1	2	End of quarters 3	4	year
	£000	£000	£000	£000	£000
Payments:					
Remuneration	1 000	1 100	1 200	1 250	4 550
Materials	1 200	1 300	1 560	1 300	5 360
Overheads	300	350	400	450	1 500
Total operational payments	2 500	2 750	3 160	3 000	11 410
Fixed Assets	50	40	40	1 200	1 330
Dividends		120			120
Taxation		140			140
Total payments	2 550	3 050	3 200	4 200	13 000
Cash at beginning	100	150	(100)	(1 300)	100
Change in period	50	(250)	(1 200)	(700)	(2 100)
Cash at end	£150	£(100)	£(1 300)	£(2 000)	£(2 000)

Action taken

1. At the end of the second quarter the surplus of receipts over operational payments is more than absorbed by payments for fixed assets, dividends and taxation. Taxation must be paid and the dividend will be expected by the shareholders. Consequently, arrangements are made with the bank for an overdraft facility of £100 000 to cover the cash shortage. If the actual shortage becomes greater than £100 000 then it is proposed to meet the deficiency by deferring payments to creditors or realizing temporary investments.
2. In the third quarter a substantial cash shortage is expected to arise as a result of lower sales due to seasonal influences, and the stocking up of materials in anticipation of future increased turnover. Also to be taken into account is the additional shortage of £700 000 in the fourth quarter from the heavy expenditure on fixed assets required for future development. Accordingly, a finance house is to be approached for a loan of £2 000 000 repayable in three years and receivable in the third quarter. The overdraft facility is retained for contingencies.
3. The cash forecast is amended to include the loan of £2 000 000 in the receipts of the third quarter, giving a balance of £700 000 cash in hand at the end of that quarter, and a nil balance at the end of the year.

Long-term forecast

A five-year forecast is now prepared below. The following notes explain the basis on which this forecast has been constructed:

1. The first year is that for the short-term forecast examined above and takes account of the term loan of £2 000 000 which is repaid in year 3.
2. The operational receipts and payments are derived from the long-term budgets as influenced by the additional premises and proposed acquisition, accounted for in years 2 and 3.

3. Many of the figures are necessarily approximate but reasonable estimates have to be made for arrangements to be made well in advance for the additional premises, the acquisitions, and for the capital required to finance them.
4. Adjustments will need to be made to these forecasts in the light of actual receipts and payments and actual cash balances. These adjustments will be made when the actual cash inflows and outflows have been ascertained for each period, and the forecast will then be extended for a further period on what is known as the 'rolling' principle.
5. It is proposed that the additional funds, being of a permanent nature, shall be obtained by a 'rights issue' to existing shareholders, with part payment in year 2 and the balance in year 3.
6. The substantial cash balance predicted at the end of year 5, resulting from the development, is intended to be used for further acquisitions. Meanwhile, it will be invested in temporary and readily realizable investments.

Five-year cash forecast

	Year 1	Year 2	Year 3	Year 4	Year 5
	£000	£000	£000	£000	£000
Receipts:					
Operational	10 900	13 000	15 000	22 000	24 000
Term loan	2 000				
Capital issue		3 000	5 000		
Total receipts	12 900	16 000	20 000	22 000	24 000
Payments:					
Operational	11 410	12 000	15 000	20 000	22 000
Fixed assets	1 330	700	500	200	200
Dividends	120	150	200	250	250
Taxation	140	150	150	200	200
Additional premises		2 500			
Acquisitions			2 500		
Loan repayment			2 000		
Total payments	13 000	15 500	20 350	20 650	22 650
Cash at beginning	100	–	500	150	1 500
Change in period	(100)	500	(350)	1 350	1 350
Cash at end	–	£500	£150	£1 500	£2 850

8 ECONOMIC EVALUATION OF INVESTMENT PROPOSALS

Capital Budgeting

Promotion from salesperson to sales manager or marketing executive to product marketing manager involves greater responsibilities for spending the company's money as well as responsibility for generating an even larger volume of business. New products are not developed nor new markets researched and penetrated without heavy expenditure by the company involved. These expenditure decisions which have a major impact on the growth and future business success constitute a major challenge for sales and marketing management. In order to optimize the quality of these decisions it is important that these managers appreciate some of the considerations underlying these capital investment decisions.

A typical capital investment decision involves management committing resources today and in the near and medium future in order to generate a stream of revenue in the distant future. Indeed, at a senior management level, executives are continuously confronted with the problem of deciding if the proposed commitment of company resources is desirable in terms of the anticipated benefits. In this context capital investment may be taken to include expenditure involved in the acquisition of existing production and marketing resources by means of a merger as well as the internal expansion of the company's own facilities.

At the inception of each investment proposal, the expected costs and anticipated revenues should be calculated, albeit in the form of 'guestimates'. Generally, these rough preliminary figures will be revised several times as more effort is expended on the proposal before they are incorporated into the financial plan. Relevant marketing, engineering and financial data must be collected and collated from all the relevant departments in the company. Although the costs ultimately acquire a certain precision, there generally remains a level of uncertainty about the revenue or positive cash flows to be generated.

Cash flow is a term that is used to express the expenditure of money and the receipt of money over a period of time, usually several years. Typically expenditure occurs in the early years and revenue in the later period. The expenditure may be symbolized by: $- - - -$, and the revenues by: $+ + + +$. A 'conventional' project may be symbolized as $- - + + +$ and used to represent project A. There is only one change in the sign from negative to positive:

	Year				
	0	1	2	3	4
Project A	− 100	− 100	+ 100	+ 150	+ 200

'Non-conventional projects' have two or more changes in the signs, $- + + - + +$, implying that more expenditure is required in year 3. Project B is an example of this:

	Year					
	0	1	2	3	4	5
Project B	− 100	+ 100	+ 150	− 50	+ 200	+ 200

The Time Value of Money

It is now necessary to consider the main issue of the capital budgeting process – the economic evaluation of a project's desirability. This in turn requires the stipulation of a decision rule for acceptance or rejection of investment projects. However, before doing this it is important to consider the effect of time on the value of money spent and received over the life of a capital investment project.

In order to focus attention on the implications of the time value of money for decision-making, it is necessary to assume at this stage of the analysis that the costs and benefits of alternative investment projects are known with certainty. This is a major assumption but without it the explanation would be unnecessarily difficult. Even where the magnitudes of the relevant cash flows are known, particular attention must still be paid to their timing when considering the desirability of an investment proposal.

This will become clear when an example is worked through. Consider a project which requires an immediate investment of £1000 and which returns £1100 exactly one year later. Is this a worthwhile investment for the company? Clearly the answer depends on the alternative uses that exist for the £1000 – if the business can earn 12 per cent by depositing the money in a bank and receive £1120 at the end of the year, it is not a particularly good idea if the investment has been made simply for immediate financial return. If, on the other hand, the bank is only paying 8 per cent interest (£1080), i.e. less than £1100 from the investment, it might be a good idea.

Clearly, an intelligent investment decision requires the comparison of alternatives. Assume that the return which can be earned in the market by the symbol k (which is really k per cent) is independent of the investment decision under consideration.

The relationship between k and the future value of £1 one year in the future may be expressed as:

$$FV_1 = 1 \times (1 + k)$$

where FV_1 denotes the future value of £1 at the end of year 1. If $k = 10$ per cent we have

$$FV_1 = 1 \times (1 + 0.10) = 1 + 0.10 = £1.10$$

In the second year an additional 10 per cent will be earned on the £1.10, so the algebraic expression is:

$$FV_2 = 1.10 + 0.11 = £1.21$$

where FV_2 denotes the value at the end of two years, or in symbols:

$$FV_2 = 1.(1 + k)(1 + k) = 1 \times (1 + k)^2$$

In general, the future value of £1 at the end of n years will be:

$$FV_n = 1 \times (1 + k)^n$$

Consider another example, to calculate the future value of £1000 after five years assuming that k is again equal to 10 per cent. At the end of two years the future value is of course the same as that using the formula for £1 (multiplied by 1000) (1.21 × 1000 = £1210). Similarly, the future value after three years may be expressed as:

$$FV_3 = FV_2(1 + 0.10) = 1210 \times 1.10 = £1331$$

The formula to calculate the investment may be expressed:

$$FV_5 = V_0 \times (1 + k)^5$$

where V_0 denotes the amount invested at the beginning of the first year. Hence:

$$FV_5 = 1000 (1 + 0.10)^5$$

The easiest way to calculate this is to look up the compound interest figure for 10 per cent over five years in Table 8.1. Therefore $FV_5 = 1000 \times 1.611 = £1611$.

Table 8.1 · Compound future value of £1

Years hence	1%	2%	3%	4%	5%	6%	7%	8%	9%	10%
1	1.010	1.020	1.030	1.040	1.050	1.060	1.070	1.080	1.090	1.100
2	1.020	1.040	1.061	1.082	1.102	1.124	1.145	1.166	1.188	1.210
3	1.030	1.061	1.093	1.125	1.158	1.191	1.225	1.260	1.295	1.331
4	1.041	1.082	1.126	1.170	1.216	1.262	1.311	1.360	1.412	1.464
5	1.051	1.104	1.159	1.217	1.276	1.338	1.403	1.469	1.539	1.611
6	1.062	1.126	1.194	1.265	1.340	1.419	1.501	1.587	1.677	1.772
7	1.072	1.149	1.230	1.316	1.407	1.504	1.605	1.714	1.828	1.949
8	1.083	1.172	1.267	1.369	1.477	1.594	1.718	1.851	1.993	2.144
9	1.094	1.195	1.305	1.423	1.551	1.689	1.838	1.999	2.172	2.358
10	1.105	1.219	1.344	1.480	1.629	1.791	1.967	2.159	2.367	2.594

It requires only a minor extension to the compound interest formula to derive a formula for the present value, which is:

$$FV = \frac{FV_n}{(1 + k)^n}$$

Applying this formula to the one-year example and assuming that the firm's alternative rate of return is given by k = 10 per cent:

$$PV = \frac{FV_1}{(1 + k)} = \frac{£1.10}{1 + 0.10} = £1$$

This means that the present value of £1.10 to be received at the end of one year is £1 where k = 0.10.

Similarly, the present value of £1.464 to be received at the end of four years is equal to £1:

$$\frac{FV_4}{(1+k)^4} = \frac{1.464}{(1+0.10)^4} = \frac{1.464}{1.464} = £1$$

The calculation is quite straightforward because the future value is given and k can be looked up in Table 8.1 along the four-year line for the value of 10 per cent.

Net Present Value (NPV)

An investment proposal's NPV is calculated by discounting the cash receipts at a rate k which reflects the value of the best alternative use of the funds. The discounted values are then added together. Finally the initial outlay is subtracted to give the NPV of the project.

Below is an example of the calculation for a project where the initial investment is £1000 and the net receipts in each of four subsequent years are £400, £600, £300 and £400. A k value of 10 per cent has been used and the values may be found in Table 8.2.

Year	Net receipt	Discount factor (k)	Present value of cash flow
	£		£
1	400	0.909	363.60
2	600	0.826	495.60
3	300	0.751	225.30
4	400	0.683	273.20
			1357.70
	Less initial investment		1000.00
		NPV =	+ £357.70

The basic decision rule is that if the NPV is positive, i.e. greater than the initial investment, then the project is worthwhile and should proceed. If the NPV is negative, that is less than the original investment, then there is no sound financial reason for proceeding with the project.

Table 8.2   Present value of £1

Years hence	1%	2%	4%	5%	6%	8%	10%
1	0.990	0.980	0.962	0.952	0.943	0.926	0.909
2	0.980	0.961	0.925	0.907	0.890	0.857	0.826
3	0.971	0.942	0.889	0.864	0.840	0.794	0.751
4	0.961	0.924	0.855	0.823	0.792	0.735	0.683
5	0.951	0.906	0.822	0.784	0.747	0.681	0.621
6	0.942	0.888	0.790	0.746	0.705	0.630	0.564
7	0.933	0.871	0.760	0.711	0.665	0.583	0.513
8	0.923	0.853	0.731	0.677	0.627	0.540	0.467
9	0.914	0.837	0.703	0.645	0.592	0.500	0.424
10	0.905	0.820	0.676	0.614	0.558	0.463	0.386

The Internal Rate of Return (IRR)

The internal rate of return is another method of calculating a project's worth that applies to a time discounted value for the cash flows. The IRR is defined as that rate of discount which equates the present value of the stream of net receipts with the initial investment in the project. Alternatively it may be regarded as the value for k which makes the NPV = 0.

The calculation of the IRR requires an iterative or 'trial and error' approach. The computational procedure is as follows: given the cash flow and investment outlay, choose a discount rate at random and calculate the project's NPV. If the NPV rate is positive, choose a higher discount rate and repeat the procedure. If the NPV is negative, choose a lower discount rate and repeat the procedure. That discount rate which makes the NPV = 0 is the IRR.

Table 8.3 gives an example of such a calculation. Using the 8 per cent discount factor the NPV is positive (+ 135.56) so a higher rate, 14 per cent, is chosen. This, however, results in a negative NPV (– 62.90), so that a discount rate that is lower than 14 per cent but higher than 8 per cent is required. At 12 per cent discount rate the project's NPV is zero, so by definition the project's IRR = 12 per cent.

The IRR decision rate must take the minimum rate of return k explicitly into account:

If IRR is greater than k accept the project.
If IRR is less than k reject the project.

The possibility of IRR = k is ignored, where the firm would be indifferent to the project.

The Payback Method

The payback method of investment appraisal measures the period of time it takes for the project to repay the original investment. For example, in project G below the payback is three years:

Project G:			
0	1	2	3
– £3000	+ £1000	+ £1000	+ £1000

While this is quite interesting, it is unbelievably simplistic for two reasons: it ignores the time value of money, and secondly it takes no account of the returns from a project once the return from the original investment has been made. Thus, according to the payback method, project H would be preferred to project I:

	0	1	2	3	4	Total return
Project H	– £2000	+ £1000	+ £1000	+ £1000	+ £1000	£2000
Project I	– £2000	+ £500	+ £500	+ £5000	+ £5000	£9000

The most favourable comment that may be made about the method is that it has some use as a supporting criterion to other more comprehensive and powerful techniques.

Table 8.3   Calculation of the IRR for a project

Year	Net cash flow	Discount factor	Present value of cash flow
First attempt at 8%:			
1	904	0.926	837.10
2	1000	0.857	857.00
3	556	0.794	441.46
Present value of cash flows		=	2135.56
Less: initial investment			2000.00
		NPV =	+ 135.56
Second attempt at 14%:			
1	904	0.877	792.80
2	1000	0.769	769.00
3	556	0.675	375.30
Present value of cash flows		=	1937.10
Less: initial investment			2000.00
		NPV =	− 62.90
Third attempt at 12%:			
1	904	0.893	807.27
2	1000	0.797	797.00
3	556	0.712	395.87
Present value of cash flows		=	2000.14
Less: initial investment			2000.00
		NPV =	0 approx.

NPV versus the IRR

It should be abundantly clear by now that the NPV and IRR as methods of selecting capital investment proposals are closely related. They are both capable of measuring the cash returns from projects in a way that takes into consideration the timing of the cash flows. Both methods also have a decision framework for deciding whether a proposed investment is sufficiently profitable to be worth pursuing. However, unless the two criteria inevitably lead to identical decisions, it becomes impossible to avoid the necessity of choosing between the two methods.

This section of the chapter will analyse and compare the two sets of rules in various situations in order to determine the optimal criterion for a business pursuing a policy of wealth maximization. Also, in order to focus on the key issue, any essence of risk will again be ignored. It will be assumed that the anticipated cash receipts associated with any project would happen with absolute certainty.

NPV v. IRR Independent Projects

In the case of conventional projects (those with only one change from negative to positive − + + +) which are economically independent of one another (this is where the selection of one project has no relational effect regarding the choice of another) both the NPV and the IRR lead to identical decisions to accept or reject a project. This may be proved both mathematically and diagrammatically. For a mathematical proof the authors would refer the reader to *Capital Investment and Financial Decisions* by Haim Levi and Marshall Sarnat.* The diagrammatic evidence is provided by Fig. 8.1 which graphs the NPV of an investment project as a function of the discount rate. The intercept, a point R, is where the NPV is equal to zero and as previously explained this is where the NPV is equal to the IRR because by definition the percentage figure for the IRR may only be calculated at the point where the NPV is equal to zero. The graph shows that where the NPV is positive (i.e. giving a decision to accept), for example using a discount rate (cost of capital) of k_1, R is greater than k_1. The NPV, which is measured by the height of the line connecting k_1 with the NPV function (the curved line AB), is clearly positive. This is because the function slopes downwards as the discount rate increases. For every increase in the discount rate the present value of the positive cash flow is decreased (i.e. 14 per cent will give a lower PV than 8 per cent). While the initial investment only remains unchanged, the

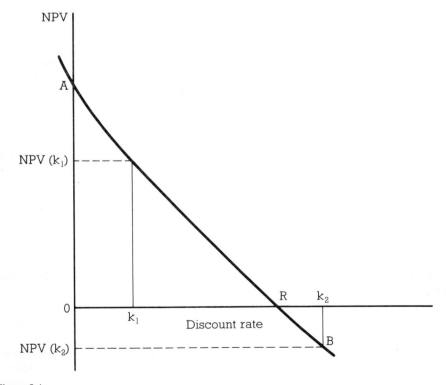

Figure 8.1

* Published by Prentice-Hall International, 3rd edition, 1986, pages 58–9.

project NPV declines until it reaches zero at point R. All projects less than R (to the left of R) should be accepted according to the NPV decision rules. According to the IRR decision rules, projects where R is greater than k_1 should be accepted. Thus both rules agree. Conversely, in the example of k_2 the NPV is negative so the project should not be pursued. Also, R is less than k_2 so according to the IRR rules the project should be rejected. Consequently, managers in companies evaluating totally independent projects need not get embroiled in the debate over where the NPV is to be preferred to the IRR or vice versa.

NPV v. IRR Dependent Projects

However, a direct confrontation between two methods of profitability analysis cannot be avoided once the assumption of independence is cast aside. In fact this is in reality the most likely situation to occur because financial resources are finite, or really only one new factory is required, or only one new product to extend the line. The problems raised by such dependency may be illustrated by the following example of two one-year projects:

	Initial investment outlay	*Net inflow at the end of the year*
Project A	− 10 000	11 800
Project B	− 15 000	17 550

Since both projects have one-year durations their IRRs can be calculated directly, using the formula without recourse to present value tables (as it is only one year):

$$\sum \frac{S}{(1 + R)^t} = I_O$$

where S is the sum received from the investment, R = the IRR, I_O = investment outlay

$$\frac{11\ 800}{1 + IRR_A} = 10\ 000, \text{ hence } IRR_A = 18\%$$

$$\frac{17\ 550}{1 + IRR_B} = 15\ 000, \text{ hence } IRR_B = 17\%$$

Assuming a cost of capital K = 10% (discount factor = 0.909), the NPVs of the two projects are given by:

	Net inflow		*Discount factor*	*Less initial outlay*		*NPV*
Project A	11 800	×	0.909	− 10 000	=	726.60
Project B	17 550	×	0.909	− 15 000	=	952.95

Thus, despite the fact that project A has the higher internal rate of return, project B has the larger net present value:

	IRR	NPV
Project A	18%	726.60
Project B	17%	952.95

If the projects are independent, both A and B are clearly acceptable using either the NPV or IRR decision rules. The difficulty arises when a choice must be made for one or the other of the projects, i.e. they are mutually exclusive. The choice of decision criterion assures considerable importance where the IRR and the NPV rank alternative projects in a different order of precedence, since only the highest ranked project is likely to be chosen.

Table 8.4   Comparing the NPV and the IRR for a specific project

Discount factor:	NPV		IRR	
k = PV factor	Project A	Project B	Project A	Project B
10% = 0.909	726.60	952.50	18%	17%
12% = 0.893	537.40	672.15	18%	17%
14% = 0.877	348.60	391.35	18%	17%
15% = 0.870	266.60	268.50	18%	17%
16% = 0.862	171.60	128.10	18%	17%
17% = 0.855	89.00	5.25	18%	17%
18% = 0.847	−0.54	−15.15	18%	17%

Table 8.4 shows clearly that the NPV ranking is dependent on the chosen discount rate. For costs of capital of 16 per cent or greater there is no contradiction as both the NPV and the IRR rank project A the highest (although in the example only 16 per cent and 17 per cent seem inherently attractive as at 18 per cent the choice is based on loss minimalization). However, for discount rates of 15 per cent or less the two methods of decision criteria result in different project rankings; project B has the higher NPV while project A provides the highest IRR score. Consequently, the marketing manager or business investor is still not provided with a clear-cut decision framework with which to select business projects from several possibilities when only one may be chosen. Further deliberation is therefore necessary. One very relevant factor so far ignored is the absolute size of the different investments and their returns.

Differences in the size of the alternative investments

Consider the following example:

	0	1	2	3
Project A	− 1 000	+ 550	+ 550	+ 550
Project B	− 11 500	+ 5000	+ 5000	+ 5000

The NPV for project A assuming a 10 per cent discount factor is:

$$£550 \times 0.909 + £550 \times 0.826 + £550 \times 0.751 - £1000$$
$$= £499.95 + £454.30 + £413.05 - £1000$$
$$= £367.3$$

Similarly the NPV for project B is:

$$£5000 \times 0.909 + £5000 \times 0.826 + £5000 \times 0.751 - £11\ 500$$
$$= £4545 + £4130 + £375.5 - £11\ 500$$
$$= £930$$

The IRR of project A is calculated using the special formula where the cash flows are identical in each year. This is a slight variation to the IRR formula used previously on page 110 $(1 + R)$, which represented the IRR, and is rewritten as Q, the discount factor, taking into account the number of years (n) for which a return is received which is necessary for calculating the percentage return over a period of time:

$$Q(n, R) = \frac{I_0}{S} = \frac{1\ 000}{550} = 1.818$$

where S = amount received per year
     n = the number of years
     I_0 = the initial investment.

Looking for the value 1.818 on the three-year line of the present value of asset of annuity tables shows 1.816 under the 30 per cent column. Consequently the IRR of project A is 30 per cent. Using the same formula, the IRR of project B is:

$$Q(n, R) = \frac{11\ 500}{5000} = 2.3$$

Again, looking up the value along the three-year line of the present value of a set of annuity tables, 14 per cent is 2.322 and 15 per cent is 2.283, therefore the IRR is very nearly $14\frac{1}{2}$ per cent. The position may be summarized:

	NPV	IRR
Project A	£367.3	30%
Project B	£930.0	$14\frac{1}{2}\%$

If the projects are mutually exclusive, then there is the old problem that the different investment rules provide different decisions. A way around this difficulty and one which takes the marketing manager towards an acceptable practical solution is to consider the incremental cash flow represented by such a choice:

	0	1	2	3
Project B	£11 500	5000	5000	5000
Project A	£1 000	550	550	550
'B minus A'	£10 500	4450	4450	4450

The IRR of 'B minus A' is:

$$Q(n, R) = \frac{10\ 500}{4450} = 2.36 = 13\%$$

Effectively this means that the marketing manager has a new set of projects to choose from: using the IRR criterion, project A would be chosen. However, project 'B minus A' also provides an acceptable IRR providing a return of 13 per cent where the cost of capital is 10 per cent. That is for a second investment of £10 500 an additional £4450 is produced each year for three years. This in fact leads the firm to choose A and 'B – A' which is effectively B. Thus the IRR rule, when used incrementally indicates the decision to select project B, which is precisely the project with the higher NPV. While this example has served to explain the superiority of the NPV over the IRR as a decision criterion for the selection of investment projects, it is important to note that where the cost of capital is greater than 13 per cent in our example it would not be financially feasible to proceed with the hypothetical project 'B – A'.

To conclude, the NPV method, by automatically examining and comparing the incremental cash flows against the cost of capital, ensures that managers will choose the optimal financial investment. The IRR criterion is ultimately rejected because it focuses on percentage rather than absolute returns. Thus the IRR method will always prefer a 50 per cent return on £1 to a 17 per cent return on £1 million.

Risk and Uncertainty

Risk and uncertainty are at the very centre of the capital investment decision. Ignoring their existence is both naïve and foolhardy; however, incorporating them within the decision-making framework adds another layer of calculations to what is already a complicated analytical process.

A company's expectations of the future gains from an investment project are usually based upon details of past performance coupled with forecasts of future events and the company's expectations of deriving a financial advantage from the antici- pated conditions in the market. Consequently, management decisions at the very best rest on estimates of a range of future costs and revenues and estimates of the relative chances of deriving a profit or making a loss.

Certainty

Absolute certainty should really only be used in calculations where the expectations about the future outcomes of an event are unanimous: in short, there is only one predictable result. In practice this is rarely possible; however, three-month Treasury bills are an exception because they produce an exact return on redemption.

Risk

Risk may be used to describe a situation where the return on an investment is not known in advance with absolute certainty, but where a range of alternative outcomes may be predicted each with an assigned subjective probability as to the likelihood of their happening. Consequently, the investment decision may then be based upon the expected profit which takes into account each possible outcome with its estimated probability. Consider the following three projects:

The maximum expected NPV criterion:

Project A		Project B		Project C	
NPV	*Probability*	*NPV*	*Probability*	*NPV*	*Probability*
10	1	− 2	0.30	− 20	0.40
		4	0.35	0	0.10
		16	0.35	40	0.50

The NPVs of projects B and C are calculated by multiplying each expected outcome by the estimate of the probability of its occurrence.

The expected profit of A $= 10 \times 1 = 10$

$$\begin{aligned}
\text{The expected profit of B} &= (-2 \times 0.3) + (4 \times 0.35) + (16 \times 0.35) \\
&= \quad -0.6 \quad + \quad 1.4 \quad + \quad 5.6 \quad = 6.4
\end{aligned}$$

$$\begin{aligned}
\text{The expected profit of C} &= (-20 \times 0.4) + (0 \times 0.10) + (40 \times 0.50) \\
&= \quad -8 \quad + \quad 0 \quad + \quad 20 \quad = 12
\end{aligned}$$

The projects may be ranked thus: C 12.0
A 10.0
B   6.4

Having calculated the expectations of each of the three alternative projects, it is now possible to choose that project with the highest expected NPV, i.e. C.

However, the fact that the maximum expected NPV criterion may be applied does not necessarily mean that it should always be used. Indeed, it may quite often be inappropriate because it does not explicitly take risk into account. Two projects may have the same expected NPV but one may be inherently riskier than the other because the range of expected outcomes is larger (project C goes from − 20 to + 40) where there is a 40 per cent (0.4) chance of a large loss. The maximum downside risk should be considered. Also, one project may be more prone to adverse economic conditions. This should also be taken into consideration when deciding between alternative projects.

9

THE BALANCE SHEET CAPITALIZATION OF BRAND NAMES

The Valuation of Brand Names

In 1988 and 1989 a number of leading companies (among them Ranks Hovis McDougall, Grand Metropolitan and United Biscuits) included in their balance sheets, or as notes to their balance sheets, the values of their brand names. This development represented a significant innovation in the presentation of the accounts, and resulted in large additions to the capital employed previously shown for the companies concerned.

Two distinct kinds of valuations were made: (1) the value of the brand names acquired by the takeover of other companies, or of a majority interest in other companies, and (2) the values of internally generated, or domestic, brand names. Some companies were content to value acquired brand names at the (historical) cost of acquisition, this cost being part of the goodwill paid for when a company with valuable brand names was taken over. Other companies valued both acquired and domestic brand names. In a number of cases these additional values increased net assets by many millions of pounds. For example, Guinness valued acquired brand names at £1.7 billion; United Biscuits reported that its leading brands had been independently valued at over £1.0 billion, but only included in its balance sheet acquired brands at a value of £107.0 million.

The two kinds of valuation mentioned above require somewhat different accounting treatment. Consider first the brands obtained by a takeover operation. The value of the brands acquired would, presumably, be included in the consideration given for the shares taken over, that consideration consisting of cash and/or an exchange of shares. If the total consideration exceeded the value of the net assets acquired, then the difference would be treated as an asset and called 'goodwill'. The value of the brand names acquired would form part, and probably a substantial part, of the figure of goodwill. It would be customary to write off goodwill against reserves or profit either immediately on completion of the takeover or within a few years thereafter. Thus when the decision was made to enter the value of the brand names acquired, this would involve, in effect, reinstating the appropriate proportion of the goodwill written off with a corresponding entry to increase the reserves, or, if the goodwill had not been written off, by reducing it by the value of the brand names which it included.

It would not be possible to calculate the cost of internally generated brand names in the same way. These would therefore be assessed by a valuation methodology. All the running in this area has been made by Interbrand Group plc, whose formula has been accepted by the auditors of RHM, Grand Metropolitan and United Biscuits. The entry in the balance sheet of the value of internally generated brands (only RHM did this) would involve an equal addition to reserves, i.e. increasing the shareholders' interest in the company.

The provisional advice of the Accounting Standards Committee was that, pending further considerations of this development, only acquired brand names should be entered in the balance sheet, and the value attributed to them shall be their cost. The value of other brand names could be shown as a note to the balance sheet. However, events have moved rather more quickly.

Buying International Market Share

The prospect of the ownership of Rowntree changing hands at a price of 25 to 30 times its current annual earnings in the Suchard-Nestlé takeover battle in the summer of 1988 served to focus the attention of managers, financiers and speculators on the hitherto unappreciated value of some big-name consumer brands.

Previously when one company seemed to pay rather 'too much' for ownership of another, the analysts and journalists attempted to justify the predator's action as a defensive one – to keep it out of the hands of a competitor. However, when Martini Rossi paid FFr 1.1 billion for Benedictine (135 times the 1987 earnings) it was explained by many as simply a unique opportunity to buy a 600-year-old brand.

In reality the companies were purchasing market share. The reason was that they might derive the benefits of dominating specific product markets in particular parts of the world. These benefits are essentially economies of scale, whereby certain overheads may be apportioned over greater production volumes, and tactics whereby attacking a competitor in his home market may keep him sufficiently preoccupied to limit activity in other markets.

The Application – Balance Sheet Repair

Some companies have been very quick to appreciate the benefits of valuing their major brands and adding this sum to the asset side of their balance sheets under the heading of 'intangibles'. The advantage to these companies is the partial elimination of the problems associated with the accounting treatment of goodwill which frequently arises on the acquisition of another company. Until the issue of ED47, which seeks changes to SSAP 22, a company which acquired another at a high premium on the value of its net tangible assets (called goodwill) was likely to see its consolidated reserves subsequently fall dramatically. This has two major disadvantages:

1. It reduces the balance sheet value of the new consolidated business, which in turn restricts the new consolidated business's predatory activity. Under the Stock Exchange rules a company cannot mount a takeover bid for another that exceeds the value of 25 per cent of its net assets without referring the plans to the shareholders. This has the disadvantages of delay, loss of secrecy and possible veto.
2. It confuses many of the ordinary shareholders who are not quite sure exactly whether they are 'better off' or 'worse off' after the takeover.

An example should make the situation clear:

Company A takes over Company B (figures in £ millions)

(Pre-takeover valuations)

	Company A				Company B		
	£m		£m		£m		£m
Ordinary		Fixed		Ordinary		Fixed	
shares	1000	assets	1200	shares	95	assets	100
Reserves	300	Working		Reserves	5	Working	
Loan		capital	150	Loan		capital	20
capital	50			capital	20		
	£1350m		£1350m		£120m		£120m

Company A pays £400 million for Company B: the bid being financed by a £50 million 'rights issue' and £350 million loan capital.

Company A takes over Company B

Consolidated balance sheet after takeover

	Company A (including B)		
	£m		£m
Ordinary shares	1050	Fixed assets	1300
Reserves	300	Goodwill	280
Loan capital	400	Working capital	170
	£1750m		£1750m

An important feature of the takeover is the change in the gearing ratio of company A.* The company has moved from a position of very low gearing to one of quite high gearing by many standards.

$$\text{Before takeover:} \quad \frac{50}{1300} = 3.85\%$$

$$\text{After takeover:} \quad \frac{420}{1350} = 31.11\%$$

The impact of this on the financial position of Company A is that the fixed interest charge has dramatically increased which will be a drain on future profits until the advantages of the takeover are realized. As a consequence, the earnings per share will go down if the directors do not write off goodwill. This of course will in turn affect the stock market valuation of the shares. Consequently, there is considerable pressure

* Gearing ratio = $\dfrac{\text{Borrowed capital}}{\text{Shareholders' funds}}$ %.

to write off the goodwill from the acquisition. This will in turn further weaken the consolidated balance sheets.

According to accounting guidelines this writing off should take place in the year of the acquisition or soon after.* Indeed, considerable pressure may be brought to bear by the auditing accountants and informed opinion. The goodwill is written off against capital reserves to effect the balance. However, companies with established f.m.c.g. (fast moving consumer goods) brands will be in the fortunate position of being able to capitalize the brands and put the values in the balance sheet. This may compensate to a greater or lesser extent for the amount of goodwill written off and serve to 'repair' the balance sheet.

Company A takes over Company B

Consolidated balance sheet after writing off goodwill

	Company A (including B)		
	£m		£m
Ordinary shares	1050	Fixed assets	1300
Reserves	20	Working capital	170
Loan capital	420		
	£1470m		£1470m

The new gearing ratio is 420/1050 = 40 per cent, which is high by most standards.

Grand Metropolitan, after it acquired Heublein (famous for the brand Smirnoff Vodka) for $1.3 billion, was obliged to write off £600 million from shareholders' funds. The gearing ratio, which had been 45 per cent before the acquisition, rose to an incredible 106 per cent afterwards.

There is clearly much scope for dual interpretation of SSAP 22, although until recently the conservative approach of writing off the amount of goodwill (or purchase premium) against reserves in the first year prevailed. Paragraph 13 of SSAP 22 offers further encouragement for those companies keen to repair their post-takeover balance sheets. It states that 'separate net assets may include identifiable intangibles such as those specifically mentioned in the balance sheet formats in the Companies Act 1981, i.e. "concessions, patents, licences, trademarks and similar rights and assets" '. Identifiable intangibles such as these form part of the separate net assets which are recorded in the acquiring company's net accounts. This is the statement that was used by Grand Metropolitan to justify adding £588 million to its balance sheet, valuing major brands it had acquired in the three years to September 1988.

However, Grand Metropolitan's decision still represented a major step forward from the common practice which recognized only tangible assets on the balance sheet. It also opened the door for Ranks Hovis McDougall to revalue its existing

---

* The Statement of Standard Accounting Practice 22 (SSAP 22) Accounting for Goodwill, as issued by the Institute of Chartered Accountants' Accounting Standards Committee, recommends that goodwill is either to be written off immediately to reserves (the preferred option) or capitalized and amortized over its useful life. Paragraph 30 of SSAP 22, on the other hand, requires that 'goodwill' should not include any value for separate intangibles. The amount of these if material should be included under the appropriate heading within intangible fixed assets in the balance sheet. ED47 now proposes that purchased goodwill be recognized as an asset, carried in the balance sheet and amortized over 20 years. Internally generated goodwill should not, however, be treated in this way.

brands by £678 million in December 1988, taking its balance sheet asset value from £254 million to £932 million.

The Case for Capitalization of Home-Grown Brands

It is, however, the decision of RHM to capitalize home-grown brands that has really caused the controversy. The actions of Nestlé, Martini Rossi and Grand Metropolitan were seen as a progressive movement by companies in an appreciation of the true value of some well-established f.m.c.g. brand names. Many marketing specialists and corporate financiers, accepting that perhaps the earnings potential of certain major brands had been underestimated in the past, were sympathetic to this progressive approach. However, very few people were ready for RHM's 370 per cent increase in the valuations of its assets. The reason for the revaluation was clearly not balance sheet repair, but a pure defensive tactic against the threat of a hostile takeover.

At the time of writing this chapter it is probably true to say that most managers are in the process of digesting RHM's actions. Corporate opinion is essentially conservative. The controversy is more about the fact that the valuation of home-grown brands represents a new development in marketing strategy rather than outright ideological criticism.

Until now, the combination of conservative accounting standards and the complexities of asset valuation has meant that many companies have excluded their most valuable assets from the balance sheet. This in itself has always caused some concern, as a balance sheet is supposed to show the underlying financial strength of a business. Consequently, it may be stated that the principal benefits of incorporating brands in the balance sheet are as follows:

1. For many established f.m.c.g. companies, a balance sheet which includes brand valuation provides a more realistic picture of the assets owned by the business.
2. Recognizing the value of brands separately at the time of an acquisition reduces the amount of goodwill that traditionally should be written off against reserves. This immediate write-off has a detrimental effect on consolidated reserves and confuses the real value of the acquisition.
3. The alternative and less common annual amortization of a proportion of the goodwill presents a continuing and unrealistic drain on future profits.
4. Valuation of brands facilitates better financial comparisons between companies operating in similar markets where the mix between home-grown and acquired brands may vary considerably. It is difficult to justify separate treatment for balance-sheet purposes since both can be equally valuable as assets to their corporate owner.
5. Capitalization of brands may very well assist companies in their expansion plans because it will reduce the amounts written off against reserves on consolidation of the balance sheets and have a lesser impact on the capital gearing ratio.

The Implications of Capitalization

Where brands are successful and seem likely to continue so for the foreseeable future, any discussion of amortization is clearly superfluous. However, should for some reason a brand suffer a reduction in value or be perceived to have a finite life, then clearly provision should be made for the brand's replacement in accordance with the provision for the replacement of any other asset.

Depreciation is likely to remain a contentious issue in the debate on brand capitalization simply because the value judgments will be made by sales and marketing specialists, although for more than a decade the accountant's considerable agility has been shown in upward revaluation as well as depreciation of certain fixed assets.

It may be necessary to move towards some definition of what constitutes a leading brand or have some criteria regarding age for reaching a qualifying maturity. Most sales and marketing professionals should accept that a leading brand only dies if it is allowed to (which suggests incompetence in the skills of selling and marketing). Clearly, if demand changes, the astute professional repositions the leading products and brands the better to satisfy the needs of the consumer. In this context, it would be interesting to know what happened to draught Double Diamond: a lot was spent promoting this brand in the 1960s and early 1970s. Indeed, what has happened to Woodbine, Capstan, Riley, Wolseley and many other 'household' names?

Capitalization Methodology – the Interbrand Group Plc Formula

The lead in this debate has been taken by Interbrand Group plc and Ranks Hovis McDougall. Their methodology, which was the first to have been accepted by accountants in their capacity as auditors, is based on the following concepts:

1. The method must consider all the marketing, financial and legal aspects of the brand.
2. Fundamental accounting concepts must be followed in the calculations.
3. The requirements of the Companies Acts should be adhered to.
4. The method should make allowances for any future revaluations that may be required.
5. The techniques used should be equally applicable to home-grown and acquired brands.

The Interbrand methodology is only concerned with the valuation of a brand as an ongoing product that is being sold in the market-place. It is not designed to calculate the 'break-up' value of a company. The calculations follow a logical pattern that starts with the brand's historical profits and then proceeds to compute a future earnings multiple based on the product in its present form. No attempt is made to include possible extensions to the line or any fanciful licensing deals.

Brand Profitability

The most important factor determining the value of a brand is its profitability over a period of time. However, calculating the balance sheet value is not just a multiple of the post-tax profits. Where, for example, a brand is very dependent on an exclusive distribution for its sales, a discount factor should be applied to reflect the elements of profit that are not related to the brand itself. Care must also be taken not to include an unrepresentative year's profits that may be higher or lower than the norm. Interbrand used a three-year weighted average of the post-tax profit figure for RHM.

Brand Strength

The multiple that is applied to the weighted average brand profit figure is derived from an in-depth assessment of the brand's strength. This is based on a composite of seven weighted factors, each of which is scored according to clearly established and consistent guidelines.

1. Leadership

A brand which dominates its rivals in the market or market sector is a far more valuable property than one lower down the order. Generally, first is best, second is acceptable and any other position is marginal, although there are exceptions.

2. Stability

Long-established brands which command consumer loyalty and have become part of the fabric of their markets are particularly valuable. For example, a brand such as Adidas, which is currently third in the sports shoe market but has a much longer track record than Reebok and Nike, might be given a higher multiple. Any major repositioning of the brand can diminish the value attributed to its longevity. Thus, for example, if Croft, launched in 1876 (see Table 9.1), had been a budget-priced product until 1978 it would lose much of the benefit of 102 years' post-registration.

Table 9.1 shows the age of some of the leading brands from two of the companies at the centre of this debate. Cadbury's, who were not so directly involved, did, however, own the products in the Premier Brands stable until Paul Judge organized a management buy-out. Paul Judge's objective was to maximize the sales potential of those leading Cadbury brands that were being used to finance other divisions of the company and in the process being allowed to fade and ultimately die.

Table 9.1 Can supported brands last for ever? Ten leading brands from three major consumer goods companies – and each brand's birth date

Ranks Hovis McDougall[1]		Grand Metropolitan[1]		Cadbury's[2]	
Cerebos	1894	Croft	1876	Dairy Milk	1905
Hovis	1895	Gilbey	1876	Bournville	1908
Bisto	1927	Ruddles	1911	Fry's Turkish	
Mothers Pride	1936	J&B	1937	Delight	1914
Granary	1936	Holsten Diet Pils	1949	Milk Tray	1915
Sharwood's	1947	Malibu	1973	Flake	1920
Nimble	1956	Holsten Export	1978	Creme Eggs	1926
Mr Kipling	1969	Foster's	1981	Fruit and Nut	1928
(Energen) One-		Webster's Yorkshire		Fry's Crunchie	1929
cal	1974	Bitter	1982	Roses	1938
McDougalls	1986	Budweiser[3]	1984	Fudge	1948

1 First UK trade mark registration.
2 When brand first appeared on market.

Source: Marketing, 2 February 1989.

3. Market

Brands in markets such as food and drink are intrinsically more valuable than brands in the high technology or ladies' clothing market sectors. The latter are most vulnerable to rapid changes and it is very difficult for a single company to lead over an extended period of time when the technology changes every two or three years and ladies' fashions every few months.

4. Internationality

Brands which are international are inherently more valuable than national or regional brands. To qualify, brands need the same name in their different international markets: thus Unilever's range of fabric conditioners would not score highly as 'Comfort' is called 'Snuggle' in the United States and 'Fa Fa' in Japan. Not all brands, of course, have the required international appeal, but brand owners have in the past ignored the opportunities that may exist for their products in other markets. Satellite broadcasting, media overlaps and cheap travel all contribute towards the internationalization of consumer taste and expectations. 'Heineken, Chanel and McDonalds sacrifice none of their brands' distinctiveness to cater for local tastes. The power of these brands resides in the consistency of their product, packaging, price, positioning, image and appeal.'*

5. Market Trends

The overall long-term trend of the brand is an important measure of its ability to remain contemporary and relevant to its customers' requirements. RHM's 'Bisto' and Cadbury's 'Dairy Milk' would score well in this category although the very highest scores would go to brands which are growing in their market share in a growing market. This is clearly difficult to do over a period of half a century.

6. Support

Brand names which over the years have received consistent investment and focused support from advertising campaigns and sales promotions must be regarded as more valuable than those which have not. The quality of the support for the campaign is thought to be as important as the amount actually spent on the advertising. A case in point is British Telecom, who advertise very heavily on television that their customers are important to them, and regularly follow up with a telephone survey to monitor the degree of consumer satisfaction.

7. Legal Protection

This is more of a minus if brands do not have a trade mark or logo or symbol that has been registered. Brands without this protection are not counted in any balance sheet valuation unless there is some very well-established common law precedent.

* Extracted from 'The role of brand valuation in marketing strategy' by Tom Blackett and Christine Berry of the Interbrand Group. The paper was obtained by the authors from Interbrand Group plc and is not known to have been published at the time of writing this chapter.

Similarly, sales and profits in countries where legal trade mark protection is weak would generally not be included in this calculation.

The brand under valuation is scored for each of the above factors according to the weightings attributed to them and the resultant total, known as the 'brand strength score', is expressed as a percentage. The Interbrand methodology is thought to be consistent, logical and capable of verification.

Determining the Multiple

The relationship between brand strength as shown by the brand strength score and the multiple of earnings to be applied may be shown graphically as an S curve. In fixing the multiples to be applied to the brand strength score the following must be taken into account:

1. A brand with no strength is not a true brand and has no value.
2. The closest available analogy to the return from a notional perfect brand is the return from a risk-free investment. However:
   (a) the perfect brand does not operate in a risk-free environment;
   (b) the return from a risk-free investment is capital free whilst part of a brand's earnings result from the capital employed in producing the product.

   Allowances for these factors must be taken into account in determining the multiple to be applied for a brand operating in a real business environment. Thus the highest multiple that can be applied will be somewhat lower than that for a risk-free investment and may vary from business to business and industry to industry.
3. The multiples at the high end of the scale will probably be greater than the average P/E ratio of the sector in which the company operates. Those at the low end of the scale will be below this ratio.

The multiple to be applied to each brand is determined by its brand strength score. The shape of the S curve is justified for the following reasons:

1. As brand strength increases from virtually zero (an unknown or new brand) to a position as number 3 or 4 in a market, the value increases gradually.
2. As the brand moves into the number 2 or particularly the number 1 position in its market and/or becomes known internationally, there is an accelerated increase in its value.
3. Once a brand has become a powerful world brand, the growth in value no longer increases at the same rate.

An Example of Brand Valuation

In this example four food brands with different marketing strengths are going to be considered though each makes the same brand profit of £10 million.

Brand W is an international brand (registered 1932) that is maintaining its market share.
Brand X is a leading national brand (registered 1921).
Brand Y is a secondary national brand (registered 1954) with a declining market share.
Brand Z is an own-label product (registered 1988).

Strength factors	Maximum Score	Brand W	Brand X	Brand Y	Brand Z
Leadership	25	19	19	10	0
Stability	15	11	12	8	0
Market	10	8	7	7	0
Internationality	25	21	5	1	0
Trend	10	8	8	4	0
Support	10	7	8	7	0
Protection	5	5	4	4	0
Brand strength score	100%	79	63	41	0
Brand profits[1] (after tax, etc.)	–	£10m	£10m	£10m	£0m
Multiple applied	–	17	13.5	6.5	0
Valuation	–	£170m	£135m	£65m	£0m

1. This brand premium profit is due to the intrinsic value of the brand over and above the basic product.

The Importance for Sales and Marketing Management

Attributing a financial value to a particular brand can give the brand an entirely new and enhanced status in the eyes of the company's marketing and financial managers. Even if the brand valuation is not capitalized by including it in the assets of the business listed in the balance sheet, it is still a company asset which must be efficiently managed to generate future revenue. The successful application or otherwise of these management skills can be measured by any increases or decreases in the subsequent valuation.

This confers a new form of accountability on sales and marketing managers, because the valuation process isolates the elements of a brand's profitability which can directly be attributed to the actions of its managers. One of the criteria for evaluating tactical and strategic decisions relating to the brand after valuation will clearly be: 'What are the implications on the value of the brand?' In the future, a brand manager's performance may be assessed on the increase in value of a brand that is his or her responsibility in the same way that sales managers are judged on the volume of goods sold by their team of salesmen and the profit from those sales.

The following points, however, need to be borne in mind when interpreting accounts which contain valuations of brand names:

1. The objectivity of the balance sheet as a statement of unexpired cost is eroded by introducing valuations of intangible assets such as brand names. Nevertheless, those valuations will be justified if they provide more useful information to readers of the accounts.
2. The balance sheet will become more of a mixture of historical cost and assessed current values. This will be particularly so where purchased brand names are shown at cost whilst those internally generated are shown at their estimated present worth to the business.

Furthermore, the values attributed to the brand names will not be immutable since they will depend on the success of the business.

3. The consequent increase in reserves will reduce the profit as a percentage of capital employed. Thus it will be difficult to compare results with those of previous years before the brand names were valued. Likewise difficulties will arise in comparing the results with the profitability of companies where brand names are not valued.

GRAND METROPOLITAN PLC showing the difference to the balance sheet and the gearing ratio of capitalising leading brands:

	1989	
	Including brands	*Excluding brands*
	£bn	£bn
Fixed assets	6.6	4.0
Other assets (net)	(0.2)	(0.2)
Borrowings	(3.6)	(3.6)
Shareholders' funds	2.8	0.2
Gearing	128%	1800%

Source: Grand Metropolitan plc.

PART THREE

Market Planning

10 MARKET MEASUREMENT, SALES FORECASTING AND TARGETING

The uniqueness of marketing amongst all the professional skills that are part of the world of business is the extent to which it focuses on the customer's real needs. Before the marketing concept was widely understood, many businesses made those goods and services which they had the knowledge and resources to produce. Once the products were completed, the salesforce was turned loose on the unsuspecting population. Sales people and managers were given their targets or quotas and accountants calculated the breakeven point, carefully allocating overheads in the preferred manner.

However, in very few instances was any serious attempt made to quantify the size of the market in terms of what the consumer needed or wanted or to calculate the volume of sales that might be achieved over a period of time. All the skills and effort had been applied internally to the organization without attempting to consider two very important factors: the consumer, and the competition.

This chapter is going to examine the marketing concept of segmentation which is used to measure or estimate the size of a market. This approach is then supplemented with practical financial and numerical techniques for increasing the accuracy of sales forecasting and then focuses attention on the most profitable options for the business to pursue.

Market Segmentation

To examine the total market for a product or service is to paint a picture with a very broad brush and generally only serves as a starting point in the analysis, the reason being that the demand specification is so generalized as to be particular to only a very small percentage of buyers. A major feature in Western developed market economies is freedom of choice. As the economies are developed, many consumers are seeking to purchase additional benefits above and beyond the basic product.

The market for housing in Great Britain can be used as a very good example (albeit somewhat out of its usual context) because of the vast amount of precise analysis that has been done on this subject. First thoughts might put this market as the total population (some 54 million people). Then one might consider the fact that some people prefer to live in towns, while others live in rural areas. Other variations occur in the type of accommodation (house or flat) and whether the inhabitants are the owners, in the process of purchasing the property, or tenants.

Indeed, so much work has been done in this area that 'A Classification of Residential Neighbourhoods' (ACORN) has gained widespread acceptance as a market

Table 10.1   1981 ACORN profile Great Britain: ACORN groups.

		1981 population Thousand	%
A	Agricultural areas	1811	3.4
B	Modern family housing, higher incomes	8667	16.2
C	Older housing of intermediate status	9420	17.6
D	Poor quality older terraced housing	2321	4.3
E	Better-off council estates	6977	13.0
F	Less well-off council estates	5033	9.4
G	Poorest council estates	4049	7.6
H	Multi-racial areas	2086	3.9
I	High status non-family areas	2248	4.2
J	Affluent suburban housing	8515	15.9
K	Better-off retirement areas	2041	3.8
U	Unclassified	389	0.7

Source: ACORN User's Guide, CACI Market Analysis Division.

segmentation grid. The rationale is that similar neighbourhoods will have similar demographic and social characteristics representing similar life-style features. These in turn will be translated into purchasing habits.

Table 10.1 shows the 12 basic 'ACORN groups' and Table 10.2 gives a list of 39 relatively homogeneous 'ACORN types', made by subdividing the groups on a local basis.

Bases of Segmentation

In the previous section segmentation was presented as an approach for measuring demand in a realistic way by attempting to distinguish between different types of consumption in the market for housing. In this section, the generally accepted alternative methods for segmentation will be examined; for consumer markets they are: geographic, demographic, psychographic and behavioural.

Geographic Segmentation

This is a method of dividing a total market based on significant regional differences that will have an effect on consumer requirements. This method is generally of lesser significance in European countries than in the United States of America, because demographic divisions based on nationality differences tend to override the geographic distinctions. For example, differences in the market for package holidays between France and Germany are probably more to do with custom and national characteristics than geographical location.

However, in Great Britain the following factors are relevant: rural and urban in terms of home central heating, for example, with oil being used in rural areas and gas in urban areas. This may be explained by the fact that laying a gas main in high population density urban areas is a sound economic proposition. Furthermore, many

Table 10.2   ACORN types

			1981 population	
			Thousand	%
A	1	Agricultural villages	1376	2.6
A	2	Areas of farms and smallholdings	435	0.8
B	3	Cheap modern private housing	2210	4.1
B	4	Recent private housing, young families	1649	3.1
B	5	Modern private housing, older children	3121	5.8
B	6	New detached houses, young families	1405	2.6
B	7	Military bases	282	0.5
C	8	Mixed owner-occupied and council estates	1880	3.5
C	9	Small town centres and flats above shops	2157	4.0
C	10	Villages with non-farm employment	2463	4.6
C	11	Older private housing, skilled workers	2920	5.5
D	12	Unimproved terraces with old people	1352	2.5
D	13	Pre-1914 terraces, low income families	762	1.4
D	14	Tenement flats lacking amenities	207	0.4
E	15	Council estates, well-off older workers	1916	3.6
E	16	Recent council estates	1393	2.6
E	17	Council estates, well-off young workers	2615	4.9
E	18	Small council houses, often Scottish	1052	2.0
F	19	Low rise estates in industrial towns	2538	4.7
F	20	Inter-war council estates, older people	1668	3.1
F	21	Council housing for the elderly	827	1.5
G	22	New council estates in inner cities	1080	2.0
G	23	Overspill estates, high unemployment	1730	3.2
G	24	Council estates with overcrowding	868	1.6
G	25	Council estates with worst poverty	371	0.7
H	26	Multi-occupied terraces, poor Asians	204	0.4
H	27	Owner-occupied terraces with Asians	578	1.1
H	28	Multi-let housing with Afro-Caribbeans	387	0.7
H	29	Better-off-multi-ethnic areas	916	1.7
I	30	High status areas, few children	1129	2.1
I	31	Multi-let big old houses and flats	822	1.5
I	32	Furnished flats, mostly single people	297	0.6
J	33	Inter-war semis, white collar workers	3054	5.7
J	34	Spacious inter-war semis, big gardens	2677	5.0
J	35	Villages with wealthy older commuters	1534	2.9
J	36	Detached houses, exclusive suburbs	1250	2.3
K	37	Private houses, well-off elderly	1200	2.2
K	38	Private flats with single pensioners	842	1.6
U	39	Unclassified	389	0.7
Area total			53557	100.0

Source: ACORN User's Guide, CACI Market Analysis Division.

flats in urban areas would find it a nuisance to make room for a 500-gallon oil storage tank which in rural areas fits conveniently into an obscure corner of the garden.

Demographic Segmentation

This is probably the easiest concept to understand: essentially it means that consumption is examined under all the categories included in anti-discrimination legislation and a few more (yet to be included?) (age, sex, family size, family life cycle, income, occupation, education, religion, race and nationality). Another advantage of demographic segmentation is the availability of the information from census data. It is also substantially accurate, although clearly there is degradation as the data tends towards being ten years old.

Multivariable demographic segmentation is an extension of this, and offers some interesting prospects for analysis. This is partially demonstrated in Table 10.3.

Table 10.3   Types of entertainment consumers want to have in a pub (base: 647 pub visitors)

					Acorn Group				
	All	AB*	C1	C2	DE	E,F,G	I,J,K	C,D	Other*
	%	%	%	%	%	%	%	%	%
Food bar (for snacks and pub meals)	54	72	62	46	47	42	65	55	54
Separate play room for children	40	32	38	42	42	32	42	42	45
Beer garden	39	38	46	34	38	34	43	34	45
Live music (say two or three times a week)	32	17	32	33	36	37	25	36	29
Play area outside for children with swings, apparatus, etc.	31	31	30	32	32	28	30	26	42
Juke box	24	11	21	24	31	29	19	27	17
Dart board	23	13	21	26	27	31	17	21	23
Pool table	23	16	17	21	31	32	16	21	19
Board/table games, e.g. dominoes, draughts, chess, Trivial Pursuit	17	11	19	18	18	21	13	16	18
Video juke box	14	5	11	16	20	21	10	12	11
Large screen TV set	10	1	10	11	14	14	7	16	5
Other types of pub games, e.g. bar billiards	10	4	8	11	12	13	6	12	8
Fruit machine	9	7	7	10	12	16	5	8	7
Games machine, e.g. Pacman and Atari types	7	3	6	8	8	11	4	7	5
None of these/don't know	9	10	10	8	10	10	13	8	7

* Denotes low sub-sample.

Source: BMRB/Mintel.

Clearly, target groups would have been more precisely identified, and their requirements understood and the appropriate product marketing plans effected, if the
ACORN and socio-economic classification (A, B, C1, C2, D, E) had been overlaid
on the age, gender and family commitments classifications as illustrated in
Table 10.4.

Table 10.4   Frequency of pub visiting (base: 938 adults)

	2–7 days a week %	About once a week %	Less often than once a week but at least once a month %	Less often than once a month %	Do not visit nowadays/ don't know %
ALL	20	16	13	20	31
Men	29	19	11	16	25
Women	11	13	11	16	36
Housewives	7	11	16	28	38
Other women*	34	23	10	6	26
Married	15	16	15	25	29
Unmarried	28	15	10	12	35
Child	23	19	12	21	25
No child	17	14	14	20	34
15–24	37	20	11	11	21
25–34	25	24	14	18	19
35–44	16	20	19	25	21
45–54	19	9	13	32	26
55–64	13	10	12	26	38
65 +	5	10	10	14	61
AB	18	10	18	21	34
C1	21	17	13	26	22
C2	19	21	16	18	27
D	22	14	9	22	33
E	17	13	11	14	47
ACORN Group					
E, F, G	21	19	10	14	36
I, J, K	24	11	14	20	31
C, D	18	18	17	23	25
B	17	13	13	26	32
Other	10	17	19	27	29

*Denotes low sub-sample.

Source: BMRB/Mintel.

Psychographic Segmentation

This recognizes that demographic segmentation can have serious limitations because not all people in the same demographic group behave in the same way or have the same purchasing preferences. Psychographic segmentation attempts to look at consumers in terms of social class, life style and personality.

A study by William Wells* distinguished between eight male life-style groups: the quiet family man, the traditionalist, the discontented man, the ethical highbrow, the pleasure-orientated man, the achiever, the he-man and the sophisticated man. 'The ethical highbrow' is described as 'a very concerned man, sensitive to people's needs. Basically a puritan, he is content with family life, friends and work, interested in literature, religion and social reform. As a consumer he is interested in quality, which may at times justify greater expenditure. He is well-educated, middle or upper socio-economic status, mainly middle-aged or older'.

A different study † by Daniel Greene identified five female life-style groups: the home-maker, the matriarch, the variety woman, the Cinderella and the glamour woman.

Behavioural Segmentation

This is the approach where buyers are divided into different groups according to when, how or why they use or purchase a product or service. Most types of travel are divided into business and leisure (purchase occasion), with further subdivisions according to budget. Segmentation according to the benefits sought from a product has been applied to many consumer products, but perhaps toothpaste is one of the better-known examples where some people select their toothpaste brand in the hope of preventing bad breath whereas others are more concerned about preventing dental decay.

User status (non-users, potential users, first-time users and ex-users) is another useful basis of segmentation. Usage rate is also commonly used and the analysis shown in Table 10.3 is a good example taken from a report produced by Mintel called 'Leisure Intelligence'.

The overriding importance of segmentation is that it provides an analytical framework for managers to develop a strategy and prepare budgets that reflect likely levels of purchase response.

Measuring the Segments and Calculating the Future Demand

Having decided on the most relevant segmentation strategy, calculating total potential demand is the next stage in the analysis. However, forecasting potential demand is not the ultimate objective: it is merely a stage in the process. What is of fundamental interest to businesses is the demand for *their products* and *when* that demand will be. In most markets there are several suppliers, therefore it is reasonable to assume that each supplier will obtain a share, however small, of that market.

* *Journal of Marketing Research*, May 1975, pp. 196–213.
† *Journal of Marketing Research*, February 1973, pp. 63–9.

Estimating the size of that share of the market over several time periods is the object of this exercise.

Measuring the segments is in fact frequently much less difficult than may initially be imagined. This is because it is likely that much of the work may have already been completed. Indeed, the task in question may be that of finding out where this information can be obtained, rather than engaging in new primary research.

There are a number of very good sources for tracking down this information, all of which can be found in a good specialist library which may be part of a university or polytechnic or the reference department of a public library. Examples of these in London are:

> The Postgraduate Business School Library, in Sussex Place, Regent's Park
> The Polytechnic of Central London Library, in Riding House Street, W1
> The Westminster Central Reference Library, in St Martin's Street, WC2.

It is also a good idea to become familiar with the various sources of the data; a very comprehensive guide is included in Chapter 4 of *Marketing Research for Managers*,* which includes details about government, company, industry and market sources. There is also the *Marketing Surveys Index†* which is a monthly publication listing all published marketing reports and surveys.

When measuring the segments in any market, there are likely to be three primary sources of data or marketing intelligence:

1. an omnibus survey (if one exists) giving the basic data on market characteristics related to product attributes. The Market Research Society will have details;
2. syndicated research services providing ongoing research and audits of certain markets, sponsored by 'syndicates' of businesses interested in the particular market;
3. secondary desk research, much of which will be available in the specialist libraries and through on-line databases, of which there are currently some 3000 in the United Kingdom. Many of the specialist business libraries subscribe to one or more of these databases.

It is probably easiest to explain this using a real example. In September 1987, one of the authors was involved in an analysis of the market for coin-operated amusement machines. Fairly quickly this was identified as some 70 000 public houses (28 000 free and 42 000 tied houses) operated by five large national and 62 regional breweries and an unknown number of other outlets. How to identify them, quantify them and obtain their names and addresses easily and cost-effectively? The answer was to approach *one* direct mailing list broker who was able to supply all the details in Table 10.5 except the fast-food outlets, which came from a secondary source – a total of 133 600 prospective customers neatly segmented by type of outlet.

Calculating the Future Demand

Having examined the various ways of optimally segmenting the target market and analysed published data about the identified groups' purchase profiles, it is now the moment to do the 'fine tuning' by new, very specific research. There are four very practical ways of obtaining the information:

---

* *Marketing Research for Managers* by Sunny Crouch published in paperback by Pan 1985 and hardback by Heinemann 1984.
† Published by Marketing Strategies for Industry of 32 Mill Green Road, Mitcham, Surrey CR4 4HY.

Table 10.5   The market for coin-operated amusement machines

Clubs for sports, recreation and entertainment, etc.	
Aero clubs	153
Amusement arcades	759
Art galleries and museums	1 357
Billiard halls	178
Bingo halls	400
Bowling clubs	2 156
Camping sites	1 421
Caravan sites:	
All	5 200
Over 75 berths	1 781
Cinemas	619
Concert halls and theatres	1 154
Entertainment Offices:	
Municipal	163
Film producing companies	134
Studios	59
Football clubs:	
Professional	130
Golf clubs:	
All	1 822
(Leading)	780
Greyhound tracks	60
Gymnasia and health clubs	393
Holiday camps	178
Leisure centres	299
Leisure parks	20
Leisure and recreation:	
Offices – municipal	476
Marinas and moorings	195
Night clubs and discotheques	528
Outdoor pursuit centres	67
Political party headquarters	870
Radio and television companies (including Branches)	142
Record companies	228
Recording studios	40
Riding holiday centres	36
Skating rinks	87
Squash clubs	1 499
Stately homes	832
Swimming pools	383
Ten-pin bowling alleys	45
Theatrical training schools	122
Working men's clubs	3 073
YMCA/YWCA	319
Yacht and sailing clubs	1 307

Table 10.5   continued

Youth clubs	1 307
Youth hostels	353
Zoological gardens	27
Other prospective buyers	
British Rail Area Boards	27
Wine bars*	1 013
Hovercraft and hydrofoil operators	3
Shipping lines	188
Fast-food outlets*	7 173
Residential homes – elderly	5 026
Residential homes – handicapped	346
Restaurants	17 084
Nursing homes – private	327
Universities and colleges	204
Colleges of technology, art and further education	632
Building and engineering colleges	273
Teachers' training colleges	172

Source: Key Postal Advertising Ltd, direct mail brokers who can supply the names and addresses printed on labels or envelopes for a rental fee.

**Source*: Business Database Ltd.

1. Surveys of buyers' intentions
2. Obtaining the opinion of the salesforce
3. Obtaining the opinions of experts
4. Test marketing.

Surveys of buyers' intentions for industrial products can frequently be undertaken by the in-house marketing department. A market research agency is probably better for consumer products because samples will be taken from a much larger buying population (a major difference in the techniques of consumer and industrial marketing reflects the smaller number of consumers in the latter).

The buying intention surveys are likely to include both qualitative and quantitative research. Qualitative research is usually exploratory or diagnostic, involving relatively small numbers of people. They will often be selected to represent the previously identified segments. The survey will attempt to obtain impressions regarding the group's response to the product. Quantitative research is concerned with larger numbers of people. The results obtained are quantified on a previously agreed basis to indicate the numbers and proportions of sample members who fall into different response categories. A degree of statistical significance is then attributed to the results within the confines of a known margin of error.

Asking the salesforce their opinion has a number of attractions. First, successful salespeople have a very precise appreciation of their market and its requirements. Without this they are not successful. Second, it will have good motivational implications. All too frequently the salesperson is presented with a product that has clearly been dreamed up in some ivory tower with scant regard for the highly competitive sales environment. However, this is not to say that the salesforce comments should be taken down and etched in stone, because they are likely to be highly subjective, representing an individual's requirements in his or her sales territory at that particular moment in time. However, checking the salesperson's story with selected customers, particularly when matched against an appropriate 'lost order report', can verify the testimony.

Companies can also obtain input to their demand calculations from experts. These may be specialists employed by the City institutions, universities, marketing consultants, dealers and the appropriate trade associations. This can be a particularly valuable input, especially when the various opinions are compared and the opinion of one party commented on by another.

The fourth approach, test marketing, is mentioned in Chapter 12 on appraising the development of new products.

Forecasting Potential Sales

The first consideration is macro-economic influences, such as government legislation (for example, forced wearing of seat belts, pensions legislation): will it affect these particular business sectors? Secondly, there are industry trends to be examined: is demand for this type of product increasing or declining? Thirdly, the reputation of the company should be considered: does the name mean quality?

Next, examine the sales territory and segment either geographically, by product type or by major account – whichever makes the most sense – and start to identify potential buyers. Make a list of their names, what you think they will buy, and how much of it. For example, a Ford car salesperson might have these prospects:

Customer	Expected sale	Order value
ABC Ltd	Granada	£14 000
HLM plc	2 × Escort	£15 000
RTY Ltd	4 × Sierra	£36 000
ICK Ltd	2 × Fiesta	£10 000
KLN plc	6 × Orion	£41 000
	Total	£116 000

Any salesperson presenting the above as a *sales forecast* would be very naïve for two reasons: one, there is no indication when the sale will take place, and two, there is no assessment of the certainty with which the forecast is made. Regarding timing, most businesses operate a forecast in months for the immediate future and quarters further ahead. Consequently, the anticipated sales figures might be more usefully presented as shown in Table 10.6.

The next step is to make an attempt to estimate as accurately as possible the degree of certainty with which the anticipated orders may be received. Failure to record any value for the potential sale is to understate the worth of a large amount of sales effort that has been expended. Similarly, recording the potential sale at its full value before a firm and legally binding contract has been signed is seriously to overestimate the value of the business prospect under consideration.

The percentage chances of obtaining the business should be according to company

Table 10.6   Anticipated sales figures

| Customer | Expected sale | Order value (£000) | | | | | | |
		Jan.	Feb.	Mar.	Qtr 2	Qtr 3	Qtr 4	Total year
ABC Ltd	Granada			14.0				
HLM plc	2 × Escort		15.0					
RTY Ltd	4 × Sierra				36.0			
ICK Ltd	2 × Fiesta	10.0						
KLN plc	6 × Orion					41.0		
		£10.0	£15.0	£14.0	£36.0	£41.0	–	£116.0

Table 10.7   Suggested order chance indicators for capital products.

Not more than 5%	Vague interest. Second meeting arranged.
Not more than 10%	Firm interest. Agreement to continue with investigation.
Not more than 15%	Confirmation of interest at board level.
Not more than 20%	Terms of reference and basis of decision agreed.
Not more than 30%	Investigation completed and findings agreed with customer.
Not more than 35%	Proposal submitted.
Not more than 50%	Short-listed.
Not more than 60%	Verbal confirmation of intent.
Not more than 70%	Board approval.
Not more than 80%	Letter of intent.
Not more than 90%	Contracts submitted for signing.
Not more than 100%	Order signed.

guidelines (see, for example, Table 10.7), and when the business is, say 60 per cent likely, you multiply the likely order value by the success factor, so £14 000 for the Granada goes in the forecast as £8400 (£14 000 × 0.60). This may be called the 'expected value factor'.

The reworked Table 10.8 clearly shows the situation when this chance factor has been included in the calculations.

Targeting Objectives

It is now time to integrate the rather specific thinking about a particular product market into the overall company or corporate plan. Decision-making in a sophisticated environment involves direction-orientated behaviour which implies the existence of a goal or goals. In the absence of any objectives, a company's directors and

Table 10.8 Revised anticipated sales figures

Customer	Expected sale	Chance factor	Jan.	Feb.	Mar.	Qtr 2	Qtr 3	Qtr 4	Total
ABC Ltd	Granada	60%			8.4				
HLM plc	2 × Escort	60%		9.0					
RTY Ltd	4 × Sierra	20%				7.2			
ICK Ltd	2 × Fiesta	60%	6.0						
KLN plc	6 × Orion	80%					32.8		
			£6.0	£9.0	£8.4	£7.2	£32.8	–	£63.4

Expected order value (£000)

managers would lack a criterion for choosing between alternative marketing and financial strategies.

This begs the question, what are the goals of a company? 'The maximization of long-term profits' will roll off the tongue of any former student of economics. However, a closer analysis of this statement produces certain ambiguities: which definition of profit; what is the balance between maximizing profits over two years and ten years, given that maximizing the former might trip the latter? Also, problems of a practical nature come to mind: accurate information about the profit attributable to a certain transaction may only be available some three or six months after the sale has taken place.

There are also other things to consider. While technically a firm may be owned by shareholders whose objective may be long-run (secure) profit maximization, the business is controlled by professional managers. These managers are for the most part extremely hardworking individuals dedicated to progressing their careers by achieving their own targeted objectives in a complex pattern of personal power relationships. Herbert Simon is one of the best known proponents of the psychological components of behaviour in complex organizations. In Simon's view the decision-making mechanism is imperfect because managers are often confronted with the necessity of making choices without knowing the outcome of each alternative.

Robert Lanzilloti's search for some empirical evidence* produced some interesting results (see Table 10.9). Analysis shows four frequently occurring goals:

1. target returns on investments;
2. stabilization of prices and margins;
3. target market share;
4. 'meeting' or preventing competition.

Although not every company mentioned all four points, a majority included these as principal or secondary objectives. In practical terms this means that sales and marketing executives should address some or all of these goals when directing their departments' efforts. Consider for example a small computer company for which the 1987–8 results were as in Table 10.10.

Clearly, some sectors of the business are more profitable than others. (Consultancy

* 'Pricing objectives in large companies', *American Economic Review*, **XLVIII**, December 1958, pp. 924–6.

Table 10.9   Pricing goals of seventeen large industrial corporations

Company	Principal pricing model	Collateral pricing goals
Alcoa	20% on investment (before taxes); higher on new products (about 10% effective rate after taxes)	(a) 'Promotive' policy on new products (b) Price stabilization
American Can	Maintenance of market share	(a) 'Meeting competition' (using cost of substitute products to determine price (b) Price stabilization
A & P	Increasing market share	'General promotive' (low-margin policy)
du Pont	Target return on investment – no specific figure given	(a) Charging what traffic will bear over long run (b) Maximum return for new products – 'life cycle' pricing
Esso (Standard Oil of NJ)	'Fair-return' target – no specific figure given	(a) Maintaining market share (b) Price stabilization
General Electric	20% on investment (after taxes); 7% on sales (after taxes)	(a) Promotive policy on new products (b) Price stabilization on nationally advertised products
General Foods	33⅓% gross margin: ('one-third to make, one-third to sell, and one-third for profit') expectation of realizing target only on new products	(a) Full line of food products and novelties (b) Maintaining market share
General Motors	20% on investment (after taxes)	Maintaining market share
Goodyear	'Meeting competitors'	(a) Maintain 'position' (b) Price stabilization
Gulf	Follow price of most important marketer in each area	(a) Maintain market share (b) Price stabilization
International Harvester	10% on investment (after taxes)	Market share: ceiling of 'less than a dominant share of any market'
Johns-Manville	Return on investment greater than last fifteen-year	(a) Market share not greater than 20%

Table 10.9   continued

Company	Principal pricing model	Collateral pricing goals
	average (about 15% after taxes); higher target for new products	(b) Stabilization of prices
Kennecott	Stabilization of prices	
Kroger	Maintaining market share	Target return of 20% on investment before taxes
National Steel	Matching the market-price follower	Increase market share
Sears Roebuck	Increasing market share (8%–10% regarded as satisfactory share)	(a) Realization of traditional return on investment of 10%–15% (after taxes) (b) General promotive (low margin) policy
Standard Oil (Indiana)	Maintain market share	(a) Stabilize prices (b) Target return on investment (none specified)

Source: Haim Levy and Marshall Sarnat, *Capital Investment and Financial Decisions*, 3rd edn, Prentice-Hall, 1986, based on work by Robert Lanzilloti.

Table 10.10   Financial results of small computer company

	Sales value £000	% of total sales	Contribution £000	%	% of total contribution
Solutions sales (hardware & software)	199.5	25.6	26.8	13.4	17.2
Hardware only	295.3	37.9	43.9	14.9	28.1
Software only	98.1	12.6	29.4	30.0	18.8
Consultancy	33.2	4.3	16.2	48.8	10.4
Service contracts	83.4	10.7	25.4	30.5	16.3
Consumables	51.2	6.6	9.1	17.8	5.8
Rental income	18.0	2.3	5.3	29.4	3.4
	£778.7	100.0%	£156.1		100.0%

has a 48.8 per cent contribution, service contractors 30.5 per cent contribution and software sales 30 per cent. They account for 45.5 per cent of the total contribution but their percentage of total sales is only 27.6 per cent.) The other parts of the business may be less profitable but make nevertheless a vital contribution to the overall success of the business. While the management would want to develop those more profitable areas as a priority, it may be that there are outside constraints and consequently the greatest possibilities for expansion lie with the less profitable areas. (This topic is further discussed in Chapter 14 on the sales and marketing plan.)

11 PLANNING SALES AREAS AND TERRITORIES

It is a sad but true fact that many salespeople on their first day in a new job are given a set of car keys, a packet of product brochures, some assorted 'sales leads' and shown the door which goes to the car park. The 'leads' may be contact names and addresses from the last trade exhibition, returned coupons from a (hopefully recent) newspaper advertising campaign or sheets from a telephone enquiry pad.

It is also unfortunately true that past, current and potential customers are unlikely to be documented in any uniform way. There will probably be no written sales plan to inherit and the only customer records as such will be the carbon or file copies of any past correspondence. The new incumbent probably has as much time as his or her predecessor (some three or four months) to achieve some level of sales before he or she too is involuntarily in receipt of a P45.

The Partitioning of Responsibility

The sales and marketing director of a company is charged with the responsibility for achieving a predetermined volume of sales. In sophisticated businesses this amount will be represented by the numbers of different product items to be sold, the total value (pounds sterling in the UK) and the budgeted contribution of each product category towards the fixed costs of the business.

The sales and marketing director divides the responsibility for achieving these sales among the various sales managers who in turn allocate 'targets' or 'quotas' amongst the salesforce. This process may be considered as the partitioning of responsibility for achieving a volume of sales. Clearly, this partitioning or division process involves some element of calculation as to how it is to be achieved.

Table 11.1 Partitioning the sales and marketing director's target among the line sales managers (Stage 1)

	Target £000	
Sales Manager A	3 250	
Sales Manager B	2 850	
Sales Manager C	3 700	
Sales Manager D	2 100	
Sales Manager E	2 900	
Sales total	14 800	(112% of director's target)
Director's target	13 200	

Because under-achieving a budget is a very serious matter and very disruptive in terms of a company's overall performance, it is usual for the sum of the sales managers' budgets to exceed that of the director (see Table 11.1, Stage 1). Similarly, at Stage 2 (see Table 11.2), the sum of the salesmen's quotas will exceed their sales manager's volume target. Over-achievement of sales on the other hand is frequently rewarded by bonuses. At management levels this is dependent also on the achievement of acceptable levels of profit or contribution. However, this is not to say that over-achievement of sales doesn't cause problems for the production planning and distribution departments.

Table 11.2   Partitioning the sales manager's target amongst the sales force (Stage 2)

	Target *£000*	
Salesperson A1	500	
Salesperson A2	675	
Salesperson A3	625	
Salesperson A4	575	
Salesperson A5	725	
Salesperson A6	500	
Sales total	£3 600	(110.8% of manager's budget)
Sales manager A's target	£3 250	

Salesforce Size

In the above example the figures are arbitrary and their allocation has been made in a similar manner. Clearly, however, in practice this would certainly not be ideal. So what criteria can be used in order to partition the sales manager's budget?

Seniority and Responsibility

One way might be to have different grades of salesperson with different scales for basic salary, commission, sales targets and total earnings or benefits package. A system like this has a number of advantages: senior and/or successful salespeople are given more difficult challenges, but receive much higher rewards. Conversely new and less experienced salespeople are not expected to 'run' before they have mastered 'walking'. It also gives the company the opportunity to attract and reward high achievers and at the same time beginners are given an opportunity to master the skills and techniques of the job, because in theory they cost the employer less. Consider, for example, the following earnings packages for salespeople at different grades:

	Basic *salary*	*Sales* *target*	*Commission* *at 2.5%*	*Total* *earnings*
Sales grade 1	£10 000	£150 000	£3750	£13 750
Sales grade 2	£13 000	£225 000	£5625	£18 625
Sales grade 3	£16 000	£375 000	£9375	£25 375

This method of structuring also provides an attractive career structure for the salesforce, at the same time offering good value to the company. Consider the direct costs of achieving sales of £375 000:

	Basic salary	Sales target	Commission at 2.5%	Total earnings
Sales grade 1	£10 000	£150 000	£3750	£13 750
Sales grade 2	£13 000	£225 000	£5625	£18 625
	£23 000	£375 000	£9375	£32 375
Sales grade 3	£16 000	£375 000	£9375	£25 375
Saving to employer				£7 000

The reduced costs of the 'high achievers' are even greater when one considers that only one car will be required (perhaps saving £3500 per annum), only one set of expenses (perhaps £3000 per annum) and one amount of employer's national insurance and pension contributions (perhaps saving £5000). This makes a total saving of £20 500 by using one Grade 3 salesperson rather than a Grade 1 and a Grade 2, whose combined sales target is the same size.

Given these calculations, it is easy to understand why, for example, in the computer industry there is a continuous demand for experienced high-achievement salespeople commanding large salaries. Secondly, there are companies that ideologically decline to accept this scenario and consequently have continuous intakes at the Sales grade 1 and Sales grade 2 levels. The salespeople tend to leave the 'nursery companies' when they have the experience and track record to command Sales grade 3 salaries which in the example above would be £46 000 for achieving a target of £1 200 000, a basic of £16 000 plus £30 000 commission (£1 200 000 × 2½ per cent) and a BMW.

New Business Salespeople and Account Managers

Another approach to partitioning the salesperson's budget is to allocate responsibility on a task-orientated basis. The distinction is between managing the sales in certain large accounts very effectively by allowing a salesperson to focus on them exclusively and directing his colleagues to play the 'numbers game' of finding new business opportunities. There is an inherently attractive logic to this approach which means that important or 'key' accounts receive a high level of attention and service. At the same time new business opportunities are continually sought so that the penalties arising from corporate myopia and introversion are avoided. Another advantage is that the skills of a wider profile are successfully kept within the team. The point is well made by the dialogue below between two salespeople.

Recently, two salespeople, Tom Kelly and John Curtis, had a chance to sit down over some coffee and compare notes. At one time they had worked together, but a little over a year ago, Kelly was transferred to a different division. They are good friends, but they haven't talked in a while, so they have taken this opportunity to catch up on their news.

*Paragraph
number*

(1) Tom: How are things going then, John?

John: Pretty well – in fact, very well. Yesterday I walked into a chap's office – somebody I had never met before – and an hour later, I walked out with his agreement to do £10 000 worth of business with our company. And there's the prospect of a lot more.

(2) Tom: Sometimes you amaze me, John. I don't know whether you can sell better than other people, but you can certainly sell faster. I've been in the business longer than you have, but I can probably count on the fingers of one hand the number of times I've been able to close on something in one go. As a matter of fact, I never expect it. Yet you seem to do it all the time.

(3) John: I wish I did. Actually, with the products we offer and the complexities involved, it's rare to have a chance to close right away. But if I see even a small chance, I go for it.

(4) Tom: I go about it a different way. I try to get the customers to talk about what they need or would like. Sometimes, they don't clearly know this themselves until we start talking. Almost always, there's some service they didn't know about or understand that fills that need, and they're happy to find out about it – and of course, I'm happy to sell it to them.

(5) John: That's your style, Tom – 'laid back' would be one way to describe it, I suppose. Not that I'm knocking it. You know, I've run into a lot of people you used to call on, and they really miss you. I get the feeling they regard you as a friend, someone they could count on. Sometimes I wonder whether I create the same feeling.

(6) Tom: I'm sure you do, John, but, as you say, it's a matter of technique and style. I look at it this way: everyone in business has problems and needs they don't know how to deal with, and in many cases our company has the answers they're looking for. That means that you and I, John, are walking around with information they want – or if we don't have it, we can get it. That's why I want to let them talk – or get them to talk – about what problems they see. Then we'll discuss it and see if our company can provide the solution, a solution that seems to have emerged from our discussion. In other words, the solution is not one I have to 'sell' to him – it's something we both have developed and can get enthusiastic about, as the result of mutual consultations.

(7) John: It sounds good, but I doubt if I have the patience for that. I agree that we have information other people want or need, but I want to get straight down to business. If our company has a service I think somebody can use, I tell them about it. Some people just refuse to listen and 'turn off', but there are plenty who are willing to hear the message – and I can be pretty persuasive when I want to be.

(8) Tom: I know you can – your record proves that. I'm not saying my approach is better; it's just different. I guess I don't rely so much on my powers of persuasion; instead, I want to be seen as an adviser. I want my visits to be seen as problem-solving sessions. And when it works, I feel I've done more than find a new customer for our company; I've built a personal relationship that will continue.

(9) John: Well, from what your customers tell me, that's exactly what you do. And I have to admit there are a couple of areas where your approach might help me. For instance sometimes prospects will drag up the craziest objections to what I'm

trying to present – wild ideas with little or no relation to reality. Sometimes I react badly, especially if the prospect seems to be a bit stupid, and before you know it, we're in what sounds like an argument. I'm trying to fight that tendency.

(10) Tom: I think you should. Remember that when people raise objections, the chances are they're just looking for information about things they genuinely are not sure of. And even though they seem hostile or stupid, when they get the facts or see the total picture, they'll be satisfied – and they'll say so.

(11) John: I'm afraid I'm always looking for that 'go ahead' signal, and when it seems far away, I may push a little too hard towards it; and if I don't see it at all, sometimes I'm not sure what to do.

(12) Tom: That's true of all of us, John, and maybe if the rest of us pushed for the goal line as hard as you do, we'd get there faster. Still, there are plenty of times when the best thing to do is just to move toward it five or ten yards at a time, which means trying to get the customer to commit to some step – another meeting, a visit to the home office – anything that will move you closer to the goal line.

Source: ICL sales training programme 1983.

Workload Approach

This is the approach favoured by many sales managers because it is relatively straightforward to operate, and uses sales-orientated logic and information that should be available to any well-managed unit. The first step is to list existing and known potential customers in a sales manager's area, and against each allocate a banded category based on an estimate of the volume of business that might be achieved. This might be:

Large potential   £20 000 plus
Medium potential   £10 000–£19 999
Small potential   £500–£9999

(We may assume in this example that business of value less than £500 is left to sales over the counter or by mail order.)

The next step is to decide how regularly each category of potential sales should receive a visit from a salesperson. For example, those prospects of large potential might merit a visit every week, medium potential once every two weeks and the small potential prospects a regular telephone call and only a visit when the salesperson thinks he can close the sale. This may for the purposes of this calculation be once every eight weeks.

If there are: 50 large potential prospects
130 medium potential prospects
200 small potential prospects

Then the number of required customer visits is:

$$50 \times 44^* = 2200$$
$$130 \times 22 = 2860$$
$$200 \times 5\tfrac{1}{2} = 1100$$

Total number of visits   6160

* Four weeks' holiday entitlement, two weeks' bank holiday, one week's training and sales meetings, one week's sickness/compassionate leave, i.e. $52 - 8 = 44$ weeks.

The number of salespeople required is 6160 divided by the number of sales calls it is thought that the salesperson can make, allowing for the amount of time that needs to be spent travelling and writing letters, proposals and tenders. If it is:

10 visits per week: 6160 divided by 10 × 44 = 14.0 salespeople†
15 visits per week: 6160 divided by 15 × 44 = 9.18 salespeople
20 visits per week: 6160 divided by 20 × 44 = 7.00 salespeople

Productivity Approach

This is the method likely to be chosen where a company is managed by tight financial budgets designed to meet precise corporate objectives specified in financial terms. A sales manager may be targeted with making a specific net profit. The following calculation is a practical way of approaching his objective:

	£	£	£
Territory sales budget			300 000
Gross profit @ 40%			120 000
Less:			
Direct sales costs:			
Salary	15 000		
Commission	5 000		
Car lease	3 000		
Expenses	3 000	26 000	
Indirect sales costs:			
Office furniture	410		
National insurance	2 090		
Pension contribution	1 000		
Office space (100 sq.ft. @ £20 per sq.ft.)	2 000		
(Quarter of a secretary)	3 000	8 500	
Overhead allocation:			
Recruitment and personnel			
Administration	4 000		
Marketing	5 000		
Finance and salaries	1 000		
Sales manager	6 000	16 000	50 500
Net profit for the sales territory (before tax)			£69 500

The territory sales budget for each salesperson is continually adjusted until the sales manager has the best estimate of what each of his or her salespeople can achieve, and the sales area as a unit can satisfy the net profit budget.

---

† Clearly in practice this might be 14, 9 and 7 salespeople respectively.

Area and Territory Management

Salespeople or sales managers should adapt their approach to the way they manage their part of the company's business according to the criteria by which they are assessed. If they are judged on sales volume alone, then clearly they will manage their business accordingly.

Table 11.3 shows a useful breakdown of the sales achieved by an area sales manager's team of four salespeople. The year's sales revenue is presented by sales territory and subdivided by product (A, B and C) and customer type (hotels, colleges and hospitals). There are totals for sales to each customer type by product and there are totals for the sales revenue achieved by each salesperson in their territory.

Table 11.3   Cumulative sales ABC plc – January to September 1988

	Eastern	Southern	Northern	Western	Total
Product A sales:	£	£	£	£	£
Hotels	100 000	150 000	120 000	110 000	480 000
Colleges	90 000	80 000	90 000	100 000	360 000
Hospitals	180 000	200 000	170 000	30 000	580 000
TOTAL	370 000	430 000	380 000	240 000	1 420 000
Product B sales:					
Hotels	110 000	100 000	90 000	120 000	420 000
Colleges	40 000	60 000	50 000	70 000	220 000
Hospitals	200 000	160 000	190 000	210 000	760 000
TOTAL	350 000	320 000	330 000	400 000	1 400 000
Product C sales:					
Hotels	20 000	30 000	50 000	30 000	130 000
Colleges	70 000	50 000	80 000	60 000	260 000
Hospitals	120 000	100 000	110 000	80 000	410 000
TOTAL	210 000	180 000	240 000	170 000	800 000
Total Hotel sales	230 000	280 000	260 000	260 000	1 030 000
Total College sales	200 000	190 000	220 000	230 000	840 000
Total Hospital sales	500 000	460 000	470 000	320 000	1 750 000
TOTAL SALES	930 000	930 000	950 000	810 000	3 620 000

Source: Examination paper on Financial and Management Accounting, Chartered Institute of Marketing Certificate, November 1987.

Presenting the results in such a manner provides the sales management with information for analysis comparison and ultimately control. Interpretation might be as follows:

Sales territory analysis:
1. Sales revenue in the Western territory is only 86.7 per cent of the mean of the other three territories: £936 666 (£930 000 + £930 000 + £950 000 divided by 3).
2. Western territory sales of product A are only 61.06 per cent of the average achieved by the other three: £393 333 (£370 000 + £430 000 + £380 000 divided by 3).
3. Western territory sales of product A to hospitals is only 16.36 per cent of the mean of the other three territories (£180 000 + £200 000 + £170 000 divided by 3 = £183 333).

Product line analysis:
1. Product C sales are only 56.53 per cent of the mean of the sales revenues achieved by products A and B.
2. Product C sales are very low to hotels: 16.25 per cent.
3. Product B sales are very low to colleges: 15.71 per cent.
4. Sales of product B to all three customer groups is highest in the Western sales territory.

Customer group analysis:
1. Hospitals are the largest customers for each product buying 40.84 per cent of product A, 54.28 per cent of product B, 51.25 per cent of product C. Overall total for hospitals 48.34 per cent of sales revenue.
2. Although sales to hospitals are larger than for any customer group, the sales in the Western territory are only 67.22 per cent of the mean of the other three (£500 000 + £460 000 + £470 000 divided by 3 = £476 666).

However, once a responsibility for profit is brought to bear, the pragmatic sales-person will adjust his control procedures accordingly. In Table 11.4, hardware sales are seen to be the biggest single group of sales at £295 300 (37.9 per cent of total sales achieved), but the contribution to fixed overheads is only £43 900 (14.9 per cent). Computer solutions (hardware, software packages and bespoke programming) at £199 500 are the second largest group of sales, but again their margin is low: £26 800 or 13.4 per cent. The salesperson or sales manager whose results are measured in terms of profit (or contributions to fixed overheads) as well as volume would be strongly advised to focus attention on increasing sales of consultancy (48.8 per cent contribution), service contracts (30.5 per cent contribution), software (30 per cent contribution) and equipment rentals (29.4 per cent contribution).

Table 11.4 Summary of 1987–8 sales for a small computer company

	Sales value £000	% of total sales	Contribution £000	%	% of total contribution
Solutions sales	199.5	25.6	26.8	13.4	17.2
Hardware	295.3	37.9	43.9	14.9	28.1
Software	98.1	12.4	29.4	30.0	18.8
Consultancy	33.2	4.3	16.2	48.8	10.4
Service contracts	83.4	10.7	25.4	30.5	16.3
Consumables/Stationery	51.2	6.6	9.1	17.8	5.8
Rental income	18.0	2.3	5.3	29.4	3.4
	£778.7	100.0	£156.1	–	100.0

The reason for this is quite straightforward: selling computer hardware, solutions and stationery is a very price-competitive business. There are many vendors in the market-place with similar products competing on price. Computer consultancy, on the other hand, may be highly specialized, and a premium may be charged. Similarly, computer software for specific businesses offers great savings in time and resources (consequently causing costs to fall), so vendors are able to make an appropriately higher margin on this.

Meeting Budget, Monitoring and Control of Sales

The reason for partitioning the responsibility for the achievement of certain volumes of sales of particular product groups to specific customers is to provide senior management with an organization structure that can be controlled very precisely.

Consider, for example, how the value to senior management of Table 11.3 would be improved if there were a percentage figure expressing the cumulative sales achieved in relation to the budget. As it stands, the question should be asked: 'Why has the Western territory progressed less successfully than the other three?'

There are perhaps three possible explanations:

Explanation:	*Remedial action:*
1. Inexperienced or less competent salesperson	Sales and/or product training as appropriate plus closer supervision
2. Greater competition	Determine real reasons for competitive success and counter using marketing group
3. Smaller prospective customer base	Consider redrafting territories on more equitable basis

However, specifically, management would want to know:

1. Why sales of product C are comparatively low – particularly to hotels.
2. Why sales of product B are very low to colleges.
3. This is particularly interesting as the *worst performing salesperson overall is performing best with product B to each customer group*.

The answer may be that the Western territory salesperson has particular experience of this product market which enables him to sell very effectively, in which case perhaps he should become a product B specialist and be groomed for product marketing management.

The value of a relatively simple table of figures can be enormous. It provides senior management with a mechanism for monitoring and indirectly controlling the volume of business achieved by particular salespeople of specific products to the various customer groups. The comparison of different levels of achievement indicates strengths and weaknesses, success and failure. This information is useful for the 'fine tuning' of the human resource base so that even higher targets may be achieved.

12 PRODUCT ABANDONMENT AND NEW PRODUCT DEVELOPMENT DECISIONS

The Product Line

A product line is a group of products that are closely related because they are perceived by consumers to function in a similar way, they offer similar benefits, are sold to the same customer groups and are marketed through the same type of outlets or fall within a particular price range.

Each item in the product line is likely to make a different contribution both to sales volume and to profits just because there are so many variables in the equation that are beyond the control of the sales and marketing departments. Clearly, companies where a disproportionately high percentage either of sales volume or profit is derived from a minority of products are in positions of considerable risk and indeed vulnerability to fierce competition. An example of this was W.D. & H.O. Wills in the late 1960s and early 1970s where more than 70 per cent of cigarette sales were from the brand Embassy. There was great concern in the sales and marketing departments lest a competitor's brand threaten Embassy's dominant position. The decision to extend the product line with Embassy Mild and Embassy King Size was an attempt to strengthen the brand's position by appealing to a wider group of the cigarette-smoking population.

Product Abandonment and the Importance of the Contribution Concept

One of the fascinating aspects of studying more than one profession or science is the realization that what is a difficult problem to resolve in subject A is quite straightforward using analytical techniques that are commonplace in subject B. A particularly good example of this is the application of the contribution concept to the situation where a company is producing a number of products of which some are being sold for a price that is less than the total cost. The question is whether those products which are apparently being sold at a loss should continue in production.

Faced with this problem, many sales and marketing managers would experience difficulty in justifying to senior management why the company should continue to produce and sell these products. Sales and marketing managers tend to be very results-orientated, and a product that sells, albeit at a temporary loss, cannot be all bad. Senior management at main board level, remote from the day-to-day contest in the market-place, views the picture from management reports which indicate a loss. Clearly, the natural inclination is to minimize the chance of this poor trading position developing into a landslide.

Sales and marketing managers are very much aware of the enormous effort that goes into selling, and accept that on occasions conditions in the market place make it difficult to maintain a high price. The reasons for this may be fierce competition from other sellers or just that the consumer is unwilling or unable to pay more. Clearly, what is needed is a technique or methodology that can be used to justify allocating resources and effort to products selling at a loss in certain circumstances.

This is extremely important because a firm's profits and future health may suffer serious depletion unless the product line is pruned. The retention of products that are not currently or foreseeably capable of making a profit contribution constitutes a significant barrier to increasing profits and lessens the firm's ability to adapt to a constantly changing environment.

The following example should serve to illustrate the point:

	Costs per unit		
	Product X	Product Y	Product Z
	£	£	£
Direct material	0.25	0.50	0.83
Direct wages:			
Dept A	0.10	0.10	0.17
Dept B	0.15	0.08	1.00
Total direct costs	0.50	0.68	2.00
Variable overheads:			
Dept A	0.13	0.13	0.21
Dept B	0.30	0.15	2.00
Fixed overheads	0.38	0.26	1.75
Total cost	1.31	1.22	5.96
Selling price	1.25	1.20	7.50
Profit (loss) per unit	(0.06)	(0.02)	1.54
Units sold	80 000	100 000	12 000
Product profit (loss)	£(4 800)	£(2 000)	£18 480
Trading profit for year		£11 680	

The question is to justify (with supporting calculations) which one of the following decisions should be followed:

1. deleting product X;
2. deleting product Y;
3. deleting products X and Y;
4. deleting no product lines.

(*Source:* Chartered Institute of Marketing examination, Finance for Marketing, June 1988.)

According to the figures above, products X and Y are being sold at a small loss while product Z is making a healthy profit. The question is whether the company should continue to produce and sell products X and Y.

The way to approach this problem is to use the concept of the contribution to fixed overheads. This is a calculation where the variable costs are deducted from sales revenue and the resulting balance (if any) is called the contribution towards recovering fixed overheads made by that particular product. Applying this to the figures above produces the following analysis:

	Product X	Product Y	Product Z
Sales revenue*	£100 000	£120 000	£90 000
Less: Variable costs†	£74 400	£96 000	£50 520
Contribution to fixed overheads	£25 600	£24 000	£39 480

The effect of deleting various products from the line is now seen to reduce overall contribution to fixed overheads and turn an overall profit into a loss:

1. *Deleting product X:* £
   Contributions from Y — 24 000
   Z — 39 480
   — 63 480
   Less: Total fixed overheads — 77 400‡
   Loss — (13 920)

2. *Deleting product Y:*
   Contributions from X — 25 600
   Z — 39 480
   — 65 080
   Less: Total fixed overheads — 77 400
   Loss — (12 320)

3. *Deleting products X and Y:*
   Contributions from Z — 39 480
   Less: Total fixed overheads — 77 400
   Loss — (37 920)

4. *Deleting no product lines:*
   Contributions from X — 25 600
   Y — 24 000
   Z — 39 480
   — 89 080
   Less: Total fixed overheads — 77 400
   Profit — £11 680

* Number of units sold multiplied by the selling price.
† Total direct costs plus variable overheads; for product X this is 50 pence plus the variable overheads of departments A and B (43 pence multiplied by the number of units sold) = 0.93 × 80 000 = £74 400.
‡ This is calculated as follows for producers X, Y and Z:
X = (0.38 × 80 000) + Y = (0.26 × 100 000) + Z = (1.75 × 12 000)
= 30 400 + £26 000 + £21 000 = £77 400.

A note on the calculations: it is important to approach the problem in the way illustrated because the fixed overhead of £0.38 for product X and £0.26 for product Y are *not fully recovered* at the prevailing selling price.

There are two more factors that should be considered in decisions for possible abandonment. They are:

1. The criteria for allocating the recovery of the fixed overheads among the various products in the line. This is relevant because a slightly different approach could mean that all three products in the above example were capable of being sold at a profit. For example, if the fixed overhead recovery figures for product X and Y were reduced to £0.30 and £0.22 respectively the figures would be:

	Product X	Product Y	Product Z
Total cost	£1.23	£1.18	£6.83*
Selling price	£1.25	£1.20	£7.50
Profit per unit	0.02	0.02	0.67
Units sold	80 000	100 000	12 000
Product profit	£1 600	£2 000	£8 040
Total profit =		£11 640	

   * The unit reduction in the fixed overhead burden for product X is 80 000 × £0.08 = £6400 plus the unit reduction of product Y £0.04 × 100 000 = £4000. £10 400 has to be reallocated to the 12 000 units of product Z at the rate of £0.87 per unit. As a result the trading profit is £11 640 and all products are individually profitable.

2. The social consequences of the abandonment decisions should also be considered; that is, the firm's responsibility to its employees as their means of earning wages, its customers as their source of supply of the products, other businesses which supply the firm with products and other businesses which supply the firm with raw materials and services. Although clearly management would be inclined to prioritize on the business's needs if the effects on the market environment were not sufficiently considered, the long-term consequences for the firm may be less than agreeable. Examples of interested parties are government departments, trade unions and consumer groups. The high additional expenditure that may result in stopping production of a product at a location where no substitute can be produced may not be limited to substantial redundancy payments, the expenditure of moving plant to other locations and, indeed, maintaining a stock of spare parts to service the existing customer base. Vast amounts of expensive management time may be involved in attempting to justify to the other interested parties that no other alternatives are available. Indeed, retaliatory action in the form of industrial action may be taken, leading to the unquantifiable lost revenue that can be the result of unfavourable publicity in the media.

Alternatives to New Product Development

In the dynamic marketing environment of the 1990s companies that fail to develop new products will risk a steadily decreasing share of their existing markets until the company becomes extinct. This is because their product profiles will not have responded to the continuous changes in consumer needs and the increasing competition, both domestic and from abroad. Superimposed on this are new opportunities and threats resulting from the continuous developments in technology.

However, the development of new products has two drawbacks that are perceived by marketing management. It is very expensive simply in terms of the amount of money required to fund the development, and secondly there is the risk that something in the question will be wrong and the resulting sales will not recover the initial investment. Consequently, companies attempt to develop strategies that keep these two aspects to a minimum. Overall there are perhaps six possible approaches, which are listed below in descending order of capital cost and inherent risk:

1. New-to-the-world products
2. New product lines
3. Additions/extensions to the product line
4. Revisions/improvements to existing products
5. Repositioning*
6. Input cost reductions.

Table 12.1 is not supposed to represent the alternative cost of any particular product strategy but to indicate the relative order of cost that might be involved. This is important because it focuses attention on the relatively cheaper alternatives to developing a totally new product, and how these lower-cost alternatives might be perceived as preferable to certain management teams, as clearly the cost of errors is considerably reduced.

New Product Development in Practice

The wave of leveraged buy-outs and hostile takeover bids that dominated the corporate scene during 1988 focused company attention on the under-capitalized value of their best-selling brands. Johnny Walker brand, owned by Grand Metropolitan, for example, has been estimated by Kleinwort Benson to be worth £1.5 bn (representing between 25 and 30 times annual earnings of the brand which is the multiple paid for the Rowntree brands by Nestlé).

This being the case, it is surprising to read in a recent survey published by Brand New (Product Origination) Ltd that Professor Peter Doyle of Warwick University is quoted as saying that:

The British emphasis in the last decade has been overwhelmingly on financial retrenchment and improving cost structure. Innovation has taken second place . . . the Japanese (in contrast) have always put long-term market domination as a priority. They have continued to invest heavily in new product development (NPD) and are now in the happy position of being market leaders in many markets . . . They believe that products have a limited life-cycle, and one of their objectives in investing heavily in innovation is to speed up the rate of change.

One of the worrying things revealed in the survey is that some 61 per cent of the 150 companies interviewed in the survey admitted to spending less than 5 per cent of turnover on NPD. Indeed, many of the 61 per cent were not even investing as much as 5 per cent, but at a level of 1 to 2 per cent. The results are shown in Table 12.2. The

---

*Repositioning a product is where the product features are significantly changed so that the appeal is directed at a different group of consumers within the total spectrum of the market-place. An example is the Ford Granada which over the last five years has been repositioned further 'up market' to compete with the BMW 5 series, Mercedes 230 and 260 and top-of-the-range Rovers.

Table 12.1 The respective costs of alternative product marketing strategies

Budget category	New-to-the world products £000	New product lines £000	Additions to the product line £000	Improvements to existing products £000	Repositioning £000	Cost reductions £000
Basic research	10 000	2000		500		
Product development	10 000	2000	750			
Test marketing	500	350	350	250	250	
Product launch:						
Advertising	1 500	1500	750	500	500	
Promotion	200	200	200	200	200	
Sales	100	100	100	100	100	
Distribution	100	100	100	100	100	
	£22 400	£6250	£2250	£1650	£1150	–

contradiction is incredible between what senior directors say they believe to be necessary and what is done in practice. These directors claim that investment in new products is their responsibility and is essential for the survival of their business. At the same time there is a definite reluctance to commit resources in the quantities necessary to succeed. The reason for this can only be that they are unwilling to accept the risk of failure which is always an unfortunate possibility – particularly where corners have been cut because of underfunding.

Executives in the companies surveyed were asked which they considered to be the most important factors in future business success: 53 per cent included NPD in the top three factors from a list of eight. The results are listed in Table 12.3, where it is shown that NPD is seen as being of greatest importance in toiletries, household goods and other manufactured goods, and regarded as relatively less important in the food and drink sector, financial services and leisure.

Table 12.2 Proportion of turnover currently invested in new products

	Total	Food & drink	Toiletries	Industry sector Household goods	Other manuf.	Fin. serv.	Leisure
Base:	150	25	25	25	25	25	25
	%	%	%	%	%	%	%
Currently							
0–5%	61	80	46	53	65	80	43
6–10%	21	12	33	32	22	–	26
11–15%	7	4	4	5	9	–	17
16–20%	3	–	8	–	–	5	4
21–25%	4	4	4	5	4	–	4
More than 25%	4	4	4	5	–	15	4
Average	7.5	4.2	8.0	8.4	5.1	10.4	9.7

Source: Brand New (Product Origination) Ltd survey.

Table 12.3 Most important factors for future business success (Top 3 aggregated)

	Total	Food & drink	Toiletries	Industry sector Household goods	Other manuf.	Fin. serv.	Leisure
Base:	150	25	25	25	25	25	25
	%	%	%	%	%	%	%
Good customer relations	70	72	60	56	52	88	92
New product innovation	53	44	68	60	68	32	48
Secure capital base	42	32	32	48	40	44	56
Good employee relations	39	32	28	36	48	52	40

Table 12.3   continued

	Total	Food & drink	Toiletries	Industry sector Household goods	Other manuf.	Fin. serv.	Leisure
Tight cost and credit control	30	44	40	12	44	20	20
Growing marketing spend	22	28	28	28	8	20	24
Greater export achievement	18	16	32	28	20	15	–
Reduction in interest rates	6	12	–	4	4	4	12

Source: Brand New (Product Origination) Ltd survey.

Factors Influencing New Product Investment

Changes in consumer demand were regarded as by far the most important reason for investing in NPD (see Table 12.4). Across the board it was regarded as more important by a factor of 3 than the second most important reason, the financial services sector being the only exception.

Technological breakthroughs were the second key criterion in every sector, with the need to maximize production quoted as third.

Table 12.4   Most important factors influencing investment in new product development

	Total	Food & drink	Toiletries	Industry sector Household goods	Other manuf.	Fin. serv.	Leisure
Base:	150	25	25	25	25	25	25
	%	%	%	%	%	%	%
Changing customer demand	58	60	60	56	60	52	60
Technological breakthroughs	22	16	20	20	32	24	20
Need to maximize production	12	8	16	20	8	8	12
Level of investment in NPD	11	–	12	8	12	24	12
Retailer pressure	9	16	8	16	4	12	–
Other	5	12	–	8	–	4	4

A few respondents mentioned two factors as equally important

Source: Brand New (Product Origination) Ltd survey.

Estimated Cost of Finding One Successful New Product

New product development is expensive and risky because the outcome is not known until the final stage of test marketing, by which time many tens or even hundreds of thousands of pounds may have been spent.

One study, conducted by Booz, Allen & Hamilton in 1969–70, produced the following results on the estimated cost of finding one successful new product (starting with 64 new ideas):*

	Stage	Number of ideas	Pass ratio	Cost per product idea $	Total cost $
1.	Idea screening	64	1:4	1 000	64 000
2.	Concept test	16	1:2	20 000	320 000
3.	Product development	8	1:2	200 000	1 600 000
4.	Test marketing	4	1:2	500 000	2 000 000
5.	National launch	2	1:2	5 000 000	10 000 000
					$13 984 000

This is interesting when compared to the acceptable NPD failure rates identified in the Brand New (Product Origination) Ltd survey given in Table 12.5, where only 2 per cent of the companies surveyed accepted the 1 in 50 success rate. The prognosis must be either that American companies are more audacious regarding NPD or that they were in different industry sectors.

Table 12.5   Acceptable new product failure rates

	Total	Food & drink	Toiletries	Industry sector Household goods	Other manuf.	Fin. serv.	Leisure
Base:	150	25	25	25	25	25	25
	%	%	%	%	%	%	%
None	39	23	17	43	50	57	48
1 in 50	2	5	–	–	4	5	–
1 in 25	3	–	4	4	–	5	5
1 in 20	3	–	4	–	–	10	5
1 in 15	4	5	–	4	4	5	5
1 in 10	20	18	21	25	17	14	24
1 in 5	7	9	17	4	13	–	–
1 in 4	6	5	13	9	4	5	–
1 in 3	8	23	13	4	8	–	–
1 in 2	7	14	13	4	–	–	14

Source: Brand New (Product Origination) Ltd survey.

* Philip Kotler, *Marketing Management, Analysis, Planning and Control*, 5th edition, Prentice-Hall, 1984.

The High Failure Rate in New Product Development

Unfortunately, many new products fail once they reach the market-place even after the most exhaustive internal selection and evaluation procedures. Clearly the reasons for this failure are not easy to establish, otherwise the groups of experienced professional marketeers involved would have taken adequate steps to avoid the unsatisfactory outcome. One hypothesis is that in practice it is very difficult to monitor and evaluate continuously some of the key variables involved:

1. perceived consumer need for the product
2. developments in other technologies
3. action by competitors.

Philips, for example, failed to find a mass market for the video disc, despite the high picture quality that it offered, because the market for video cassettes had already been established and offered one very significant additional benefit – home recording of TV programmes by the public broadcast services. After much speculation it was reluctantly admitted by the TV industry that there were no practical methods of preventing the recording of their programmes.

More than one American company has failed to take account of the differences in disposable income between the USA and the UK. A product that is very affordable in North American households is not always successful in the UK. A particular example was a toy product, 'Rainbow Brite' produced by the Mattel Corporation, that proved to be too expensive for British children, who had a relatively lower disposable income (pocket money).

Campbells, a market leader in branded soups, attempted to broaden their market profile into ready-packed chilled salads. However, they failed to acknowledge that the market was already well supplied with established brands and strong own-label products.

Sir Clive Sinclair produced an innovative piece of transport technology in the C5 (a small battery-powered motor vehicle). However, motorists were reluctant to drive it on the public highway essentially because it was thought dangerous, being so low on the ground that other vehicles could not see it.

Obviously, market research and new product development departments need to co-operate more closely to avoid these expensive failures. In response to this, quantitative research has attempted to design new techniques based on a more subtle appreciation of the communication process.

The creative and research methodology needs to focus continually on potential niches in the market that are not being supplied by the competition, yet identify with a company's skills and resources. After identifying the gap in consumer fulfilment, a product must be developed, named, packaged and positioned to meet the requirements. However, the size of this submarket needs accurate measurement, as does the susceptibilities of the target audience to the media message. Unfortunately, this process may take several years, so the market must be continually monitored to check that the mood has not passed, or been successfully addressed in the meantime by a competitor.

Strategic Elements of New Product Development

A firm's strategy for new product development involves assessing the consumption potential for a product that is currently supplied in an inferior way or is not being supplied at all. The decision to proceed with the investment involves calculations as to the size of this market and the degree of success that may be realistically anticipated by a firm with a particular resource and experience or skills. Professor Igor Ansoff* calls this 'competitive advantage'.

The analysis of competitive advantage is assisted by the classification of product-market opportunities under three headings: a breakthrough, a competitive product and an improved product. The breakthrough product offers either a major performance advantage over competitive products, a drastically lower price, or occasionally both. A competitive product offers no particular advantage over others on the market, except that it is competitive in the sense that it offers a compromise between cost and performance characteristics that is attractive to a significant demand segment. The improved product is one that is demonstrably superior to others at the same or similar price, usually as a result of technological advance.

Different types of consumer demand may also be identified. This is important because, depending upon the category in which the new product lies, are the costs that may be expected for gaining consumer acceptance of the product. Where demand for the product has already been *established*, the associated costs are those involved in 'persuading' the consumer as to the superiority of this particular brand. Clearly, the more obvious these advantages, the lower the cost.

In the *latent* demand situation the consumer has to be sold on the idea of the product. The cost of creating demand is likely to be considerably higher than the cost of bringing about a 'switch', where a product demand is already established. The situation of *incipient* demand is the most expensive because two additional tasks must be accomplished. There is no current awareness of need on the part of prospective customers. Consequently, they have to be precisely identified, which involves certain expenditure on consumer research. Secondly, the targeted groups need to be educated as to why they need this product.

A final element for consideration when attempting to measure the likely cost of developing a new product in a competitive environment is the synergy component of the strategy. When a firm's competence profile is superimposed upon the competitive profile of a product-market opportunity, the areas of reinforcement show scope for synergy in terms of individual skills, specialized facilities or management skills. An example of this is Saab, unique among companies in producing fighter aircraft and luxury cars. Their car advertising frequently features both products in an attempt to gain synergy from the reputation of their modern fighting planes.

---

* *Corporate Strategy*, published by McGraw–Hill in 1965 and Penguin Books in 1968.

13 FINANCIAL ASPECTS OF EXPORT MARKETING

Pricing for Export Markets

The first fact to appreciate about exporting is that the costs of doing the business in another country will almost certainly be higher than in the home market. Furthermore, this is normally reflected in the price at which the goods are offered for sale. Consequently, it is worth considering the levels of disposable income in those countries where it is proposed to start trading.

These additional costs generally fall into four categories: modification of the product to any prevailing foreign standards and obtaining any necessary approval (Agrément Board, for example) for selling the product in another country; the costs of packaging and insurance and transport; any import duties on entry to the other country; and, finally, the channel or distribution costs at the other end. The following example shows the calculations of extra costs for getting an industrial product to a customer in Denmark. The UK price is £640, the Danish price £1000 – 56 per cent higher. (The terms and abbreviations used are explained in Table 13.1.)

		£	£
Standard home market (ex-works)			640
Modification to Danish standards		80	
Development amortization		10	
Costs of obtaining translations and Danish acceptance board approval		10	100
Overhead allocations:			
Marketing		10	
Administration/documentation		30	
Advertising/promotion		30	70
Ex works			810
	Packing for export		50
			860
FOT	Loading		5
			865
	Transport to docks		10
	Insurance cover to docks		5

		£	£
FOR			880
	Wharfage and porterage		25
FAS			905
	Dock rates		5
FOB			910
	Port rates		10
	Sea freight to Copenhagen		35
	Landing charges in Copenhagen		15
C&F			970
	Marine insurance		15
CIF			985
	Unloading, handling and insurance cover to warehouse		15
Franco domicile			£1000

Table 13.1 Export terms and conditions of sale

Terms	Charges paid by the seller (cumulative)	Delivery takes place (at/on)	Property and risks pass (on)[6]
Loco	Nil	'Where they are'	When contract made
Ex works	Packing (unless the contract otherwise provides) and preparation for dispatch	Seller's premises or other notified warehouse	Notification that goods are at buyer's disposal
FOR}C/F	Loading on to rail/truck[1]	Rail siding or depot	Delivery to carrier
FOT}C/P	Freight to port of shipment[2]	Factory gates	
FAS	Charges to and at port of shipment up to 'alongside'	Under the ship's hooks	When vessel able and ready to load
FOB	Dock and port expenses and outward customs formalities[3]	When safely loaded	Over the ship's rail
C&F	Shipping expenses, documentation and ocean freight	On tender of bills of lading to buyer	Ditto
CIF (seller selects ship)	Marine insurance	Ditto	Ditto

Table 13.1   continued

Terms	Charges paid by the seller (cumulative)	Delivery takes place (at/on)	Property and risks pass (on)[6]
Ex ship	Inward port dues[4]	On discharge from ship	When vessel able and willing to discharge
Landed or franco quay	Cost of discharge, lighters to shore and quay charges	On landing	Landing
Franco warehouse	Dock handling charges and transport to warehouse[5]	At warehouse	Delivery to warehouse
Franco domicile	Duty, clearance and delivery to buyer's premises	Buyer's premises	Delivery to buyer's premises

1. In the USA this is called 'FOB point of origin'.
2. In the USA this is called 'FOB port of shipment'. They do not therein include railhead to dock haulage nor port or shipment costs.
3. This must not be confused with the US expression. Continental use of FOB includes all costs of loading, shipping and documentation leaving the buyer to pay only the freight and insurance charges, the seller taking out and paying for a 'freight forward' bill of lading. In the UK loading costs are paid by the ship and are recovered in the freight paid by the buyer, *but* this is not the case on a tramp ship loading under a charterparty. In such cases the seller must pay the cost of loading. There is considerable argument in the UK over the liability for port rates, dock dues and customs specification charges. The practice on this varies from port to port and trade to trade.
4. In the USA this is called 'FOB port of destination'.
5. This may or may not include customs duty and clearance charges. This should be made clear – e.g. franco warehouse duty paid.
6. If the right of disposal has been reserved, the property and (normally) the risks pass only when the seller's conditions have been fulfilled. Thus on C&F or CAD (cash against documents) the seller could be both at risk and uninsured.

The calculations below show how the retail price might be constructed for the product once it has reached the country of destination:

	£
Total invoice value (Franco Copenhagen)	1000
Plus: VAT@15%	150
	£1150

	£
Price paid by Danish wholesaler	1150
Less: VAT	150
	1000
Plus: 20% mark-up	200
	1200
Plus: 15% VAT	180
	£1380

	£
Price paid by Danish retailer	1380
Less: VAT included	180
	1200
Plus: 20% mark-up	240
	1440
Plus: 15% VAT	216
Price paid by final purchaser	£1656

Specific Country Analyses

Profitable export selling is more difficult and time-consuming than doing comparable business in the home market. The principal reason for this is the great attention to detail that is required to make absolutely certain that payment is received for any goods or services supplied. In the home market, if a customer is dilatory regarding payment, there are two positive courses of action. The first is litigation where, if the courts decide that a contract has been established and the customer has the funds to pay, the seller is likely to receive payment some 12 to 18 months later. The alternative is to go to the purchaser's place of business and talk to them, rather forcibly if necessary. Persistence frequently succeeds and there is always recourse to the law if it does not.

The difficulty with exporting is that other countries have other laws and very different attitudes to certain aspects of behaviour. For example, in some states it is not considered wrong to allow an exporter to dispatch goods, receive them and then become very dilatory over payment. This becomes extremely painful for the exporter if several hundred thousand pounds of a company's money are at stake. In the eighteenth and nineteenth centuries, the equivalent of visiting the purchaser's offices involved sending the Royal Navy, and while this was generally very successful from the British point of view, the rest of the world became increasingly hostile to the idea. Indeed, the opposite is now the case, in that the exporting company may find it very difficult to obtain payment from a state, whether sovereign, communist or a dictatorship, boasting an army, navy and airforce.

Consequently, it is worth considering the real benefits of exporting to certain countries very seriously indeed. The potential exporter should consider the questions detailed below and attempt to score and rank the difficulty or cost associated with obtaining an acceptable answer in each case. Clearly, countries or markets with a high risk of non-payment or specific and unusual expenses or lack of market intelligence should be accorded a low weighting to the nominal value of the trade, thereby reflecting the adverse conditions of doing business with these specific countries. Table 13.2 illustrates a checklist for scoring the 'cost/benefit' of specific export options.

Table 13.2   Export market potential/analysis

Factor	(A) Weight	(B) Assessment	(A) × (B) Rating

International environment:
Diplomatic relations with Country X
Tariffs in Country X
Non-tariff barriers
Currency controls
Transportation costs

Local marketing environment:
Government stability/political predictability
Economic development, growth rate
Sensitivity to business cycles
Rate of inflation
Government controls:
   Regulation of competitive practices
   State marketing bodies
   Health and safety regulations
   Product labelling, standardization
Local business culture:
   State control or free market
   Extent of cartelization
   Respect for contracts
   Business ethics
Marketing infrastructure
   Data availability and
   reliability
   Marketing research agencies
   Literacy
   Advertising media
   Advertising agencies
   Public warehousing facilities
   Extent of telephone and postal systems
   Transportation facilities and costs

Marketing structure and demand analysis:
Consumer buying behaviour
Distributors and margins
Price range
Product variation
Competitive strategies (fierce or lax)
Potential competition (domestic/foreign)
Local stage of product life cycle
Market potential, short and long term

Table 13.2   *continued*

Factor	(A) Weight	(B) Assessment	(A) × (B) Rating
Financial estimates:			
Size of initial investment			
Investment by third party availability			
Sales volume (x years)			
Profitability (y per cent)			
Long-term return on investment			

International Environment

Are relations between the Home Office and a particular Country X cordial? Is there a history of cultural and political entente that is still strongly felt by both governments? Is the country under consideration a co-member of a free trading union or are there tariffs on certain imported goods? Are there non-tariff barriers such as quotas, difficult technical specifications, compensation (reciprocal) trading, licensing and contract manufacture joint-venture arrangements? Are there controls on the availability of hard currency such that it is difficult for the exporter to be paid in a negotiable form of money? (Generally this means sterling, American dollars, German marks, French francs or Japanese yen.) How high are the transportation costs as a percentage of the total cost? Transporting low-value, large-volume and heavy items long distances can be very expensive.

Local Market Environment

Is the government of the country stable? Many Third World governments are notorious for disclaiming responsibility for debts incurred by their predecessors in power. How predictable is public policy? Sudden token-payment nationalization of a company's overseas assets can be an expensive mistake for the business concerned. Has the country a steady rate of economic growth, is inflation under control? Does the government have effective regulation of competitive practices (EC rules for example)? Are the health and safety regulations comparable to Western standards? Are there particular requirements regarding labelling of product contents or different size standardizations for packaging?

The local business culture is also very important, particularly regarding business ethics and respect for the binding nature of the law of contract. Is the local market dominated by established cartels or other restrictions to free trade that are outlawed in many Western economies?

Other topics of concern are the sophistication of the business infrastructure: availability and reliability of market data, reliability of the telephone and postal networks, transportation facilities and their costs, media infrastructure (national newspapers, television) and the availability of secure warehousing facilities.

Market Structure and Demand Analysis

The prospective exporter should also take steps to obtain information on consumer buying behaviour in the country under consideration and whether any variations on the basic domestic product are required. Indeed, can the exporting company make an acceptable profit in the new market?

The exact method of reaching the ultimate consumer needs to be evaluated (local distributor or joint-venture with a national organization, for example). Prudence would suggest that a detailed analysis of the existing and potential competition, both foreign and domestic, be undertaken.

The maturity of the market might also be examined. Perhaps they are some years behind the UK and there is the future potential for selling what is an increasingly obsolete production-line in the home market. Perhaps the overseas economy is rapidly expanding and these exports might well result in economies of scale in the home market too.

Sales Channel Costs

Decisions about the sales channels to be used are amongst the most important taken by sales and marketing managers. These decisions must necessarily be medium or long term because they take time and considerable sums of money to implement. They also impact across the whole spectrum of a company's sales and marketing strategy.

The task facing the international seller is that distribution systems within foreign countries vary dramatically and that these local variations must be superimposed upon the alternatives that already exist as a result of the product's perceived characteristics (perishability, unit value, weight, size) and consumer purchasing practices (e.g. is the product a necessity or a luxury with a regular or infrequent purchase cycle?). In addition, some countries impose certain legal restrictions on the distribution of products within their domain. Finally, the activities of any competition should also be considered.

The final choice between the various alternative sales channels will generally be a balance between budgeted distribution costs on the one hand versus the degree of control of the sales and marketing effort on the other. Channel costs quite typically fall into two types – the capital or initial investment cost, and the cost of managing and maintaining the system or network, of which a major element is the margin taken by the intermediaries.

There are four principal types of overseas sales channel, although most are capable of some local variation. The relative costs and benefits of each are outlined in Table 13.3.

Generally, where the value of an individual order is high, perhaps in excess of £250 000, and particularly where the product is technically complicated, a company is likely to sell direct using its own sales and marketing expertise with a local agent. Where the potential for the level of business is greater, a joint venture or subsidiary might seem preferable and a worthwhile investment. High-value, high-volume orders of consumer retail products can also qualify.

Table 13.3   Alternative export sales channels

	Initial investment	Recurring costs	Degree of control	Profitability	Timing of payment to UK company
Indirect export	None	High distribution margins	Low	Generally low or modest	Immediate
Direct export	Low	Low corporate costs and dealer margins	Some	Modest	Several months depending on sales cycle
Joint ventures	Low	Training/ quality control	Some/more	Modest (licence fees are normally between 2 and 7%)	6 or 12 monthly licence payments
Overseas manufacturing subsidiary	High	The idea is that these should be modest	Absolute within local government sanctions	Potentially high, though repatriation may be restricted	Annually

Indirect Export

This generally involves institutions called 'export houses', which are organizations specializing in the handling and financing of British exports and international trade not connected with the UK, though they themselves do not manufacture. There are three main types, each offering a slightly different service.

Export merchants resemble domestic wholesalers with overseas interests and methods of distribution which can include agents, salespeople and sometimes local offices. The advantage to the manufacturer is that the merchant takes legal title to the goods and is responsible for all the documentation and risk.

A confirming house finances the export transaction by paying the seller before the goods leave the UK. In return, a commission is received by the confirming house for taking the short-term credit risk that was unacceptable to the producer. Manufacturers' export agents take care of the distribution in the export market but the principal must handle the export finance, the credit risk, shipping, insurance and documentation.

Sometimes an established company will allow another to use its own overseas distribution network in exchange for a commission payment. This is called complementary marketing.

Direct Export

It is not essential to use an intermediary: indeed, many types of industrial products are sold direct to overseas countries, such as those types of consumer goods that can be sold through a department store group or a mail-order house. Sales to local and national governments are also frequently done direct.

Where a company does not have its own overseas offices, a commission agent is freuquently used in addition to the corporate sales and marketing team. The advantage to the exporter is the agent's local knowledge and experience at a low initial investment cost. Another alternative is to use a distributor or stockist who purchases and then resells the exporter's products. As the volume of business increases, a branch office might become financially feasible, depending upon the restrictions imposed by local law, particularly employment legislation and the implications of local contract law. The branch office does, however, involve initial capital expenditure and a continuing overhead irrespective of the subsequent short-term volume of sales.

Joint Ventures

This term covers five different types of 'partnership' with an overseas organization: licensing, franchising, industrial (manufacturing) co-operation, contract manufacture and management contracts. The major advantages to the exporter are the avoidance of market entry barriers (import quotas or tariffs), a reduction in freight charges and a much reduced cost of initial investment.

Licensing permits overseas organizations to use a UK company's knowledge and technical know-how (whether or not covered by a patent) in return for an agreed remuneration. The disadvantage of this from the licenser's viewpoint is that the licensee may become a competitor at the end of the agreement.

Business format franchising requires the franchisee (local operator) to carry on a particular business under a format or system established by the franchisor (UK company in this case). The franchisee can use the franchisor's trade name, trade mark, goodwill and know-how, while the franchisor is entitled to exercise continuing control over the way in which the franchisee carries on the business. The franchisee is not only expected to make a substantial personal investment in the business but pay the franchisor a regular percentage (usually 10 per cent) of the turnover. The financial advantages and disadvantages are similar to those for licensing.

Industrial co-operation agreements are generally long-term specialization agreements entered into by two companies from different countries with the object of sharing the costs of a certain project. Well-known examples are Concorde, the European Airbus, the Westland helicopter issue and the Channel Tunnel.

Contract manufacture is a financial halfway point between licensing and a direct investment in an overseas manufacturing or process capability. It is a long-term contract for the manufacture or assembly of a product. A particular financial advantage is the limited local investment which is free from the subsequent risk of nationalization or expropriation.

The management contract is similar to a long-term consultancy agreement where an overseas operation is managed in return for fees and sometimes a share of the profits.

Overseas Manufacturing Subsidiary

Manufacturing a product in another country is likely to involve a substantial capital investment and a higher element of risk than generally exists in the home market. Unilateral nationalization without adequate compensation is perhaps greatest in certain developing nations.*

Considered sequentially the first decision must be whether to invest abroad or not. Clearly a number of product-market possibilities will present themselves with various rates of return and net present values (see Chapter 8). All these alternatives which meet or exceed the corporate criteria for such decisions (rate of return, market share) should then be ranked in descending order according to the country or product combination.

The second decision, which product should be manufactured in which country, should receive consideration above and beyond strict financial return. The topics presented in Table 13.2 might equally well be adapted to provide input to this decision.

Subsequent decisions revolve around the nature of the manufacturing capability, assembly or the complete manufacturing process. Assembly close to the market offers for many companies an attractive compromise between exporting and a complete overseas manufacturing capability. The advantages are frequently lower freight costs, cost advantages reflecting lower rates of pay in the overseas market, lower or no import duties and indeed a certain amount of official patronage in some circumstances.

The fourth decision revolves around whether there are additional benefits from a joint venture with an organization indigenous to the market. In some Third World countries this is the only effective option available as 100 per cent foreign ownership is discouraged. In some circumstances this is a very convenient and practical way to reach the market at a reduced capital cost. However, in other situations it can be a veritable minefield of intrigue, deviousness and outright skulduggery – or so it may appear to the British or European partner.

A variation on this, representing effectively the fifth decision, is whether to buy a going concern in the overseas country or start up an entirely new operation. The former may be financially attractive if a suitable candidate can be discovered and a minimum amount of ill-feeling generated by the takeover.

Government Support for Exporters

The Export Credit Guarantee Department (ECGD) is a government department whose function is to provide assistance to exporting companies. It has two main roles:

1. In broad terms the ECGD insures companies against the risk of not being paid – whether through default of the buyer or other causes, such as the cancellation of valid import licences or restrictions on the transfer of currency.
2. ECGD provides guarantees of 100 per cent repayment to banks who have advanced money to overseas buyers of UK companies' goods and services.

---

* The Export Credit Guarantee Department does provide insurance against this eventuality in certain circumstances though usually for a maximum of 15 years and for 90 per cent of any loss.

The objectives of ECGD services are to insure exporting companies against the risks of non-payment and thus hopefully pursue a bolder marketing strategy. Secondly, the ECGD support for export finance is designed to help British exporters to offer competitive terms and win contracts that would otherwise elude them.

Comprehensive Short-Term Insurance

Generally, exporters allowing the ECGD to insure all their export business will have a better chance of qualifying for cheaper premiums. This is because ECGD aims at a wide spread of risk with as much sound business in the portfolios as possible to minimize the department's vulnerability to massive claims.

Specific Insurance

The principle of comprehensive insurance cannot, however, be applied to contracts for the supply of capital goods or construction projects because they may be 'one-offs'. These contracts are therefore underwritten individually and may incur higher premiums.

Guarantees for Supplier Credit Finance

ECGD does not itself provide finance for export credit, but for goods and services sold on credit of two years and more it will provide a range of direct guarantees to the banks providing export finance over the whole field of exports.

Guarantees for Buyer Credit Finance

ECGD supports loans made by banks in the UK direct to an overseas borrower at fixed preferential interest rates for up to 85 per cent of the value of contracts for major projects and capital goods where the UK content (for either goods or services) is valued at £1 million or more.

Underwriting the Buyer

Where the contracts involve the sale of heavy capital goods or major projects, the ECGD will investigate the financial position and business representation of the buyer in the course of underwriting the contract.

Underwriting the Overseas Market

The country risk is of crucial importance, and so the ECGD maintains an up-to-date intelligence file of the political and economic developments in 180 countries. Four different business categories of countries exist, reflecting the perceived risk of trading with them. This is of course reflected in the premium charged for underwriting the bank loan to the overseas buyer.

Percentage of Cover Given

It is an ECGD requirement that the policyholder (the exporter) carry a small part of any loss. The maximum percentages covered are 90 per cent for buyer risks and 90 per cent of 95 per cent for market risks.

ECGD Premiums

The premium paid by the exporter under the comprehensive Short-Term Guarantee is paid in two ways. First, a non-refundable premium is paid at the beginning of each insurance year. This is fixed for each policy individually. The amount payable depends partly on the size of the policyholder's export turnover and partly on the degree of use made of the ECGD credit limit service.

Secondly, a premium is paid monthly on exports declared in that month at a flat rate for each policy fixed at the beginning of each year of insurance. Where a company has insurable exports of less than £25 000 a year an inclusive annual premium is payable.

Premium rates for specific business and for comprehensive business covered under the Supplementary Extended Terms Guarantee are determined contract by contract, based upon the length of the period during which the ECGD is at risk and the ECGD grading of the market where the business is done.

Overseas Investment Insurance Scheme

ECGD's Overseas Investment Insurance Scheme is designed to encourage new investment in developing countries throughout the world. It enables UK companies to invest more confidently in the knowledge that they are protected against losses arising from expropriation, war or restrictions on remittances back to the UK. Other specific political risks, such as breach of contract by the host government, may also be insured.

Once cover is issued, ECGD will maintain that cover for the full agreed term of the insurance (normally 15 years). Cover is renewable annually and premiums are fixed from the outset of the insurance.

Invoicing in Foreign Currency and Foreign Exchange Procedures

In the past a large part of world trade was conducted in sterling and there was no need for British traders to operate in any other currency than sterling. The very fact that one party, whether buyer or seller, was operating in sterling meant that the other party had to operate in what was for them foreign currency. As a consequence those countries which are now Britain's keen competitors have always been accustomed to dealing in other currencies.

Sterling no longer enjoys the same predominance, and the British firm trading overseas should now be prepared to consider conducting business in foreign currency. A company which is prepared to quote prices and invoice in the buyer's currency can gain some advantage. In the first place it has a marketing attraction because it simplifies the whole transaction for the buyer, telling him immediately what is the cost. Secondly, because most sales are made on credit terms there is a possible extra profit available by selling the expected currency receipts on the forward exchange market. Most of the principal currencies (US dollar, German mark, Japanese yen) are at a premium for future delivery which means that when sold forward those currencies realize more sterling. Operations in foreign currency present few problems because the banks are fully equipped to provide all the information and facilities required. Indeed, the London foreign exchange market is the most efficient and comprehensive in the world. Any foreign currency received in payment of exports can be readily sold through the exporter's bank.

The Forward Market

When goods have been sold at a price expressed in a foreign currency and the credit terms have been granted, payment will not be received until some future date. The prudent exporter will cover the risk of changes in the exchange rate by selling the expected currency forward. The exporter has only to inform his bank that he expects to receive a certain sum in a foreign currency on such a date and establish with the bank a 'forward' contract. The bank will now quote a rate at which it will buy the currency on the date when the currency is received. The exporter thus knows exactly how much sterling he will receive when the payment is made.

Forward rates are quoted in the press daily for the principal currencies, usually for one, two, three and six months ahead. For some of the major currencies it is possible to get quotations for up to twelve months and in the case of US dollars a period of up to two years can be arranged. The quotations show a small premium or discount on the spot rate (the prevailing rate at the date and time in question).

Where the exporter cannot be certain as to the exact future date when payment will be received, an 'option forward' contract can be arranged. The 'option' is not whether to proceed or not but merely flexibility as to the exact date of delivery of the currency. Where, for example, an exporter has sold on 90-day terms but expects the buyer to be a little dilatory, the currency can be sold forward for three months fixed, with the option of up to a further month if necessary. The currency may then be delivered any time from the end of three months up to the end of the fourth month.

Examples of Forward Rate Calculations

Example 1

Suppose an exporter has sold to Germany on 1 February goods on 90-day terms and asks the bank to arrange forward currency cover. The rate quoted by the bank will be calculated as follows. If on 1 February the bank's spot rate for deutschmarks is 3.10½–3.11½, and one month forward is at a 3–2 Pf premium and three months forward is at a 9–8 Pf premium, the exporter will be selling deutschmarks to the bank, therefore the bank will apply its buying rate based on spot 3.11½ (3.10½ is the selling rate which is lower).

The deutschmark payment is expected in three months' time, so the bank will calculate on the basis of the three months forward rate 9–8 Pf premium. The forward rate is at a premium, i.e. dearer, in the future, so the rate will be lower and the premium deducted from the spot rate. But the bank is buying, so will wish to keep the rate as high as possible (i.e. wanting more deutschmarks for the amount of sterling it provides) and will therefore deduct the smaller premium, i.e. 8 Pf. The forward rate would therefore be: 3.11 ½ less 0.08 = 3.03 ½.

If, on the other hand, the exporter is expecting payment some time during March and wishes to cover forward, he will cover one month fixed, with an option one further month. The one month fixed takes him to 1 March, and he can receive the benefit of the one-month premium, but as payment may be received any time between 1 March and 31 March, he cannot receive the benefit of any extra premium for the second month, and so the rate will be: 3.03 ½ less 0.02 = 3.01 ½. This means that the bank will give the exporter one pound for every DM 3.01 ½.

Example 2

In this example, the exporter has also sold goods to Spain on 90-day terms and wishes to cover forward on 1 February. The bank's rates on that date are: spot 196.10–196.40; one month forward 20–70 c discount; three months forward 90–130 c discount. Again the bank will base the calculation on the spot buying rate of 196.40 and the three-months forward rate of 90–130 c discount. In this case, however, the forward rate is a discount, i.e. cheaper forward, and therefore the rate will be higher and the discount added to the spot. The bank, wishing to keep a buying rate as high as possible, will add the larger discount, i.e. 130 c. The forward rate would therefore be: 196.40 + 1.30 = 197.70.

If the exporter is expecting payment during March or April he can still only obtain a fixed forward rate for one month, i.e. to 1 March, with an option for a further two months. As payment may be received any time from 1 March to the end of April, i.e. three months, and as the forward rates are at a discount, the bank will take the maximum discount and apply the three-month rate. So the forward rate will be the same as above: 196.40 + 1.30 = 197.70.

14 THE SALES AND MARKETING PLAN

Dwight D. Eisenhower is attributed with having said: 'Plans are nothing, planning is everything.' This is clearly stating that the systematic process whereby objectives are agreed and the strategy for achieving them calculated and implemented has a greater importance than the printed document recording the fact. The most obvious explanation for this is that the dynamic process of planning is responsive to change whereas a plan that was formulated under conditions which are now obsolete is of little practical use. However, it is essential that the latest thoughts and proposals for the business are recorded in print for effective communication to the managers charged with implementing them. This document must be the blueprint for measuring performance until a new version is produced in response to market developments and changes in environmental conditions.

Corporate Objectives and the Mission Statement

A business should decide on its objectives in order that the planning process might have a target that can provide directional guidance for the efforts of the management and staff. Furthermore, a time profile needs to be fixed for the achievement of these objectives.

The mission statement usually combines several objectives together in one succinct paragraph attempting to balance the following:

1. certain financial objectives, such as a return on investment or a profit target, either expressed as a percentage on an absolute amount in pounds sterling;
2. certain marketing objectives relating to market share or the achievement of entry into a geographical or product market;
3. certain strategic objectives such as preventing Company X or Country Y from achieving certain specific objectives that are against the interests of the company making the plan.

Analysis of the Previous Trading Year

Having carefully prepared a list of corporate objectives it is important to have a clear picture as to the company's present business position. Primarily it is important to know:

1. sales revenue and profitability or contribution by each product/service market;
2. an analysis of how the business was obtained (this will depend on the type of business, but will indicate clear guidelines for future marketing strategy).

In order to give this explanation a certain realism, an actual example will be used based on a sales and marketing plan produced for a computer services company in September 1988.

The first step was to analyse all the sales achieved in the year 1987–8. This was done under seven separate headings:

1. Computer solutions
2. Hardware sales
3. Software sales
4. Consultancy
5. Service contracts
6. Sales of consumables/stationery
7. Rental contracts.

The first product group was computer solutions sales with a revenue of £198 970, making an average contribution of 13.5 per cent, as shown in Table 14.1. All the other product/services revenues were analysed in a similar manner until Table 14.2 could be produced, summarizing the year's sales revenue.

Another very important aspect of producing a sales and marketing plan is to examine how the sales were introduced to the company. Good sources of introductions must be nurtured and kept informed as to the company's continually evolving skills capability. Low-productivity activities should be evaluated for possible improvement, kept as a marginal low-cost activity or discarded as being a relative waste of time. Table 14.3 shows the analysis of our company's revenue by source of

Table 14.1   Computer solutions sales

Client	Business type	Source of introduction	Order value £	Contribution %	Contribution £
J.R. Esq	Translator	Personal contact	6 950	10	690
PYY Syndications	Greetings ards	KSA*	11 950	20	2 390
Mr X	Engineer	Personal contact	11 950	5	590
CXX Services	Pathology services	Personal contact	15 000	20	3 000
A.D.W. Esq	Accountant	Personal contact	16 310	7	1 140
PY Finance	Finance company	KSA*	18 550	8	1 480
St K's	Hospital	Personal contact	5 110	10	510
Institute of Z	Professional institute	KSA*	113 150	15	16 970
			£198 970	13.5	£26 770

* Keith Steward Associates Limited (sales, marketing, computer and financial consultants).

Table 14.2   Summary of 1987–8 sales revenue

	Sales value	% of total sales	Contribution £	%	% of total contribution
Computer solutions	198 970	25.6	25 290	12.7	17.2
Hardware	295 330	37.9	43 970	14.9	28.1
Software	98 130	12.4	29 440	30.0	18.8
Consultancy	33 250	4.3	16 175	48.8	10.4
Service contracts	83 410	10.7	15 405	30.5	16.3
Consumables/Stationery	51 240	6.6	9 140	17.8	5.8
Rentals	18 020	2.3	5 260	29.4	3.4
	£778 350	100.0	£145 180		100.0

Table 14.3   Sales analysis by source of introduction

	£
Directors' personal contacts	288 450
Marketing consultants (KSA)	208 930
Software supplier X referrals	95 480
Hardware supplier Y referrals	100 500
Software supplier Z referrals	19 870
Software supplier Q referrals	23 050
Advertising in journals	22 100
Direct mail campaigns	19 950
Total	£778 330

introduction. Quite clearly software suppliers Z and Q and direct mail campaigns need to be examined for greater productivity. In the case of nominal advertising the cost of producing £22 100 worth of business needs to be checked to see whether value is being received.

Interpretation of the previous year's results

Analysis of the 1987–8 results shows that consultancy, service contracts, software sales and rentals achieve a very satisfactory contribution towards the overheads of running the business. Unfortunately as shown in Table 14.4, their share of the total amount of business obtained was rather low (29.7 per cent).

Consultancy

Clearly, the most profitable product market segment is consultancy (with an average contribution of 48.8 per cent). Unfortunately it only produces revenue of £33 250. A very substantial increase is needed in this type of business if the company is going to make satisfactory profits.

Table 14.4 High contribution business sectors

	Sales value	% of total sales	Actual contribution	% of total contribution
	£		£	
Consultancy	33 250	4.3	16 175	10.4
Service contracts	83 410	10.7	15 405	16.3
Software	98 130	12.4	29 940	18.8
Rentals	18 020	2.3	5 260	3.4
		29.7	£66 780	48.9

Table 14.5 Prospective new business

(A) Prospective chart	(B) Potential value of consultancy	(C) Estimated % chance of obtaining work	((B) × (C)) Expected value	Source of introduction
University X	16 000	80	12 800	Institute C
Y Ltd	40 000	70	28 000	Institute D
Z Viewdata Services	20 000	50	10 000	Institute F
Q Insurance	10 000	35	3 500	Institute D
W Transport	30 000	15	4 500	Institute D
	£116 000		£58 800	

Table 14.5 shows current position for prospective new business. This is already showing a distinct improvement over the previous year's £33 250 (a 56 per cent increase). If this level of consultancy business is to be sustained, the closest possible contacts must be maintained with the various professional institutes. Furthermore, all work undertaken must be to the very highest professional standards to ensure that nothing is done to interrupt the flow of referrals.

Service Support Contracts

Of this business 42 per cent comes from St W's Hospital and is a direct result of one of the director's personal contacts (having worked there for many years prior to forming a limited company). This is a difficult business segment to develop quickly without changing the main thrust of the business.

Software Sales

This business is attractive both in terms of volume and profitability and is achieved substantially as a result of leads from the software companies themselves. As with all referral business nothing succeeds like success. This business is entirely dependent upon maintaining a strong technical and sales capability. When the volume becomes too much for the existing team additional people must be recruited and trained to the present high standards.

Rentals

This is for clients without the cash flow to purchase or the long-term commitment to lease. It will never amount to a major part of the business, but clearly a gap through which custom might be lost.

Consumables and Stationery

At 6.6 per cent of total sales, this is a useful additional client service. It will only be expanded by additional sales and marketing effort – which means extra staff.

Hardware Sales

Sales of computer hardware account for 37.9 per cent of the sales revenue and as such it is the mainstay of the business, but in a very price-competitive business it is almost impossible to make more than a 20 per cent contribution. This is common knowledge and companies selling computer hardware must either go for large volume or supplement the profit from this business sector with complementary high margin services.

Strengths, Weaknesses, Opportunities, Threats (SWOT) Analysis

This is now a well-known method for appraising a company's standing!

Strengths

1. Dr Jones is a computer scientist with a European reputation:
   (a) ROMTEC dealer panel member
   (b) Tutor to MSc students at the R University
   (c) Tutor to PhD students at University O
   (d) St W's Hospital reputation.
2. The business has agencies for many hardware products; consequently it can advise without the bias of single supplier dealerships. The range of computer processors that the company sells extends from the BBC Micro (at the lowest price end of the market) to DEC, VAX and Altos networks at £100 000 plus at the top of the range.
3. The staff have been especially selected to provide specialist knowledge in a number of areas:
   (a) The use of transputer technology
   (b) Financial packages
   (c) Desk-top publishing
   (d) Relational databases
   (e) Commercial estate agency systems
   (f) Foreign language capability (German, Norwegian, Swedish and Danish).

Weaknesses

Small size and low turnover £778 330 (net of VAT). Only eleven full-time staff:

MD
Technical director
1 Financial sales consultant
3 Sales executives
2 Programmer/analysts
2 Programmers
Secretary

Opportunities

1. Offering specialist high technology computer and marketing consultancy in conjunction with KSA Ltd.
2. Computer consultancy to small accountants' practices.
3. St W's Hospital – unique reputation as a supplier of small- and medium-size computer systems.
4. Scandinavian companies with offices in the UK as the company has a Norwegian speaking employee.
5. The companies for which hardware and software agencies are held are aware of the expertise available to support their products despite the relatively small size of the business.

Threats

The greatest and only real threat is that the volume of business achieved in 1989 will not sustain a staff of fifteen (eleven now plus budgeted four extra to manage additional business) in NW1 offices.

Sales and Marketing Plan

Table 14.6 shows the directors' targeted objectives: essentially they wish to take the company to the position where its turnover is £2 million and the contribution to fixed costs exceeds £500 000, using the 1987/8 contribution figures.

Marketing Strategy

The following potential markets (Markets 1, 2 and 3) were identified by the directors of the company. Markets 4, 5, 6 and 7 are the recommendations of the sales and marketing consultants (KSA Ltd).

Market 1: NHS Teaching Hospitals

Of the company's business 16.7 per cent came from St W's Hospital with additional small orders from the Royal Z and the M Hospitals. Clearly, if this level of business could be obtained from the other postgraduate teaching hospitals, the company would have a very secure future. Unfortunately this is unlikely to happen, because

Table 14.6   Directors' targeted objectives

	Sales objectives £	Increase over 1987–8 %	1987–8 % contribution	Contribution £
Computer solutions	400 000	49.7	13.4	53 600
Hardware	500 000	59.1	14.9	74 500
Software	250 000	39.3	13.4	31 000
Consultancy	600 000	554.2	48.8	292 800
Service contracts	125 000	66.7	30.5	38 130
Consumables/stationery	100 000	51.2	17.8	17 800
Rentals	25 000	72.1	29.4	7 350
	£2 000 000			£515 180

the St W's success is based on a level of personal contact that it would be impossible to achieve without spending ten years working as a member of the hospital staff.

Market 2: Commercial Estate Agents

The commercial estate agents package was originally designed for Dobson & Dobson but they later chose a competitive product. However, another company has since shown interest. Completion date is scheduled for 1 October 1988 with acceptance on 1 November. Although there are some 400 commercial estate agents in the Greater London area, the product is not expected to be a major seller as this market shows great reluctance to invest in business technology.

Market 3: Accountants – Small Practices

The advantage of computerizing a company's ledger and accountancy system is the comparative ease with which management accounts can subsequently be produced. Most accountants would now agree with that. Unfortunately, if they qualified more than five years ago, they are unlikely to have had a great deal of practical computer training.

The idea is to offer advice and guidance to small accountancy practices not able to afford a full-time computer specialist. A salesperson with a sound knowledge of accountancy and computer systems has been recruited. The first task has been to select two accountancy software packages for retailing and to transfer the company's accounts to one of these systems, thereby gaining the appropriate practical experience.

Market 4: Consultancy Referrals from Professional Institutes

Over the past year, the Institutes of D and C have referred a number of computer and high technology marketing assignments to KSA. On a number of these, the computer and technical input has been provided by the company. This is proving so successful that the two companies believe that a niche has been identified for this almost unique combination of specialist consultancy:

Client/prospect	Application	Original source of business introduction
1	Designing a computerized prospect recording and evaluation system using artificial intelligence	The Institute of D
2	Supply of a network of PCs for WP in the conference office	KSA Ltd
3	An audit of the market for full text retrieval and identification of niche opportunities	The Institute of C
4	Identification of potential European dealerships for transputer products	The Institute of C
5	Produce a sales and marketing plan for a viewdata-based information service	The Institute of D
6	Prospect recording system and desk-top publishing	The Institute of D
7	Design of customer records database with output files for management accounting	The Institute of D

The strategy is for the company to obtain a similar high profile with other professional bodies.

Market 5: Hardware and Software Suppliers

As a priority, meetings should be arranged with the appropriate Dealer Sales Manager of the following:

(1) Hardware manufacturers or software authors:

Company	Product
Software	A
Publishing Corporation	B
ABC	C
Disk Associates	D
Pineapple	E
U Systems	F

(2) Multi-vendor distributors:

Company	Product
Maws	G
Normtec	H
Mersey Systems	I
Electronics	J
Wizz Ltd	K
Back-up Systems	L

They should be interested because the biggest problem facing Dealer Sales Managers is dissatisfied end-users. This problem occurs where the dealer, not really understanding the agency product, exaggerates its capabilities. If the company can expand its reputation for doing 'good clean business', it has to be in the principal's interest to forward leads to the company.

Expanding the theme of receiving sales leads from principals, it is worth considering (1) extension of the software product line and (2) some tactics to locate prospects for the software products already being sold.

At an 'idea-generation' meeting in early August, two product lines were identified for a major effort:

(1) accounting packages for use by one type of business;
(2) desk-top publishing for a particular market sector.

The specific sectors have not been identified for reasons of confidentiality.

Market 6: Desk-top Publishing

Desk-top publishing is both technically and commercially a logical extension of wordprocessing. Effectively, it involves bringing black on white artwork, lettering and graphics into the normal sales office that already has a desk-top computer. The additions are a typesetting software package at about £1000 and a laser printer costing from £1500.

The benefits are improved document quality for proposals, reports and tenders, giving a really professional image. A wider choice of lettering in both style and size (founts ranging from 4 to 127 points) is available than if using wordprocessing software alone. Furthermore, there is the ability to do extensive graphics (lines, boxes, circles, pie charts, histograms and other shapes, including half-tones), which the user can define using the 'paint-brush' or 'spray-gun' facilities. Effectively, the system as specified (appropriate software and laser printer) offers platesetting without the ability to reproduce good-quality artwork and colour. A consultation from a graphic designer can provide both the fine tuning on layout and the bromide transparencies for original artwork with the recommended Pantone colours. Clearly, this brings brochure layout and design as well as customer history profiles within the company, and offers saving in time, effort and cost. The only limitation is the inability to use colour artwork.

Market 7: Scandinavian Companies Based in the UK

Having a senior member of staff with Scandinavian nationality as well as accounting and computer expertise, it seems sensible to take advantage of this 'unique' combination of skills and address this market niche. An appropriate list has already been obtained from the Norwegian embassy.

The detailed work that resulted in the final sales and marketing plan (Table 14.7) resulted in figures falling a little short of the £2 million revenue target and the £500 000 contribution objective. The plan is extremely ambitious and it will be very interesting to monitor progress throughout 1988/9.

Table 14.7 1988/89 Sales Plan

	Computer solutions	Hardware	Software	Consultancy	Service Contracts	Consumables/ stationery	Rentals	Total
1. Vertical market segmentation								
NHS teaching hospitals		150 000		10 000	80 000	20 000		260 000
Commercial estate agents	100 000				5 000	20 000	25 000	150 000
Accountants	150 000	50 000	50 000	75 000	10 000			335 000
2. Segmentation by source of introduction								
Professional institutes' referrals				415 000				415 000
Hardware suppliers		100 000						100 000
Software suppliers		50 000			20 000			70 000
3. Segmentation by application								
Desk-top publishing		100 000	100 000		10 000			210 000
Other	100 000		50 000			40 000		190 000
4. Segmentation by demography								
Scandinavian companies in the UK	50 000	100 000				20 000		170 000
Projected revenue	£400 000	£550 000	£200 000	£500 000	£125 000	£100 000	£25 000	£1 900 000
Projected contribution	53 600	81 950	26 800	244 000	38 125	17 800	7 350	469 625

PART FOUR

Controlling the Performance

15 PRICE DETERMINATION AND PRICING POLICY

The determination of the price of a product or service is the particular prerogative of the marketing manager. The price at which a product is placed on the market has a critical influence on the profit made by a business, and a small difference in price can have a large effect on the return on capital, as shown by the following example:

	A	B
Price per unit	£1.00	£1.05
Turnover in units	100 000	100 000
Sales	£100 000	£105 000
Total cost	95 000	95 000
Profit	£5 000	£10 000
Capital employed	£40 000	£40 000
Return on capital	$12\frac{1}{2}\%$	25%

Of course, the example is somewhat simplified because the higher price may in practice cause a reduction in turnover, or require an increase in marketing and selling costs in order to sustain the higher turnover.

Numerous considerations will influence the marketing manager in deciding on the 'right price' for the product. In the case of a highly competitive market, the over-riding factor will be the price at which products are being, or are likely to be, sold by competitors. All products are to some extent subject to competition for there is always a substitute, or an alternative choice for a buyer making a purchase. There is, however, usually a limited range of prices acceptable to the market, and a somewhat higher price than those of competitors can only be sustained by superior selling effort, better product quality, and/or superior standards of customer service.

For many consumer products, sales turnover is elastic in relation to price. This means that the higher the price, the lower the volume, but a reduction in price would increase sales volume. There are exceptions, however, such as prestige goods where too low a price can arouse suspicion as to quality and deter potential buyers. Profit is maximized by selecting the optimum combination of price and turnover in the manner set out on pages 190–192.

Cost is usually held to be a significant factor in setting prices. Indeed, there is a common tendency to increase prices when costs rise. This practice can be successful if it is carried out by the market leader and smaller traders follow suit. However, the existence of substitutes – gas for heating instead of electricity, for example – may result in cost-plus pricing causing reduced sales and a subsequent lower profit.

Standard Cost Pricing

Standard cost pricing is a supreme example of misusing valuable management information. The costs associated with producing a product or service are important only for determining the minimum price at which it is commercially feasible to sell that product. The price that is ultimately selected must be based upon totally different criteria that relate to the conditions prevailing in the market-place, not those in the seller's factory.

The standard cost is essentially the average cost of producing a certain volume of products over a period of time in what is thought to be normal conditions. It is then used as a measure for future production performance. Differences from the standard are known as variances which may be 'favourable' or 'negative'. It is a useful concept for measuring production efficiency but as a basis for pricing it is about as relevant as yesterday's weather forecast.

Cost-plus System of Pricing

The most important thing about this method is that the supplier at least has a better chance of staying in business because the selling price is calculated on the basis of all the costs plus a percentage profit margin agreed between the buyer and the seller. It is used in certain industries for major contracts, of which the most widely publicized have been between the Ministry of Defence and its suppliers. When buying using this system, the purchaser usually likes to audit the seller's accounts to verify that the costs allocated are justified. However, the system has a number of major disadvantages, particularly to the buyer:

1. It is difficult to know the costs in advance and consequently the purchase price; this makes planning and budgetary control difficult.
2. The difficulty of allocating specific costs to particular projects is a serious drawback.
3. The competitive element of the market-place is totally disregarded.
4. No distinction is made between the 'not otherwise recoverable costs' (R&D) and the variable costs of production.

Market-related Pricing Tactics

These pricing tactics are concerned with pricing products to achieve specific marketing objectives. Once these have been achieved the price will almost certainly be changed to achieve subsequent objectives.

Market Penetration Price

This is a technique based on pricing a product below that of other similar products in the market-place in order to gain market share. To be certain of success with this method a company needs large financial resources because the effect of making a small profit without substantial increases in volume can be disastrous (see Table 15.2 later). Secondly, a company indulging in this practice needs a competitive edge that stops other companies following suit and creating a price war. This may be unique technology, a large and well-established retail chain, or a prestige company name that commands a loyal consumer base. Thirdly, when embarking on this path, it is necessary to 'cut deep', 40, 50 or 60 per cent for consumer durables – it must be a sensational buy to attract the large volume of customers required to make this work.

Market Skimming

This tactic is based on the fact that there are always a small number of people who are willing to pay a high price for an exclusive product. This tactic is frequently used for 'new-to-the-world' products, particularly where they are based on new technology (videotape recorders, laser printers). The prices subsequently fall as the competition responds to this new product with their own similar products.

Another area where this method of pricing can be used is where demand exceeds a finite supply. Examples of this are the Glyndebourne Festival, Centre Court tickets at Wimbledon (particularly on the days of the singles finals) and luxury motor cars made by small specialist producers (Morgan, Bristol).

Changes in Volume Costs and Selling Price

Even slight changes in the cost of producing and marketing a product, or in the price at which these sales are made, can have major implications for product profitability. It is surprising how most companies put all their effort into increasing sales volume when far greater increases in profit can be made by slight adjustments to the selling price or the level of costs incurred.

Consider the situation in Table 15.1. A 10 per cent increase in sales volume with selling prices and costs unchanged produces quite reasonably a 10 per cent increase in profit. However, a 5 per cent price increase produces a startling 50 per cent increase in profit and a 5 per cent cost reduction-an impressive 45 per cent increase in profit. This is of course on the assumption that sales volume remains unchanged with the increase in the selling price. In practice this would not always happen. There is for most products a fall in demand following a price increase, though as consumers become accustomed to the new price levels, volume tends to rise again over the few months following the increase in prices.

Table 15.1   Effect on profits of volume, price and cost

	Original	Volume +10%	Price +5%	Costs −5%
	£	£	£	£
Sales	100 000	110 000	105 000	100 000
Costs	90 000	99 000	90 000	85 500
Profit	£10 000	£11 000	£15 000	£14 500
% increase in profit		10%	50%	45%

In Table 15.2 two alternative pricing tactics are examined with assumed responses in consumer demand. In the first instance, sales volume remains unchanged; in the second, volume falls by 10 per cent following a 5 per cent price rise. The third case shows the disastrous effects that can be created by reducing price in an attempt to increase sales volume, where the subsequent increase is only modest – in this case 10 per cent.

Table 15.2   Effect on profit of volume changes following an increase or decrease in selling price

	Price + 5% Sales volume unchanged	Price + 5% Sales volume – 10%	Price – 5% Sales volume + 10%
	£	£	£
Sales	105 000	94 500	104 500
Costs	90 000	81 000	99 000
Profit	£15 000	£13 500	£5 500
Change in profit	+ 50%	+ 35%	– 45%

Clearly, the tactics employed are absolutely crucial for the profitability of this product. The most advantageous tactic (or the least damaging) depends on two factors:

1. The magnitude of the customer reaction to a change in the status quo of the product price – because clearly 5 per cent adjustments up or down do not uniformly cause 10 per cent increases or decreases in demand.
2. The relative size of the variable costs to the fixed costs of the products involved in the analysis.

Table 15.3 demonstrates the effect on profit of various levels of reduction in sales volume after a price increase. In the example shown in the table a price rise of 5 per cent will produce substantial extra profits even with a considerable reduction in consumer demand. This is because costs represent 90 per cent of the selling price and these costs have so far been assumed to be 100 per cent variable costs. If there were a fixed cost element, the reduction in sales revenue would more quickly have the effect of eroding the additional profit arising from the price increase. This effect is demonstrated in Table 15.4.

The existence of fixed costs at the level of £20 000 is sufficient to show a reduction in profit when sales volume falls by 15 per cent after the 5 per cent price increase. This is contrasted with the situation where all the costs were assumed to be variable (Table 15.3) where there was still a 20 per cent increase in profits following the price increase although sales volume was also reduced by 20 per cent.

If we return to the situation briefly considered in Table 15.2 where a price reduction is favoured as the tactic for increasing profitability, the increase in sales volume must be substantial if the reduction in price is not to have the opposite to the desired effect, i.e. to reduce profits. Consider the outcomes to a price reduction displayed in Table 15.5.

Table 15.3   Effect on profit of various sales volume changes following an increase in price

	Price + 5% Sales volume unchanged	Price + 5% Sales volume − 5%	Price + 5% Sales volume − 10%	Price + 5% Sales volume − 15%	Price + 5% Sales volume − 20%
	£	£	£	£	£
Sales	105 000	99 750	94 500	89 250	84 000
Costs	90 000	85 500	81 000	76 500	72 000
	£15 000	£14 250	£13 500	£12 750	£12 000
Increase in profit	+ 50%	$+ 42\frac{1}{2}\%$	+ 35%	$+ 27\frac{1}{2}\%$	+ 20%

Table 15.4   The effect on profit of various reductions in sales volume following a price increase but where there exist certain fixed costs

	Price + 5% Sales volume unchanged	Price + 5% Sales volume − 5%	Price + 5% Sales volume − 10%	Price + 5% Sales volume − 15%	Price + 5% Sales volume − 20%
	£	£	£	£	£
Sales	105 000	99 750	94 500	89 250	84 000
Variable costs	70 000	66 500	63 000	59 500	56 000
Contribution	35 000	33 250	31 500	29 750	28 000
Fixed costs	20 000	20 000	20 000	20 000	20 000
Profit	£15 000	£13 250	£11 500	£9 750	£8 000
increase[1] or decrease	50%	$32\frac{1}{2}\%$	15%	$(2\frac{1}{2}\%)$	(20%)

1. Refers to original situation in Table 15.1.

Table 15.5

	Original position	Price − 5% Volume + 10%	Price − 5% Volume + 20%	Price − 5% Volume + 30%	Price − 5% Volume + 40%
	£	£	£	£	£
Sales	100 000	104 500	114 000	123 250	133 000
Variable costs	70 000	77 000	84 000	91 000	98 000
Contribution	30 000	27 500	30 000	32 500	35 000
Fixed costs	20 000	20 000	20 000	20 000	20 000
Profit	£10 000	£7 500	£10 000	£12 500	£15 000
Increase or decrease in profit	–	(25%)	–	+ 25%	+ 50%

The Optimum Selling Price

The optimum selling price for a product is that which yields the maximum contribution. Different combinations of selling price and the volume of sales achieved at that price may produce a range of contributions. However, in practice, there is normally a limited range of prices at which a product is likely to be acceptable to a particular segment of the market-place. The problem is to determine the optimum price within this range, and where the combination of price and sales volume will produce the greatest contribution. Consider the information presented in Table 15.6.

Table 15.6   The optimum selling price

(a) Selling Price per unit	(b) Estimated Probable units	(c) Total Revenue (a) × (b)	(d) Variable Cost at £4.4 per unit	(e) Contribution (c) − (d)
£		£	£	£
5.00	1000	5000	4400	600
6.00	860	5160	3784	1376
7.00	650	4550	2860	1690
8.00	500	4000	2200	1800
9.00	380	3420	1672	1748
10.00	300	3000	1320	1680
11.00	250	2750	1100	1650
12.00	180	2160	792	1368

Clearly, the optimum selling price in strict financial terms is £8, which produces a contribution of £1800 to fixed costs with estimated probable sales of 500 units. However, if the objectives of the company lay in obtaining a sizeable market share, some contribution might well be forsaken in order to achieve additional sales. For example, consider what happens when the selling price is £6 or £7:

Selling price	Estimated probable sales	% increase in sales volume	Revenue forsaken
£7	650	+ 30%	£110
£6	860	+ 72%	£424

Clearly, the practical application of this concept requires two things:

1. Accurate market research regarding the price-sensitivity of demand for the product.
2. The calculation of average variable cost for a range of probable volumes of sales.

Pricing and the Profitability of the Product Line

In most cases, the gross margin or profit expressed as a percentage of the sales revenue for each product in the line will provide a good guide to the relative profitability of each product.

Consider the following example of the product line A, comprising products A_1, A_2 and A_3.

	A_1	A_2	A_3
	£	£	£
Selling price	100	125	150
Direct material	40	50	60
Direct labour	10	15	20
Other expenses	15	20	20
Total variable costs	65	85	100
Contribution	£35	£40	£50
Profitability ranking	3	2	1

Product A_3 is the most profitable product when it can be sold at a price of £150 per unit. However, if there is a limit to the availability of one of the factors of production, perhaps the most relevant measure of product profitability may be the contribution per unit of limiting factor. The amount of the various key factors of production used by each product is:

	A_1	A_2	A_3
Direct labour (hours)	20	30	40
Bottleneck machinery (hours)	1	1	1
Prime raw material (lbs)	10	22	20

This produces the following contribution per unit of limiting factor:

	A_1	A_2	A_3
Contribution per labour hour	£1.75	£1.33	£1.25
Profitability ranking	(1)	(2)	(3)
Contribution per machine hour	£35.00	£40.00	£33.00
Profitability ranking	(2)	(1)	(3)
Contribution per lb of material	£3.50	£1.78	£2.50
Profitability ranking	(1)	(3)	(2)

What are the implications of this information for product-line pricing policy? The first thing is that information will clearly be of more immediate relevance in some industries than others, for example any item comprising largely one commodity (tea, coffee, sugar, cocoa) that is processed and packaged into a consumer product. If this commodity becomes particularly expensive or in short supply, product A_2 might be pinpointed as being a candidate for an adjustment in price to reflect certain short-term marketing tactics. It might be dropped altogether under certain circumstances.

The Recovery of Heavy Research and Development Expenditure

Research and development (R&D) is a truly 'sunk' cost, representing money that has been spent some time in the past when there was no certainty that any revenue would result. R&D may represent a high proportion of total expenditure in many industries involving advanced technology, such as defence systems, computers and the oil and pharmaceutical industries.

In some situations, especially those involving government contracts, R&D is remunerated on the basis of cost, although a somewhat flexible financial limit to the expenditure is normally imposed. For accounting purposes, where the recovery of the expenditure is assured, the cost can be carried forward in the balance sheet as an asset until it is reimbursed. In other cases R&D should be written off in the profit and loss account each year as it is incurred. This is a prudent rule which may appear to conflict with the principle of matching expenditure against income, but is justified on the grounds that it is virtually impossible to predict the amount of revenue which an R&D project is likely to produce.

However, in management accounts, R&D is often written off over a short period, maybe three years, against the relevant sales. In theory the writing-off period – frequently called 'amortization' – should be based on the time which is expected to elapse before further substantial research will be required, or on the estimated life of the product, whichever occurs sooner. The inclusion of apportioned R&D in product profit statements is a reasonable attempt to show the profit or loss derived from a line of sales after charging all relevant costs. But such a statement is history, and the price of the product must be decided before it is put on the market. That price, as in all pricing decisions, should be the figure which, combined with the appropriate turn-over, will produce the greatest contribution after charging variable costs. R&D expenditure, which has been spent before the product is marketed represents past not future outgoings, and should not therefore be brought into account in the pricing decision; future R&D costs to develop or modify the product are, however, relevant. The calculation should be made over the expected life of the product. The levels of turnover used in the calculation will be limited by the market potential, the share of the market which can be obtained and the capacity of the plant. Such a calculation is, of course, dependent on forecasting skills, and in many cases the ultimate price in the long term will emerge from trading experience.

Example

An airways corporation has indicated to an aircraft manufacturer that it is interested in obtaining 20 aircraft a year of an advanced type and specification. With this encouragement the manufacturer engages in a programme of research and development which has cost £120m by the time the first prototype is produced. It is intended that the production shall be carried out in a separate factory which can be obtained and equipped for £320m. The manufacturer's cost of capital is 12½ per cent but an extra 5 per cent is assumed necessary for risk, making a profit target of 17½ per cent of £320m = £56m. For the purpose of determining a price for the production of 20 aircraft a year, the average annual costs are estimated as follows:

	£m
Variable costs	60
Fixed costs	100
	160
R&D to be written off over 3 years: $\dfrac{£120m}{3}$	40
Total costs	£200m

Adding the profit target of £56m the management arrive at a price per aircraft of:

$$\frac{£200m + £56m}{20} = 12.8m$$

However, on the basis of expected revenues and operating costs of the aircraft, the airways corporation assesses the maximum price they can pay at £10.4m per aircraft. At this price the annual income of the manufacturer will be $20 \times £10.4m = £208.0m$, and with variable and fixed costs at £160m, the surplus of £48m will be insufficient to write off R&D costs over the three years stipulated and to provide more than marginal interest on capital. Being unable to obtain a higher price than £10.4m per aircraft, the manufacturer proposes to cancel production of the aircraft and sell the factory for an estimated £200m. They hope for some 'spin-off' from the R&D to develop other products. Is this decision correct?

The decision needs to be taken after considering the marginal costs of producing the aircraft, and the basic question in so doing is the extent to which future income will exceed future outgoings. The R&D costs which have been spent are irrelevant but allowance must be made for future R&D, such as for necessary modifications. The past R&D costs represent a loss of capital which has occurred in prior years.

In this situation most of the fixed costs will be marginal to the extent that they represent future outgoings for making the aircraft: for instance, adequate staff must be retained and paid, plant maintained and the usual business services provided. Depreciation should be replaced by provisions for replacing the assets. Assume that, on a marginal basis, the future annual cash inflow and outflow is estimated as follows:

	£	£
Sales: $20 \times £10.4m$		208
Total variable and fixed costs adjusted to future cash outflow	165	
Annual further R&D	3	
		168
Surplus		£40

The surplus is now sufficient to remunerate capital at a basic rate of 12½ per cent, but further income may be obtained from modifications commissioned by the purchaser, other purchasers may be found, and 'spin-off' from the research is likely to be valuable. The alternative of selling the factory and its contents would incur a one-off loss of £320m – £200m = £120m, and interest on the proceeds at the basic rate would yield only 12½ per cent of £200m + £25m p.a. The conclusion is that the manufacturer should ignore the accumulated R&D expenditure and proceed to manufacture and sell the aircraft.

Pricing to Absorb Production Capacity

In most businesses the marketing function is under continuous pressure to increase turnover. One reason is that, except possibly in the smallest business, the increase in the size of a business enhances the prestige of the managers and, probably, the remuneration they can command. The more specific reason is that, up to certain limits, the additional turnover adds little or nothing to fixed costs and thus improves the rate of profit. The effect of increasing turnover is indicated by the following specimen figures:

	Existing sales	*Additional sales*	*Total*
	£	£	£
Sales	500 000	100 000	600 000
Variable costs (60% of sales)	300 000	60 000	360 000
Contribution	200 000	40 000	240 000
Fixed costs	100 000	–	100 000
Profit	£100 000	£40 000	£140 000
Percentage of sales	20%	40%	$23\frac{1}{3}\%$

There are, of course, many qualifications to this simple illustration. On the one hand the additional output may produce economies of scale in the form, for example, of fewer working hours per unit of output and larger discounts on purchases, such factors tending to reduce the rate of variable costs. The additional turnover may, however, necessitate some additions to fixed costs, such as in space, administration and equipment. The effect of these changes in rates of cost and overheads will be minimal where resources are not fully utilized.

However, there are many cases where a commercial enterprise is not fully utilizing its capacity because the market where it operates has declined. Nevertheless, a number of possibilities exist for enlarging turnover and so absorbing the under-utilized resources. If the existing market has permanently shrunk, and the business is incapable of producing another product in another market, then the organization must be cut down to an economical size. This is a drastic procedure which has had to be carried out by some very large undertakings (such as the coal industry and the rail-ways) and inevitably involves loss of capital.

There are some more positive methods available to remedy the situation. The first might be to exploit a separate market (perhaps overseas) with, if necessary, a reduced price and, maybe, higher unit costs. The second might be to take on subcontract work, not necessarily in the existing product line and possibly for a low return. Either course of action will be justified if it helps to absorb unused capacity and produces an additional net cash flow, i.e. a marginal profit.

The issues regarding selling and marketing in overseas markets have been covered in Chapter 14. The following example illustrates the benefits of undertaking subcontract work. A company undertakes maintenance services for a certain type of electrical equipment. It has a capacity to generate 200 000 direct man hours for which the ruling market price is £10.00 an hour. Its capital employed is £500 000, on which the management expect a return of 20 per cent, i.e. £100 000. Because of a downturn in sales the company is unable to sell more than 150 000 man hours in a year. The projected profit and loss budget (based on capacity working), and the expected results for the next year, are as follows:

	Budget at capacity £	Expected results £
Direct hours	200 000	150 000
Price per hour	10.00	10.00
Sales	2 000 000	1 500 000
Variable costs at £5.5 an hour	1 100 000	825 000
Contribution	900 000	675 000
Fixed costs at £4.00 per hour	800 000	600 000
Surplus before under-recovered fixed costs	100 000	75 000
Under-recovered fixed costs	–	200 000
Final profit/(loss)	£100 000	£(125 000)

If the management decide that no formula of changing price to affect volume will produce additional profit, then another proposition would be to apply the spare capacity to the servicing of another type of equipment. Of course there would be additional costs, perhaps an additional £150 000 a year would be required for equipment and training. In addition, there would be certain administrative expenses, and variable costs are calculated to rise to £5.75 an hour. The price charged will be held at £10.00 an hour in order to obtain a foothold in a new market. Assuming the spare capacity could be absorbed in this way, the expected results might be as follows for the subcontracted work in the new market:

	£
Revenue (50 000 hours at £10 per hour)	500 000
Less: Variable costs at £5.75 per hour	287 500
Contribution	212 500
Less: Additional costs of setting up*	50 000

* Prudently amortized over three years at £50 000 per year.

Contribution from new market	162 500
Contribution from existing market	675 000
Total contribution	837 500
Less: Fixed costs	800 000
Profit	£37 500

This was clearly the best course of action, although it would produce a return on capital of only 5.77 per cent.* It had the special advantage that, when the market for the existing activity revived, the contract work could be progressively diminished so far as necessary, but the availability of such work would give flexibility to the business in relation to future market fluctuations.

---

* 37 500/650 000 × 100 = 5.77%. The £650 000 is the original £500 000 plus the additional £150 000 for the equipment and training.

16 INDICATORS FOR ACTION AND BUDGET REVISION

The Basic Indicators

Control of the various activities of a business, as well as the preparation of the forward plans, is the responsibility of the managers, sometimes acting individually but more often jointly. The management team embraces all ranks of executives and supervisors, those in charge of divisions, departments and sections, as well as general management, e.g. the board of directors.

For effective forward planning and control managers need up-to-date information relevant to their needs, and much of this will consist of monetary and quantitative figures produced by the accounting service. Developments in computerization have immensely widened the scope and facilitated the presentation of the information required. The basic information is contained in the monthly accounts, but these accounts need supplementing by many detailed statements of sales, costs, assets and liabilities. It is important that the monthly accounts should be available to managers soon after the end of the month concerned, so that remedial action can be based on topical information. The accounts should show not only the results for the last month but also the cumulative results for the last twelve months, with the actual results compared with budgets or forecasts. Statements of costs which are out of line with standards may require reporting at weekly intervals.

Although the decisive figures are those expressed in terms of money, some levels of management may react more positively to quantitative statistics. Thus those responsible for selling in the field need to be informed of the volume of sales of a particular product as well as the monetary value. Likewise supervisors in the works are more concerned with operating hours and quantities of output than costs, since they have little, if any, control over rates of pay or material prices.

Figures in isolation are meaningless; they only become meaningful when they are related to pre-assessed standards or to the activity which influences their movements. For instance, a figure of profit becomes significant when it is related to capital employed or to sales; turnover needs to be compared with a budget which in turn may be based on a share of the market potential; production times are expressed in terms of units of output and the cost of the output is compared with a standard. Intuitive standards are imperfect and, if based on past results, take no account of changing conditions.

For these reasons the simplest and usually the most effective basis for appraising the operating results is to compare them with budgets reflecting the intentions of the management team. The budgets should be formulated by considering the output and services required to implement the sales target, and after having regard to the appropriate ratios or relationships between expenditure and activity. Standards, normally related to working times, should be assessed for production costs.

The rest of this chapter therefore places considerable emphasis on indicators consisting of variances between actual performance and budgets or standards. However, the great drawback of the budgetary system is that the budgets and standards frequently become unrealistic. This occurs mainly as a result of unpredictable changes in external circumstances, but may be due to budgeting errors. When uncontrollable variances occur the budgets and standards need to be replaced by forecasts until they can be thoroughly revised. In making these forecasts and budget revisions, ratios of expenditure to activity should be borne in mind, and these ratios represent supplementary indicators for appraising the results.

A suggested sequence for the appraisal of results is set out in the following sections, and the analysis is based on the specimen profit and loss account shown in Fig. 16.1. For simplicity the figures are confined to the results for the last month, although the budget and actual comparison for the last twelve months should also be considered. Whilst much of the analysis does not directly concern the marketing and selling function, it is desirable that all managers should be aware of the situation as a whole, because their activities are inevitably interrelated.

To give reality to the illustration it may be assumed that the product was a standard type of industrial belting for which a price per metre was quoted. The figures are hypothetical and have no reference to any existing business.

Indicators of Profitability

The Budget and Actual Variance

Attention will naturally first be directed to the net profit, for this is the final outcome of the operations for the period. Figure 16.1 shows that net profit has fallen below budget by £42 000. Net profit is significant to the shareholders for it represents the earnings on their capital after allowing for taxation. For the managers, however, pre-tax profit is normally of greater interest because the tax provision is outside their control. Pre-tax profit shows an adverse variance of £59 000 on the budget. The causes of these large variances need investigation and are analysed in subsequent sections of this chapter.

Profit Related to Capital Employed

The ultimate measure of the profitability of a business is the return on capital or, more specifically, the percentage of pre-tax profit to capital employed. (The nature of capital employed was examined in Chapter 2.) For the reason given above the deduction for taxation is best ignored for management control purposes. Figure 16.1 shows that the actual percentage is only 5.54 per cent compared with a target of 20 per cent, the calculations being made on the average capital employed in the period (see below). The actual percentage is, moreover, lower than any normal cost of borrowing, so that if interest on capital is regarded as a cost of doing business, the results indicate an effective loss.

	Budget	Actual	Variance
SALES	£1 000 000	£900 000	£(100 000)
Cost of sales at standard	£600 000	£480 000	£120 000
Percentage of sales	60%	53.3%	
GROSS PROFIT AT STANDARD	£400 000	£420 000	£20 000
Percentage of sales	40%	46.7%	
Standard cost variances	–	£86 000	£(86 000)
GROSS PROFIT, ACTUAL	£400 000	£334 000	£(66 000)
	£	£	£
Operating expenses:			
Selling and distribution	100 000	95 000	5 000
Administration	50 000	48 000	2 000
Research and development	150 000	152 000	(2 000)
Total operating expenses	300 000	295 000	5 000
OPERATING PROFIT	100 000	39 000	(61 000)
Non-trading expenses:			
Financial	15 000	16 000	(1 000)
Exceptional and extraordinary	5 000	2 000	3 000
Total non-trading expenses	20 000	18 000	2 000
PRE-TAX PROFIT	80 000	21 000	(59 000)
Tax provision	24 000	7 000	17 000
NET PROFIT	56 000	14 000	(42 000)
Average capital employed	400 000	379 000	
Percentage profit on capital employed	20%	5.54%	

Figure 16.1   Specimen profit and loss statement.

Notes on the Calculations

1. For the purpose of this example the capital employed at the beginning of
   the period was assumed to be: £372 000

2. The above opening figure of capital employed would have been increased over the year by
   the net profit. For simplicity it is assumed that there were no payments of dividend (which
   would have reduced the capital employed).
      The budgeted capital employed at the end of the year therefore
   became: £372 000 + £56 000 =   £428 000

      The actual capital employed at the end of the year became:
   £372 000 + £14 000 =   £386 000

3. Profit is sometimes related to opening capital employed and in this case the calculations
   would have been as follows:

	Budget	Actual
Opening capital employed	£372 000	£372 000
Pre-tax profit	80 000	21 000
Percentages	21.50%	5.65%

4. Another basis often used is to relate profit to closing capital employed, with the following calculations:

Closing capital employed	£428 000	£386 000
Pre-tax profit	80 000	21 000
Percentages	18.69%	5.44%

5. The capital employed is, however, being continually increased by the profit which arises during the period. The assumption, for simplicity, is that the profit was evenly spread over the period, in the absence of other evidence. For this reason it is considered that the use of average capital employed gives a more realistic and more consistent base for the measurement of profitability. The average capital employed is calculated as the sum of the opening and closing amounts divided by 2.

Thus, for the budget the average capital employed is:

$$\frac{£372\ 000 + £428\ 000}{2} \qquad\qquad £400\ 000$$

and the profit percentage is:

$$\frac{£80\ 000 \times 100}{£400\ 000} \qquad\qquad 20.00\%$$

The actual average capital employed is:

$$\frac{£372\ 000 + £386\ 000}{2} \qquad\qquad £379\ 000$$

and the actual profit percentage is:

$$\frac{£21\ 000 \times 100}{£379\ 000} \qquad\qquad 5.54\%$$

Although in this example the three methods of calculation produce no great variations in the percentages, they might do so in a different situation.

The question to be answered is: What has caused the fall in profit? If the account is read from the sales downwards, the gross profit is seen to be below budget by £66 000 owing to the reduction in sales and the standard cost variances. The fall in gross profit has been lessened by the operating expenses and the non-trading expenses being below budget. The variances need detailed investigation.

Sales and Gross Profit Variances

Sales Variances

It will be noted in Fig. 16.1 that the actual sales are £100 000 below budget. This variance is, however, made up of two elements: the amount due to the change in price and the amount due to the change in the volume compared with the budgeted figures.

Where possible these two elements of the total variance need to be calculated because price and volume are often interdependent factors.

The two variances are difficult to segregate where, as is frequently the case, the turnover comprises a variety of products and different rates of price changes, compared with the budgeted prices, are applied to each product or product group. In such a situation the variances need to be calculated for each product line. Where different sizes or quantities of a particular product line are marketed, the volume variance can be calculated on the basis of a key factor common to all items sold, such as weight, length or the operating hours involved in their production.

A further difficulty arises where a price change, compared with the budgeted price, was made during the period under review, i.e. after the beginning of that period. That difficulty can be solved by calculating the price variance on the actual turnover after the price change was put into effect.

In the present example it is assumed for simplicity that the sales were of a homogeneous product, measured in metres, a price per metre was charged, and that the actual price was raised above the budgeted price at the beginning of the period.

It is not usual for sales or standard gross profit variances to be shown in the body of the profit and loss account. The following details would appear as notes to the accounts presented to management:

Sales variances

	Budget	*Actual*	*Variance*
Quantity in metres	100 000	80 000	(20 000)
Price per metre	£10.00	£11.25	£1.25
Total value	£1 000 000	900 000	(100 000)

Given the above information the price and volume variances may now be analysed as follows:

	Favourable	*Adverse*
Price: 80 000 × £1.25	£100 000	
Volume: 20 000 × £10.00		£200 000
Net adverse variance as above		£100 000

Notes on the Variance Calculations

1. *Price variance.*   The price variance is the actual quantity sold multiplied by the difference between the budgeted and actual price. If, in the above example, the price had remained as budgeted at £10 a metre the turnover would have been £10 × 80 000 metres, but was in fact £11.25 × 80 000 metres, giving a favourable variance (or increase in turnover) of £100 000.

2. *Volume variance.*   The volume (or quantity) variance is the budgeted price multiplied by the difference between the budgeted and actual quantity sold. This calculation shows the change in the value of the turnover due exclusively to the difference between the budgeted and actual quantity sold, on the assumption that no price change occurred. In this example actual sales were 20 000 metres below the budget and this figure multiplied by the budgeted price of £10 a metre produces the adverse volume variance of £200 000.

Standard Cost of Sales Variance

The favourable variance of £120 000 for the cost of sales at standard is entirely a volume or quantity variance because for both budget and actual the same standard costs per unit are used. In the example the standard costs per unit were £6 giving the following figures:

	Budget	*Actual*	*Variance*
Units sold in metres	100 000	80 000	20 000
Standard costs per unit	£6	£6	–
Standard cost of sales	£600 000	£480 000	£120 000

Gross Profit at Standard Variance

The variance of £20 000 (favourable) shown against the gross profit at standard is obviously the difference between the sales variance and the cost variance. The make-up of the figure may now be summarized as follows:

	Variances	
	Favourable	*Adverse*
Volume:		
sales: 20 000 × £10		£200 000
costs: 20 000 × £6	£120 000	
Net volume variances		£80 000
Price:		
sales: 80 000 × £1.25	£100 000	
Net favourable gross profit variance at standard	£20 000	

Percentage Profit on Sales

In the example the actual gross profit at standard as a percentage of the sales is 6.7 per cent above the budgeted percentage. This rise is obviously due to the price increase.

The profit percentage on sales could be a useful indicator in the following circumstances: (1) where the budgets had become impossible to achieve and needed revision; (2) where no budgetary control system operated; and (3) where there was no standard costing system. In these circumstances it would be helpful to show the trend of this percentage over a number of months, possibly years.

Conclusions So Far

1. The results examined so far suggest that the increase in price was a cause of the reduction in the volume of sales when compared with the budgets. This caused a loss of income because the adverse volume variance was £200 000 against the favourable price variance of £100 000.
2. The foregoing conclusion does not, however, take into account the effect of the lower volume on the cost of sales and hence gross profit at standard. The reduction in volume

caused an adverse gross profit variance of only £80 000, i.e. less than the favourable price variance. On this basis the price increase appears to have been justified.

3. However, if the reduced volume of sales caused restrictions on production, the consequence could well be adverse standard cost variances due to slower working times and under-utilized facilities. This aspect of the situation is examined in the next section.

4. Studies of the relationship between price and volume of sales (if they have not already been carried out) might indicate that a different price level would optimize gross profit.

Production Budget Variances

Before analysing the production standard cost variances it is necessary to consider how the actual output compared with the budgeted output. The figures are derived from the manufacturing account (or a similar form of account for a non-manufacturing operation). This account for the business under examination is set out in Fig. 16.2. For simplicity opening and closing production stocks and work in progress have been excluded from the statement.

The output, both budgeted and actual, is shown at standard cost, the cost variances having been extracted at the source of the transactions. The standards are expressed in operating hours as well as in quantities (in this case, metres) for each of these measures will have relevance to the analysis. The variances, or differences between budget and actual costs, therefore refer entirely to the volume of output at standard cost rates.

	Standard costs		Output at standard cost			
			Budget	Actual	Sales	Stock addition
	Per metre	Per hour				
Volume:						
Metres		2.5	100 000	90 000	80 000	10 000
Hours	0.4		40 000	36 000	32 000	4 000
Costs:	£	£	£	£	£	£
Labour	2.0	5.0	200 000	180 000	160 000	20 000
Material	1.0	2.5	100 000	90 000	80 000	10 000
Total labour and material costs	3.0	7.5	300 000	270 000	240 000	30 000
Overheads:						
Variable	1.2	3.0	120 000	108 000	96 000	12 000
Fixed	1.8	4.5	180 000	162 000	144 000	18 000
Total overheads	3.0	7.5	300 000	270 000	240 000	30 000
Total costs	£6.0	£15.0	£600 000	£540 000	£480 000	£60 000

Figure 16.2   Specimen manufacturing account.

The conclusions to be drawn from this statement are as follows:

1. The planned or budgeted output at 100 000 metres or 40 000 operating hours not only agreed with the sales budget but, in this example, was assumed to have absorbed the capacity of the plant. In practice, this ideal situation is unlikely to be achieved. If the sales requirements exceeded capacity then it must be assumed that the difference would come from stocks. If the sales requirements were less than capacity, either an increase in stocks or under-utilization of capacity would be contemplated.
2. In fact the actual output is shown to be 10 000 metres or 4000 hours short of the budgeted output. In the case under consideration this shortage of output did not reflect adversely on the production manager because he had deliberately reduced the rate of output when he became aware that sales were falling below target.
3. Even so, the actual output was 10 000 metres more than the actual volume of sales so that stocks rose by a cost of £60 000. Unless, therefore, sales can be expanded the business will continue to be increasing stocks and/or working at below capacity, with consequent idle resources and excess costs.

It should be appreciated that budget variances are distinct from standard cost variances, the latter referring to the actual production. The standard cost variances may now be analysed.

Standard Cost Variances

The standard cost variances arise from the output produced in the factory, not the output which is sold. These variances are deducted in the profit and loss account from the gross profit at standard to ensure that all costs or losses which arise are written off in the period in which they are incurred. If the variances were favourable they would be shown as added to gross profit at standard because they represent cost savings.

Labour

Assume that the actual rate of pay for the period was £5.50 an hour compared with the standard of £5.00 an hour, and the actual time taken was 0.38 a metre compared with a standard of 0.4 a metre. The total labour cost variance is calculated as follows:

	Standard	*Actual*	*Variance*
Actual output in metres	90 000	90 000	
Hours per metre	0.40	0.38	0.02
Total hours	36 000	34 200	1800
Costs per hour	£5.00	£5.50	£(0.50)
Total costs	£180 000	£188 100	£(8100)

The total variance of £8100 (adverse) has two components. One is a favourable efficiency variance due to the hours taken being below standard, and the other is an adverse variance due to the higher rate per hour.

The Efficiency Variance

This is the difference between the actual hours taken and the standard hours multiplied by the standard rate, i.e. ignoring any change in the rate of pay. The calculation in this example is:

$$1800 \text{ hours} \times £5.0 = £9000$$

The Rate Variance

This is the difference between the actual rate of pay and the standard rate multiplied by the actual hours taken, thus representing the extent to which the actual costs have increased due to the rise in pay:

$$£0.50 \times 34\ 200 \text{ hours} = £(17\ 100)$$

The net adverse variance thus becomes £17 100 – £9000 = £8100 as shown above.

In this case the causes of the variances are explained as follows: Improved working methods were introduced to reduce operating hours per metre, but in consequence rates of pay had to be increased. Whilst it was appreciated that the benefit from the greater efficiency was more than offset by the increase in pay, it was thought that working times were not yet at their optimum due to a consciousness in the works that output was being restricted.

Material

The standard quantity was 1 kg per metre but the actual usage was only 0.9 kg per metre. The standard price was £1.00 per kg but the actual price was £1.10 per kg. Assume, for simplicity, that purchases were exactly sufficient for the output actually produced. The standard and actual cost comparison is as follows:

	Standard	Actual	Variance
Actual output in metres	90 000	90 000	
Kg per metre	1.00	0.9	
Total kg	90 000	81 000	9000
Price per kg	£1.00	£1.10	£0.10
Total costs	£90 000	£89 100	£900

The total variance of £900 includes a favourable usage variance and an adverse price variance, calculated as shown below.

Usage Variance

This is the difference between the actual quantity used and the standard usage, multiplied by the standard price:

$$9000 \text{ kg} \times £1.00 = £9000 \text{ (Fav.)}$$

Price Variance

This is the difference between the actual and standard price per kg, multiplied by the actual usage:

$$£0.10 \times 81\ 000\ \text{kg} = £(8100)\ (\text{Adv.})$$

The net favourable variance is therefore £9000 − £8100 = 900.

The favourable usage variance is attributable to the improvements in production methods, but the unfavourable price variance was due to a combination of unpredicted inflation and a reduction in trade discount due to the lower volume of purchases.

Overheads

The 'actual' overheads shown in Fig. 16.2 were the result of applying the standard overhead rates to the actual production. Thus the variable overheads so applied were £3.00 an hour × 36 000 hours = £108 000. The charge for fixed overheads was £4.50 an hour × 36 000 hours = £162 000. In fact the actual expenditure was variable overheads: £150 000, and fixed overheads: £198 800. In many situations a single overhead rate of £7.50 an hour would have been charged, but the division between fixed and variable overheads is important for analysis purposes, as shown below.

The expenditure variances are the differences between the actual expenditure and the totals charged to costs through the overhead rates. For the fixed overheads there is, in addition, a volume variance which is the difference between the budgeted expenditure and the amount charged to costs by the overhead rate.

The overhead variances are set out in the following statement:

	£	£	£
Variable overheads:			
Actual expenditure		150 000	
Charged to costs at the standard rate: £3.00 per hour × 36 000 standard hours		108 000	
Expenditure variance (adverse)			(42 000)
Fixed overheads:			
Actual expenditure	198 800		
Budget	180 000		
Expenditure variance (adverse)		(18 800)	
Budget	180 000		
Charged to costs at the standard rate of £4.50 per hour × 36 000 standard hours	162 000		
Volume variance (adverse)		(18 000)	
Total fixed overhead variances (adverse)			(36 800)
Total overhead variances			£(78 800)

The variable overheads should, by definition, have remained at £3.00 an hour. The expenditure even exceeds the budget, which was based on a greater activity in working hours than was in fact generated. The overspending should be traced to its sources and the necessary enonomies put into effect. The approach to such an investigation is to calculate the percentage which each item of expense budgeted bears to the budgeted hours, and to compare the result with the percentages which the actual items of expenditure bear to the standard hours for the actual output. It is possible that some differences may arise from uncontrollable factors, such as inflation, and in this case the standard rate may need amendment.

The fixed overhead expenditure is theoretically independent of activity (at least in the short term) and should have been as budgeted. On investigation it was found that the expenditure variance was due to increases in pay for supervisory staff and, as this was considered uncontrollable (although it should have been anticipated), an increase in the budget was authorized. The volume variance was due to the actual activity in standard hours being 4000 hours below the budgeted activity. This represents a 'management loss' due to the reduction in output, and should *not* be corrected by raising the overhead rate. It is up to the management to find some means of utilizing the full capacity of the plant.

In general, the high level of adverse overhead variances emphasizes the need for stringent control of indirect costs, which tend to increase with the development of systems and automation.

Summary of Standard Cost Variances

All the standard cost variances can now be summarized in the following statement:

	Favourable £	Adverse £
Labour:		
Rate		17 100
Efficiency	9000	
Net labour variances		8 100
Material:		
Price		8 100
Usage	9000	
Net material variances	900	
Overheads:		
Variable – expenditure		42 000
Fixed – expenditure		18 800
volume		18 000
Net overhead variances		78 800
Total net adverse variances (as in the profit and loss account)		£86 000

Operating and Non-trading Expenses

Selling and Distribution

These expenses are below budget in total, as might be expected from the lower turn-over. However, a more searching analysis is necessary, achieved by segregating the fixed from the variable elements of the total, and then setting out the significant variances from budget in individual items of expense. The more detailed comparison is as follows:

| | Budget | | Actual | | Variance |
	£	% of sales	£	% of sales	£
Fixed expenses	£55 000	5.5	£50 000	5.6	£5000
Variable expenses:					
Commission	20 000	2.0	18 000	2.0	2000
Travel and subsistence	9 000	0.9	10 000	1.1	(1000)
Special advertising	10 000	1.0	11 500	1.3	(1500)
Miscellaneous	6 000	0.6	5 500	0.6	500
Total variable	£45 000	4.5	£45 000	5.0	–
Total expenses	£100 000	10.0	£95 000	10.6	£5000

The underspending on the fixed expenses was due to the deferment of a proposal to obtain an additional sales depot, thus demonstrating that savings can be made on expenses classified as 'fixed'.

The fact that the total variable expenses are on budget is not a cause for congratulation for they should have been below the budget as a result of the lower turnover. In fact their percentage to sales has increased by 0.5 per cent. Thus in this instance a simple comparison between the budgeted and actual expenditure gives an incomplete picture and needs to be supplemented by ratios of activity. By using the percentages to sales it appears that the expenditure on travelling should have been 0.9 per cent of the actual turnover of £900 000, i.e. £8100, giving an adverse variance of £1900, and the special advertising should have been 1.0 per cent of £900 000 = £9000.

Administration

The favourable variance for administrative expenses was analysed in a similar manner to that carried out for sales. The variance was found to be largely due to savings in variable expenses, such as postage, stationery and telephone calls, due to the reduced activity.

Research and Development

This expense is invariably difficult to forecast and the overspending of £2000 is small, but nevertheless requires explanation by the R&D manager.

Non-trading Expenses

The saving in exceptional and extraordinary expenses is due to errors in budgeting for these items, which are very difficult to estimate in advance. The rise in financial charges is due to higher rates of interest and a small increase in borrowings to finance the addition to stocks.

Other Indicators

Up to this point attention has been directed largely to indicators consisting of variances between actual performance and budgets or standards. It is apparent, however, that these indicators no longer represent effective bases for action when a change in circumstances makes the original budgets and standards invalid. This situation occurs in particular when, as in the foregoing illustration, a fall in turnover causes reduced activity in the cost centres, the converse being equally true. In such situations the appraisal of the results will be assisted by the use of ratios and percentages. Costs and expenses should be related to the actual activity of the operation concerned, and the ratio so calculated can then be compared with a standard ratio derived from the budget. There follows a list of the important relationships, ratios and percentages.

Financial Ratios

1. *Gearing of capital.* This is the relationship between equity interests and loan capital. The implications of a low or high gearing are discussed in Chapter 2.
2. *The ratio of fixed assets to total assets.* Is a movement in this ratio the result of exceptional additions or sales of fixed assets, or of a change in net current assets? All of these need explanation for they will affect cash flow.
3. *The ratio of current assets to current liabilities.* A primary indication of liquidity, also discussed in Chapter 2. Should be supplemented by considering the ratio of liquid assets to current liabilities.
4. *The ratio of stocks to budgeted cost of sales.* To determine whether idle funds are locked up in stocks, or whether they are adequate for future sales. Needs supplementing by an ageing statement.
5. *The ratio of debtors to past sales.* Reflects the effectiveness of credit policy and collection procedures and may also indicate idle capital. An ageing statement of debtors will be informative.

Profit Indicators

1. *The turnover rate.* This is the cost of sales divided by average capital employed. It will indicate the number of times the capital employed is 'turned over' in sales.

2. *The percentage gross profit to sales.* A basic indicator of the profitability of sales but needs to be considered in association with the turnover rate.
3. *The percentage operating profit to capital employed.* The return on capital produced by the operations.
4. *The percentage pre-tax profit to capital employed.* The return on capital after accounting for financial, exceptional and extraordinary charges and income.
5. *The earnings per share.* The profit attributable to the ordinary shareholders (i.e. after preference dividends and loan interest) divided by the number of shares.
6. *The earnings yield.* Primarily an investor's ratio, and means the earnings per share as a percentage of the quoted price per share.
7. *The dividend yield.* A ratio for the shareholders, meaning the dividend per share as a percentage of the price per share.
8. *The price/earnings ratio.* Another ratio for the shareholders and investors, calculated by dividing the price per share by the earnings per share.

Cost Indicators

1. *Percentages of costs and expenses to activity.* Production costs are usefully related by percentages to output, which may be expressed in such measures as man hours, production hours, weight, etc., as appropriate. The trend of selling expenses, especially the variable element, can be monitored by watching their percentages to sales. Variable administrative expenses may also be related to sales, but for several of these expenses more specific factors of activity are appropriate. Thus the cost of the personnel function, the wages department, security and the canteen can be usefully appraised as a cost per employee.
2. *The ratio between direct and indirect production costs.* Indirect costs are often unduly inflated by the growth of systems, mechanization and automation.

Revision of Budgets and Standards

When Budgets and Standards Become Ineffective

As mentioned in the introduction to the preceding section, budgets and standards frequently become invalid as targets of performance. This may be due to changes in markets and consumer choice, technological developments, intervention by domestic and overseas governments, or economic and social trends. In addition, it must be accepted that even the most carefully constructed system of budgets and standards is subject to human error. Furthermore, unless the system is rigorously controlled, there is a natural tendency for managers to introduce what is called 'slack' into the budgets they compile; thus budgeted costs may be overstated and budgeted sales may be understated. In addition a major cause of variances is the effect of inflation.

In situations where actual turnover exceeds the budget, greater output and more services are required to service the increased activity. Thus adverse cost and expense variances arise, but they do not necessarily indicate inefficiency. Conversely, as shown by the illustration in this chapter, lower turnover may result in a reduction in costs and expenses, but the consequent favourable variances are not always a cause for congratulation.

When budgets and standards become invalid the whole system tends to fall into disrepute amongst operating managers and it no longer acts as a motivating force, nor is it an effective basis for controlling the finances of the organization. These consequence are not, however, inevitable if prompt action is taken to revise the budgets and substitute more realistic standards.

The Remedies

The essential remedy is to revise the budgets and standards for the future, so that ideally amendments are made on a continuous basis. The problem is that operating managers cannot be expected to devote their time to, say, a monthly exercise of revising the company's forward plans; the need to prepare budgets once a year is sufficiently demanding.

For these reasons it is customary for the accounting function to extract 'revision variances' when uncontrollable differences occur between the actual results and the standards. These are useful reminders of the amendments which need to be made when next year's budgets and standards are prepared. However, revision variances leave the existing standards of performance invalid and ineffective.

Pending a major exercise of revising the budgetary and standard costing system, it is suggested that the financial function should replace ineffective standards by interim forecasts. These interim forecasts should obviously be made in consultation with the managers concerned. In formulating these forecasts many of the ratios and percentages described in the preceding section should be relevant, but not necessarily decisive. Apart from acting as temporary standards of performance or at least targets, the forecasts will be necessary for the purpose of the essential monthly revisions to the cash forecast. It will be desirable to project these forecasts for 12 months ahead.

Formal Budget Revisions

It is normally convenient for the annual budgets to cover the forthcoming accounting year. The exercise of budget preparation, involving all departments, should therefore take place in the month preceding the start of that year.

At the same time, revisions will be required to the longer-term plans, which should extend for five years ahead, or maybe longer. This means that targets need to be set for a further year ahead, on the so-called 'rolling budget' principle. The revised budgets will clearly take the place of the interim forecasts.

17 COST AND PROFIT CONTROL

Scope of the Chapter

Profit is arrived at by deducting expenditure from income. The justification for this statement of the obvious is that it leads to the conclusion that profit control has two aspects: one is to minimize cost, and the other to maximize income. This chapter deals successively with these two aspects of the subject.

Traditionally cost control has been largely concerned with production costs, particularly the direct costs of labour and material, or, as in a wholesale or retail organization, the cost of goods bought for resale. In the case of service industries such as catering, transport, maintenance, etc., the emphasis of cost control is normally on the direct operations, e.g. providing meals, running the fleet and carrying out the maintenance.

There is, however, a tendency for an increasing proportion of business expenditure to fall into the 'indirect' category, which embraces not only production overheads but also operating expenses, including those of marketing, selling and administration. The rising trend of indirect costs may be attributed to developments in automation, computerized systems, widening communications and the growth of the marketing function. It is therefore essential that cost control is applied to indirect as well as to direct costs and expenses.

In recent years the rapid advances in technology have imposed on many industrial organizations a need to expend large sums each year on capital projects. Once the money has been spent on a new or replacement asset, or on a project of research and development, it is effectively uncontrollable. For such expenditure the managerial effort must initially be applied to appraising the economics of the proposal (as discussed in Chapter 15) and then in controlling the operations to which the investment is directed. This essentially means ensuring that capital expenditure produces sales. Thus a substantial proportion of the business expenditure charged in the profit and loss account is uncontrollable; it does not represent ongoing costs, such as materials, wages, salaries and services, but consists of allocations of past expenditure (or 'sunk costs') to future accounting periods. Such costs are carried forward on the grounds that they refer to sales yet to be made.

The foregoing observations do not reduce the need for the control of current expenditure. They do, however, have two major implications for cost control in the modern environment. First, since it is only the individual managers who can take action on costs, it is essential that they are held responsible only for the costs over which they have a measure of control. Secondly, with the closely integrated framework of a modern business, many costs are the responsibility of the management as a team. For instance, a rise in manufacturing or buying costs may be directly due to a change in the specification of a product imposed by marketing requirements. Ultimately all costs are controllable at some level of management. The third implication is that operating systems, once established, cannot be easily adapted, at least without considerable effort and expense, thus imposing on the management team an increasing need for forecasting and pre-planning. The need now is not only for appraising what the market requires, but also for creating markets in what the business is set up to supply.

Information for Cost Control

General

There are four general requirements of an efficient information system.

1. *Topicality*. The figures must be up to date. If cost data is a month in arrear the situation may have changed in the meantime.
2. *Relevance*. The information must be designed to meet the needs of the manager to whom it is directed; it must be relevant to the situation for which he is responsible.
3. *Flexibility*. Although some statements will be of a routine nature, there will be a need for special reports to be prepared in relation to the changing circumstances of a business. As examples, attention might need to be drawn to the effects on unit costs of an unexpected fall in the demand for a product, of a rise in material prices, a changed specification, etc.
4. *Economy*. There are two aspects of the need for economy in the cost information service. One is to control the cost of costing itself. The other, and perhaps more important, is to avoid managers having to waste their time poring over figures which call for no action.

   There is no merit in managers being presented with lengthy tabulations of results which are proceeding according to plan; the job of the manager is to make decisions on the abnormalities, or 'management by exception'. This principle is fulfilled in particular by the presentation of only the significant standard cost variances.

The Principle of Relationships

General Considerations

A figure of cost in isolation is meaningless. Nothing of significance is conveyed by the bare statement that the cost of a product is, say, £5.00. The person receiving such a statement will instinctively relate the figure to, say, the selling price, to past costs or to the costs of similar products. Costs take on meanings of varying significance when compared with past results, related figures, or the activities which cause movements in the costs.

Comparisons with Past Figures

Some limited information is conveyed by comparing current costs with those of last month or last year. However, the change in the two figures may conceal a falling or rising trend, as indicated in the graph presented in Fig. 17.1. In this simple example

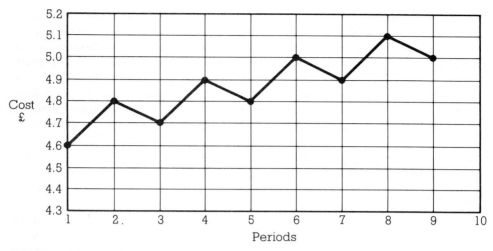

Figure 17.1 Rising trend of cost.

the importance of showing the trend is that unless remedial action is taken the cost is likely to continue to rise over the long term. The usefulness of this basis of comparison is qualified by the fact that cost movements derive from a variety of causes other than inefficiency, and these causes include inflation, changes in specifications, rate of output, buying quantities, etc.

Relationships

All accounting figures have relationships with other figures or with measures of activity. Thus it would be necessary to know to what extent a rise in a unit cost was due to an increased proportion of material, labour or other elements, and to appraise the proportions which those amounts bear to total costs. It is informative to relate the cost of a product to its selling price, or vice versa; a rising percentage of cost to price would indicate a need to reduce cost, increase price, or increase turnover.

The most meaningful relationships are those where a cost is expressed as a percentage or rate in relation to the factor which determines its movements. The labour cost in a workshop should be expressed as a rate per unit of output, the output being measured, as appropriate, by quantity, man hours, machine hours or production hours, etc.

In some industries more complex rates are established, such as tonne-miles in transport. Overhead cost may be appraised by the use of various determining factors; the costs of the canteen, the personnel department and the wages section can usefully be shown as a rate per employee. In all cases it will again be important to depict the trend of the relationship.

Comparisons with Standards

Probably the most effective form of control is based on comparisons between actual and standard costs, particularly so far as direct costs are concerned. With this form of control information the attention of the managers is directed to the controllable variances of significance and, in theory, no other information should be required. The standards are presumed to have been set up by some form of work study, but will usually also be influenced by past results, including trends, and by relationships with factors of activity. However, even a standard costing variance is not necessarily a sign of inefficiency. The actual costs may be influenced by unavoidable price or rate increases, or changes in the volume of output and working methods, apart from errors in the original assessment of the standards. The cause of a major variance therefore needs investigating, initially by the management accounting service.

Control Action

The General Approach to Cost Control

Cost information is useless unless it inspires action at the appropriate managerial level. Obviously where a unit cost variance is found to be due to excessive working times or buying prices, the remedy is to cure the inefficiency. The efficiency and rate variances on labour costs, and the price and usage variances on purchased materials, are illustrated in Chapter 4.

In many situations, however, a cost variance is not controllable at grass-roots level. Operating times and material prices may be high due, for example, to the incidence of small orders or a reduction in the demand for a product. In these situations the remedies lie within the responsibility of higher executive levels, frequently marketing management. The problem is invariably resolved by considering the respective merits of alternative courses of action, and for this purpose the relevant figures to be taken into account are the marginal or additional costs and the marginal or additional sales.

Assuming that action is taken to control operational efficiency, then the reasons for excessive unit costs are essentially the following:

1. Inadequate turnover to utilize the full resources of the undertaking, or, conversely, a level of turnover which causes the business to operate beyond its optimum capacity.
2. An uneconomic mix of products.
3. Small orders incurring high setting up time in the works and excessive overheads on selling, distribution and administration.

Inadequate Turnover

Inadequate turnover means that the resources of the business are not fully utilized. In the production or operating departments this situation results in idle or not fully occupied manpower, plant and space. The same consequences appear in the distribution and administrative departments. Whilst it may be possible to tailor most of the variable costs to the level of turnover actually being obtained, there will inevitably be an excessive cost of 'fixed' and semi-variable overheads. These overheads will include depreciation of plant and equipment and the cost of supervisors and managers, plus the costs of service functions such as maintenance, accounting and general office facilities. Apart from the effect on profit, the result will be a high cash outflow compared with the inflow, causing in turn possible high payments of interest for finance.

The situation may, in essence, be shown by the following example, where A represents the turnover and expenditure at reasonably full utilization and B the actual situation. The units of turnover may consist of quantities of homogeneous output or some key factor such as man hours or production hours. In a retail store the turnover will probably have to be expressed for the purpose by the value of the sales.

	A *(full utilization)*		B *(actual situation)*	
Turnover in units	10 000		8000	
	£	Per unit £	£	Per unit £
Variable costs	20 000	2.00	16 000	2.00
Semi-variable costs	30 000	3.00	28 000	3.50
Fixed costs	50 000	5.00	50 000	6.25
Total costs	£100 000	£10.00	£94 000	£11.75

In the above example it has been assumed that the semi-variable costs could not be reduced in direct relation to the lower actual turnover and the fixed costs have remained totally unaltered. As a result total costs per unit are substantially higher than they would be with full utilization of the resources. The marginal or differential cost of the under-utilization of capacity is shown to be £1.75 per unit.

What Are the Remedies?

In the long run, and assuming full utilization could not be achieved, the resources represented by the fixed and semi-variable costs might be reduced – in other words the undertaking would be 'cut down to size'.

This would involve disposing of some plant and equipment, possibly letting out space, and cutting down supervision and service functions. Such action would be unlikely to reduce the unit cost to the optimum level of £10.00, and would inevitably involve 'one-off' costs in losses on the sale of plant and equipment, as well as redundancy pay.

For the short term (which will probably be a period of under a year) consideration needs to be given to the possibilities of reducing unit costs, increasing turnover, and improving the profitability of the sales mix.

Reducing Unit Costs

Attention would first be given to overcoming inefficiencies in the operations. In this sense inefficiencies would embrace over-long working times, the use of high-paid personnel on low-grade work, excessive prices and quantities of material, and unnecessary marketing and administration costs. The next consideration would be whether unit costs could be reduced by changing working methods, this aspect of the remedy applying as much to administration, distribution and selling as to the direct operations. Working methods would include further or, maybe, less mechanization (in offices as well as in the workshops) and the economics of buying in parts or products instead of making them, and of subcontracting particular operations.

In calculating the comparative marginal cost of a mechanized as opposed to a manual operation, a problem arises as regards the amount to be included for the cost of the machinery, including its design and installation. The marginal cost would include these costs less any residual value at the end of the working life of the machinery. But the working life could extend for many years, whereas the assessment is likely to be made for a short period of, say, a year. For the comparative figures in a short period it would therefore be reasonable to make an apportionment of the net capital cost.

The following specimen figures indicate the calculations required:

	p.a. £
Manual operation:	
Personnel costs for the budgeted output, including national insurance, pension contributions, and other variable expenses	£100 000
Conversion to mechanized operation:	
Net cost of installing machinery – apportionment for 1 year	10 000
Maintenance of machinery	5 000
Operators and supervision	60 000
Interest on capital	6 000
	£81 000

The marginal cost saving is thus £19 000 a year, which, with a budgeted output of, say, 8000 units, represents a unit cost saving of 19 000/8000 = £2.38. If it is assumed that the output after mechanization was raised from, say, 8000 units to 10 000 units, the reduction in unit costs would be:

		£
Manual operation:	£100 000 ÷ 8 000 =	12.5
Mechanized operation:	£81 000 ÷ 10 000 =	8.1
		£4.4

Consideration might then be given to calculating whether increased cost savings could be made by buying in the product or component in question.

Specimen comparative figures are for 10 000 units as follows

	£	Per unit
Buying in:		
Suppliers' charges	150 000	15.00
Additional variable buying costs	29 000	2.9
Interest on capital	1 000	0.1
	£180 000	£18.0

Making (mechanized operation):

Machinery, operators and interest	81 000	8.10
Materials	75 000	7.50
	£156 000	£15.60

Buying in is consequently found to be more expensive than making (either by manual or mechanized methods). This would be the normal situation because the suppliers' charges would include profit. Nevertheless, buying in could be desirable for some products or components where the resources involved in manufacture, especially managerial time, could be applied to more profitable activities.

Increasing Turnover

As illustrated on page 218 above, increasing turnover, and thus the utilization of capacity, will reduce costs until the optimum level is reached. The so-called 'diseconomies of scale' will occur when higher wage rates have to be paid for overtime and shift premiums, when additional accommodation at a high cost has to be obtained, and when the cost of keeping machinery in continuous operation is unduly high. These are signs that the resources of the business need enlarging. The key consideration in all situations where turnover is expanded is the marginal profit (i.e. additional income less marginal costs) from the increased output.

In a situation of under capacity working, however, the marginal profit is likely to accelerate with increasing sales (as shown by the breakeven chart and profit graph given in Figs 5.1 and 5.2). The basic reason is that the additional turnover in such a situation does not incur more fixed costs. However, efforts to increase sales often involve marketing and selling costs disproportionate to the additional income. Expensive publicity may have to be incurred and an extension of sales areas and markets may incur heavy costs for a comparatively small return in income.

A further consequence of raising turnover is that prices have to be reduced to capture new markets or hesitant customers. It is rarely expedient for a price reduction to be confined to a particular market segment:

Present situation

Turnover:		
Units	8000	Per unit
	£	£
Sales value	96 000	12.00
Total costs	94 000	11.75
Profit	£2000	£0.25
Capital employed	£64 000	
Return on capital	3.125%	
Profit on sales	2.083%	

It is estimated that, by reducing the price to £11.50 a unit, sales can be increased by 2000 units. Additional publicity and selling cost will amount to £10 000.

The marginal profitability of the additional sales will be:

Increasing sales

	Present situation	Additional sales	New situation	Per unit
Sales: Units	8 000	2 000	10 000	
	£	£	£	£
Price	12.00	11.50		
Value	96 000	23 000	119 000	11.9
Reduction in price on present sales		(4 000)	(4 000)	(0.4)
Net sales income	£96 000	£19 000	£115 000	£11.5
Costs:				
Variable at £2	16 000	4 000	20 000	2.0
Semi-variable: at £3.50	28 000			
at £3.00		6 000	30 000	3.0
Reduction for present sales		(4 000)		
Fixed	50 000		50 000	5.0
Additional costs		10 000	10 000	1.0
	£94 000	£16 000	£110 000	£11.0
Profit	£2 000	£3 000	£5 000	£0.5

The marginal profit from increasing sales by 2000 units is £3000. This is a comparatively small amount, considering that the proposal is not free from risk, e.g. of a failure to obtain the additional turnover. However, the return on the capital employed of £64 000 has been raised from 3.125 per cent to the more respectable figure of 7.8 per cent and the profit on the value of sales has increased from 2.1 to 4.4 per cent.

Reviewing the Sales Mix

The preceding examples have, for simplicity, assumed a single product, or a range of products which could be measured in terms of a single factor, represented by the expression 'unit'. In many situations, however, the turnover will consist of a number of disparate products or sales lines, with different units costs and different profit margins. These products may be obtained from a single manufacturing unit or by a single purchasing department. The resources of the business are bound to be limited by such factors as the capacity of the plant and, ultimately, by the funds which can be made available. The capacity of the plant may be measured by key factors, otherwise known as 'limiting factors', such as the man hours or production hours that can be generated. In a retail store the limiting factor may be the counter space available; in transport it will normally be the potential tonne miles or passenger miles; in some concerns it may be the supply of a key material. In all cases, of course, the market potential will be a conclusive limiting factor, but this is frequently a fairly flexible quantity.

The maximization of profit depends upon using limited resources in the most profitable manner. In practical terms this means applying resources as far as possible where profit is highest per unit of the limiting factor. The product which shows the highest percentage profit on sales may not be the one which makes the most profitable use of the limited resources. Consider the following example where the limiting factor is the total man hours available, which is 75 000, and 'profit' is represented by the contribution on the grounds that the fixed expenses cannot be precisely allocated to individual products. For simplicity it is assumed that only three products are sold, and the man hours available can be applied to any of the products.

	Product A	Product B	Product C	Total
Units sold	10 000	20 000	5 000	
Hours per unit	0.5	1.5	8.0	
Total hours	5 000	30 000	40 000	75 000
Price per unit	£2	£3	£4	
Sales value	£20 000	60 000	20 000	100 000
Variable costs	17 000	48 000	10 000	75 000
Contribution	3 000	12 000	10 000	25 000
% on sales	15%	20%	50%	
Per hour	£0.6	£0.4	£0.25	
Possible share of market potential in units	20 000	25 000	6 000	

From the percentage contributions on sales values the order of relative profitability is C, B, A. Accordingly, marketing management propose to increase sales of apparently the most profitable product, C, up to the market potential of 6000 units obtainable at the existing price. This output will absorb 8 × 6000 = 48 000 hours, and it is proposed that the remaining 27 000 hours shall be applied to the apparently next profitable product B, product A to be phased out owing to its low percentage contribution on sales. When the proposal is evaluated, as shown below, the management are surprised to find that the overall contribution wil be reduced from £25 000 to £22 800.

	Product A	Product B	Product C	Total
Units	–	18 000	6 000	
Hours per unit	–	1.5	8.0	
Total hours	–	27 000	48 000	75 000
Price per unit	–	£3	£4	
Sales value	–	£54 000	£24 000	£78 000
Contribution % on sales	–	20%	50%	
Contribution amount	–	£10 800	£12 000	£22 800

The approach which should have been used to maximize profit was to concentrate resources in the order of the relative contributions per man hour, i.e. A, B, C. By selling up to the potential market share of A, then B and applying the remaining hours to C, the contribution will be maximized, as shown below:

	Product A	Product B	Product C	
Units	20 000	25 000	3 475	
Hours per unit	0.5	1.5	8.0	
Total hours	10 000	37 500	27 500	£75 000
Price per unit	£2	£3	£4	
Sales value	£40 000	£75 000	£13 900	£128 900
Contribution %	15%	20%	50%	
Contribution amount	£60 000	£15 000	£6 950	£81 950

The example is simplified to show the correct approach to the problem. In practical terms many other factors need to be taken into account. For instance, increasing sales of product A may involve a lower price and additional selling expenses. It may be possible to maintain the turnover of product C by raising capacity (at a cost) through overtime working or the use of subcontractors. Furthermore, proposals for increasing the sales of a product are accompanied by risk and uncertainty.

Loss Leaders and Special Offers

In the present context the term 'special offers' embraces loss leaders, gifts, gift vouchers, free entries in competitions and lotteries, and discounts for prompt purchases. A loss leader is a product associated with a main product of which it is intended to increase the sales as, for example, razors are associated with razor blades. The object of the special offer is to stimulate turnover and thus to obtain more profit than would be made without the offer.

Before a special offer is made the probable financial merits of the proposal should be assessed. The question is whether an additional *contribution* to overall profit is likely to be achieved. The contribution is the marginal (i.e. additional) income less the marginal (essentially variable) costs of the package as a whole, that is the main product and the special offer combined. The assumption is that fixed expenses will not normally be increased, so that no apportionments of those expenses should be included in the calculation. A specimen form of assessment is as follows:

Marginal profit from loss leader

	£	£	£
Additional sales of main product			500 000
Less: Marginal costs:			
Main product		£200 000	
Loss leader:			
Variable costs	60 000		
Income	50 000		
Loss		10 000	
			210 000
Additional contribution			£290 000

The major problem in preparing this forecast is the usual one of estimating the likely sales, in this case additional sales. That assessment will depend on the period of time covered by the forecast. In the case of non-recurrent sales to particular customers, such as with a new book, the period should be the duration of the offer, since subsequent sales should, so to speak, stand on their own feet so far as profit is concerned. A different situation arises with a product of which a customer makes repeat purchases such as most foods.

In the latter case a customer may buy in anticipation of future needs whilst the special offer is available. That customer's later purchases may be deferred, to the detriment of future sales. An important objective of a special offer is, however, to attract new customers for the product, in the hope that a proportion will make repeat purchases. The wider clientele should also stimulate sales of other products, but that factor is virtually unquantifiable.

The increase in sales may be limited by countermeasures taken by competitors, such as reductions in price. On the other hand, the special offer may be made not so much in anticipation of increased sales as to sustain the turnover in the face of encroachment by competitors. In this situation the additional sales included in the forecast will be those which would have been lost if the special offer had not been made.

Thus there will be many imponderables to consider in making a prior appraisal of the validity of the proposal. Nevertheless, a reasoned and cautious estimate is better than none at all. It might, for instance, disclose unsustainable costs in providing the loss leader or other incentive; it will represent a target and a standard against which the actual results can be compared. Many factors will influence sales after the special offer has expired and for this reason the assessment should be made on a short-term basis, perhaps covering no more than a few months.

As a guide to future projects of this nature it will be desirable to compare the forecast with the actual results. There should be no difficulty in recording the sales of a new product. The main problem lies in ascertaining the additional sales of an existing product over the period selected. The suggested basis is as follows: deduct from the total sales after the initiation of the offer the turnover in a normal period before the offer.

Profit Planning for Joint Products

Joint products are those which are derived from a common basic material. Thus raw coal and crude oil are processed to produce various chemicals, fuels and gases. Another typical example is where various edible products are derived from animal carcasses. A by-product is of a similar nature but is usually considered as an inevitable outcome of producing the main product.

In most cases it is impossible to allocate the cost of the main product to each of the joint products or by-products except by some arbitrary arithmetic. For example, if the cost to a meat products company of obtaining a carcass was, say, £100, by no realistic method could that cost be divided between the joints and other products offered for sale to the consumer. It would only be feasible to make realistic allocations of cost where certain quantities of the basic material were specifically applied to the production of a single product, but this is rarely the situation.

In the costing system it is customary to make arbitrary allocations of base material costs to joint products by such devices as weight or cost or sales value of further processing, but such methods can be misleading for profit planning. For the latter purpose, the marketing manager needs to be able (1) to decide on the appropriate price for each product, and (2) to compare the relative profitability of each product so as to consider where resources of processing and marketing are best applied.

The price is, of course, decided by the market. The market involves factors such as the consumer's willingness to pay, the existence of substitutes (e.g. electricity, gas, coal and oil for heating and power), competition, achievement of desired turnover, etc. The price must not, in the long run, be below cost for obvious reasons. However, the only costs which can be stated with reasonable precision are:

1. the cost of the basic material, including transportation, storing and refining (less receipts from scrap);
2. the costs of further processing to produce the individual products for sale.

The cost of the basic material, (1), above, represents the amount which must be recovered by the sum of the contributions from the sale of the products in (2) above. For both (1) and (2) the costs to be brought into account are marginal, essentially variable costs. Thus any price for a product which exceeds its variable cost will add to the overall profit of the organization, or reduce the loss. Profit planning should ensure that the resulting surplus is sufficient to cover the fixed costs of the whole undertaking and to provide adequate profit as a return on the capital employed. The profit plan may be illustrated by the following specimen figures:

	£	£	£
Product A:			
Sales	500 000		
Variable costs	200 000		
Contribution		300 000	
Product C:			
Sales	100 000		
Variable costs	20 000		
Contribution		80 000	
Product D:			
Sales	50 000		
Variable costs	10 000		
Contribution		40 000	
Total contribution from products			420 000
Less: Variable costs of basic material			200 000
Grand total contribution			220 000
Less: Fixed costs of organization			120 000
			£100 000

Since the total contribution will vary according to the inflow of basic material and the demand for the products, alternative profit plans are amenable to a system of flexible budgeting. So as to maximize profit these budgets could also show the effect of changing the mix of products by the methods indicated on page 222. For long-term predictions changes in fixed costs will need to be taken into account, and they will to this extent become marginal.

In a complex situation the various alternative courses of action may be computerized and expressed by mathematical models.

18 ACQUISITIONS, BUY-OUTS AND DISPOSALS

Introduction

Of all the events in the life of a company, few transactions represent as great a risk as a major acquisition or disposal, yet in many instances the decision to proceed is not taken on the basis of a carefully considered strategic plan. The acquisition and disposal process is complex, frequently hazardous and often goes wrong (for example the Guinness attempt on Distillers, the Blue Arrow attempt on Manpower, the Ranks Hovis McDougall merger with Goodman Fielder Wattie and the Minorco attempt on Consgold). Of those that are completed, many are subsequently regarded as being less than totally successful by the management. Yet a few are so spectacularly successful (the Hanson Trust takeover of the Imperial Group, for example) that the process of expansion is bound to continue as the potential rewards are enormous and come much quicker than home-grown growth.

Public and Private Company Transactions

The processes involved in the acquisitions and disposals of private companies are very different from those of public companies. Public companies for this purpose may be defined as those to which the City Code on Takeovers and Mergers applies, primarily those listed on the Stock Exchange or quoted on the Unlisted Securities or over-the-counter markets, or which, although they are private in the legal sense, have sufficient shareholders to require a general offer to be made for their shares. Privately owned companies are those whose shares are not available for purchase by the general public. Within this category are those companies that have been bought out by the management. Table 18.1 summarizes the differences.

Acquisitions

The first point to make is that operations of this nature are better conducted on a strictly 'need to know' basis. If other people get to hear of a company's plans for acquisition, they may decide that the target company might conveniently fit into their own plans for expansion.

Planning Expansion

Expansion strategy must follow on from the objectives stated in the corporate plan.

Table 18.1 Differences between public and private companies

	Public company	*Private company*
Shareholders	Not involved in negotiating process	Usually involved
Form	Contested or agreed	Agreed
Valuation	Quoted share price provides a floor and basis for valuation	No quoted share price
Consideration	Quoted shares, cash, loan notes or convertible, payable on offer becoming unconditional	Any form but may also include deferred or contingent consideration
Regulatory	The City Code on Takeovers and Mergers, The Stock Exchange's Yellow Book etc.	Generally unregulated save for Companies Act requirements
Accounting	No accountants' report	Usual to have an accountants' report
Legal	Circular to shareholders with Form of Acceptance and Transfer	Sale and Purchase Agreement, usually including warranties and indemnities

Source: Acquisitions and Disposals, Ernst & Young.

The proposed expansion must be aimed at the achievement of certain financial or marketing objectives. These may include adding value to the combined businesses by rationalization of production capacity, utilizing a substantial tax loss or acquiring a national distribution network. The targeted benefits should also be quantified because acquisition carries a higher risk than internal growth and the potential effects of an unsuccessful acquisition should be included in the calculations.

The differences of approach towards planned expansion are demonstrated by the previous and current Chairmen of Grand Metropolitan. Sir Maxwell Joseph's strategy for growth was based on a superb ability to spot and acquire undervalued companies. His successor, Sir Stanley Grinstead, needed to develop a more sophisticated approach to corporate development. This involved forming a strategy development team which quickly implemented a programme of asset disposal, divesting Grand Met of various peripheral businesses.

The core businesses were defined as being drinks, hotels, retailing and food. The strategy review attempted to define the company's strengths, weaknesses and opportunities and to identify any threats to the group. From this analysis two factors in particular became clear: first that Grand Met's worldwide ambitions in the hotel sector would be almost impossible to achieve without such enormous expense that the return on the capital employed would be unacceptably low. Secondly, the food sector was targeted for growth by a policy of acquisitions.

Pilsbury, the American food giant, was a favourite because it would allow faster growth. It would enable Grand Met to switch from dependence on an asset-intensive business producing relatively small profits to one with a richer cash flow. This good cash flow would increase the speed with which expansion could take place. As well as complementing Grand Met's present market strengths (food, retailing and drinks),

Pilsbury has some strong brands which could be further developed internationally (Burger King fast-food chain, Green Giant vegetables and Van der Kamp seafood). The justification for the bid was that Grand Met management could produce a greater return on the assets than Pilsbury have managed over recent years.

Reasons for Acquisition

It is possible to identify five separate objectives that may be fulfilled by an acquisition strategy. The first is the economies of scale that can result from reducing overheads, or being able to allocate existing overheads over a larger volume of production. Another aspect might be the partial elimination of the effects of seasonality for an existing business.

Vertical expansion can give a manufacturer greater presence in the market-place, for example where retail outlets are acquired. Alternatively, if sources of raw material supply are acquired, the regularity of supply may be assured. The third reason, geographical expansion, is similar: the acquisition is made to obtain new markets that have hitherto been effectively closed to the business.

A fourth motive for expansion is to buy a competitor's skills that can be used to improve the performance of the existing company. Diversification is the fifth reason for acquisition. This is where a company expands into largely unrelated activities because the existing business is declining, or showing limited potential for growth. In the late 1960s, the Imperial Tobacco Group started to diversify into food, buying Ross and Golden Wonder crisps, because public awareness of the link between cigarette-smoking and lung cancer was indicating a probable decline in cigarette tobacco sales.

Valuations

The valuation of a business in the context of its acquisition or disposal is far from being an exact science. Ultimately it is of course the price which the purchaser will pay and the vendor accept. In most circumstances this figure is reached only by negotiation, or sometimes auction in the case of private companies.

The objective information for the valuation will first comprise historic balance sheets and profit and loss accounts, their future projections and the assumptions upon which these calculations have been based. Separate valuations may need to be commissioned for certain of the assets, typically property but also various investment portfolios and stock. In the motor car industry, supplying parts of obsolete models at a very high mark-up is an important part of the business. In other industries stocks from non-current production may be almost worthless and it is important that they should be valued accordingly.

External information is then required to set the business concerned in the appropriate context. This will in part involve valuations of similar companies whose market value may be capable of more precise determination: they may have a stock market quotation, for example. Other aspects of the broader environment might include the possible effects of impending legislation on the business or clearly defin-able changes in consumption or attitudes to any sphere of the company's business.

When all the relevant information that it is possible to assemble is collated, one or more methods of valuation should be chosen. Net asset valuation provides a good guide for some types of business (property investment companies and investment trusts). However, in most trading companies, profits are more relevant than assets and the key factor is the price/earnings ratio, which is generally expressed as a multiple of after-tax profits.* Loss-making companies require a slightly different treatment, and in these cases turnover, gross margins and their future projections assume a greater importance, as do the values of the assets. In other businesses where the only asset is a future cash flow such as royalties, or a wasting asset like a mine, the discounted cash flow of the future income stream is practical.

Disposals

Strategic Aspects

The first issue when considering whether to buy another company is to understand the reasons for it being offered for sale. In a private company the most common reason is that the proprietor is retiring or needs to raise money. Because money could be raised by other means, for example by selling shares to other parties or borrowing from an institution, it may be important to understand why the owners are proposing to sell the whole business. With a subsidiary or a division, the disposal will probably result from a corporate plan which has highlighted core business areas, the sale of certain peripheral business therefore being part of a programme of rationalization.

The effects of a disposal on the shareholders need careful consideration: a holding company may wish to exchange contracts before a year-end in order to improve its balance sheet by showing greater liquidity, for example, or a higher asset value. Conversely, the individual shareholders in a family company may gain tax advantages by delaying the exchange of contracts until the new tax year.

Business disposals are usually carried out discreetly with as few people as possible involved beyond those required to canvass the sale. Inevitably, once it is known that there is to be a change of ownership, customers, suppliers and employees suffer from uncertainty.

Preparatory Steps

A company which owns freehold property would be advised to obtain an independent valuation from suitably qualified surveyors. This not only helps to substantiate the asking price, but also saves time later.

---

* The p/e ratio is calculated by dividing the quoted price per share by the earnings per share. The earnings are the profits attributable to the ordinary shareholders (i.e. after accounting for prior claims such as loan interest and the fixed rate of preference dividends). For example, a company has a capital of £100 000 comprising 2 000 000 5 p shares and makes a pre-tax profit of £200 000. The market price of the shares is 50 p.

(a) Market valuation = number of shares × Market price = 200 000 × 50 p = £1 000 000.
(b) Net the profit by deducting corporate tax, i.e. 200 000 less 35% = £140 000.
(c) Subtract loan interest and preference short dividends of £20 000.
(d) Divide the market capitalization by the sum available for dividend: £1 000 000/120 000 = 8.33.

The p/e is an expression of how many years' current profits the same share price reflects (the smaller the better).

Secondly, solicitors should be retained at an early stage to identify any possible legal impediments to the sale and to consider what warranties and indemnities may be required. Early planning can often identify and solve issues before they become problems.

Thirdly, there will be issues concerning the separating out of part of the pension fund. Fourthly, any problems with recent audits should be resolved because the purchaser will clearly require an accountant's report.

Fifthly, the attitude of potential interested government bodies should be considered. The Monopolies Commission is usually involved only in disposals where the gross assets of the company being sold exceed £30 million or where a monopoly is enhanced or created.

Finally, a selling memorandum should be prepared. This is a marketing document designed to attract would-be purchasers. Particular care should be taken not to make statements which cannot later be substantiated. A well-prepared document avoids the delays of providing information on a piecemeal basis and demonstrates a serious commitment on the vendor's part.

Categories of Potential Buyer

Buyers can fall into three possible categories: the first group are those close to the business who may be competitors, suppliers or customers in the same or a closely related industry. They will understand the business and their interest will be from the synergy they expect to gain.

Secondly, management buy-outs have become popular and successful over recent years, perhaps the most successful being Paul Judge's Premier Brands which was formerly Cadbury's food and beverage division. In three years a director's stake of £330 000 (and borrowings of £96.7 million) have multiplied five hundred times to between £160 and £170 million. This is considered in more detail on pages 233–234.

Totally unconnected acquirers represent an increasingly frequent type of corporate buyer. Their reasons vary from genuine diversification to 'turnaround' of staid traditional businesses, buying to split up and resell the components to other interested parties, or for tax considerations. Such potential buyers will demand extensive industry information.

Methods of Sale

For private companies where the likely buyer may be difficult to identify, a public auction may have obvious advantages, particularly where the business is clearly very saleable. Secrecy is, however, sacrificed.

A limited auction combines the advantage to the vendor of competitive bidding with some retention of secrecy. A few potential buyers are invited to make offers for the business as described in a selling prospectus. A clearly described timetable is imposed giving a period for negotiations and a deadline by which offers subject to contract must be received. These auctions are not public and not usually binding until a later stage of the negotiations is reached. Throughout the selling cycle the vendor should be able to retain control by managing the timetable and threatening to go to another party if a deadline is not adhered to or the offer is unacceptable.

Management Buy-outs

Many large companies have recognized that if they wish to dispose of a business that does not fit in with their corporate strategy, the best purchaser is often the resident management team who should have the greatest appreciation of the risks and potential rewards. The management buy-out offers advantages to the seller (which may be a holding company or individual or family) for whom the outcome of a sale to the management may be more advantageous than the sale to a third party. It avoids the cost both financial and social of disclosure. Secondly, the team of (usually 2–6) top managers who have the opportunity of acquiring a significant part of the business may realize substantial financial rewards if growth later enables them to sell all or part of their shareholding. Finally, the financial backers may be able to anticipate a satisfactory return on their investment given the track record of a proven management team. It is estimated that between 1000 and 1500 management buy-outs have taken place since the late 1970s.

The management buy-out requires an effective team of managers with the skills and abilities required to make a sufficient success of the business so that a future stream of profits can be used to repay the initial borrowings. There are three major situations where this may occur: the first is the rationalization of a group of businesses where parts are sold off to increase operating efficiency. This may include:

1. Products making insufficient profits.
2. Loss-making or marginal manufacturing units.
3. Operations peripheral to the main business assets which can be sold to realize capital for more attractive projects.

The second situation is buying from a liquidator or receiver a viable part of a business that may continue as a going concern. The third type of situation is that of a privately owned business where the owners, which may be a family, wish to dispose of some or all of their stake – perhaps on the retirement of the chairman or managing director.

Assembling the financial package will be part of the negotiation process of prices and terms. There are a number of ways of giving the financial backers a share in the ownership of the new business, each with different tax and repayment implications. The management team will wish to limit the financial backers to as small a percentage of the share capital as possible, while at the same time not leaving the enterprise too dependent on short- and medium-term loans from the banks and other financial institutions.

The options for financing the buy-out include the following:

1. Ordinary share capital, a minority holding.
2. Convertible preference shares or loan stock, the conversion terms often reducing as performance increases to provide an additional incentive for the management team.
3. Redeemable preference shares, giving the investor a fixed return with repayment at the end of a stated period.
4. A loan or bank overdraft.

The management team will usually be required to make a substantial financial commitment to make it more difficult for them to 'abandon ship' should things prove more difficult than was originally anticipated. Of course, the opposite can happen.

When Paul Judge organized the management buy-out of Cadbury's food and beverage division, the directors mortgaged their houses to provide £330 000 for buying the business. However, four years later, the shares of each director are worth some £15 million, with Paul Judge holding three times that amount.

The market flotation that had been planned has now had to be abandoned because a majority of the directors wish to realize their assets more quickly than would be possible from a flotation. Lazard Brothers, the merchant bank advising the company, had only recommended that each director sell 10 per cent of his equity holding.

Leveraged Buy-outs

On 30 November 1988 the Chairman of RJR Nabisco, America's 19th largest company, agreed to the company being taken over by Kohlberg Kravis and Roberts (KKR) in a leveraged buy-out. The sum involved was US$25.08 billion. This was by far the largest business deal ever: indeed, the price was higher than Portugal's gross national product.

A leveraged buy-out is the purchase of a company that is financed to a large extent by borrowings against the assets of the company. For example, an organization wishing to purchase another company might put up in equity 10 per cent of the purchase price and borrow (or leverage) 90 per cent from a financial institution with the debt supported by the assets of the company being purchased.

As a rule the lending institution would not consider the proposition unless a substantial reduction in the debt position over five years may be anticipated. From the predator's point of view the interest on the debt can be a large drain on profits until unwanted assets can be sold and the borrowing reduced.

The RJR Nabisco deal was an outstanding piece of financial engineering. KKR only invested US$15 million (about 0.06 per cent), with another US$1.5 billion coming from investors in a KKR buy-out fund. Approximately US$5.2 billion was in the form of shares redeemable at a later date, with the balance of US$18.3 billion borrowed.

Mergers

A merger is the willing and planned combination that forms one economic unit of what was previously two companies. The adjective 'willing' is important because it distinguishes the merger from the takeover type of acquisition. The merger is set in motion by one company buying the shares of the other according to a predetermined plan. Suppose there are two companies, A and B:

	Company A	Company B
Total earnings	£20 000	£50 000
Number of shares	5 000	10 000
Earnings per share	£4	£5
Price/earnings ratio	15 times	12 times
Market price per share	£60	£60

The firms agree to merge with B, the 'surviving' company, acquiring the shares of

A by a one-for-one exchange of stock. The exchange ratio is determined by the respective market prices of the two companies. Assuming no increase in earnings, the effects on earnings per share are as follows:

	Shares of Company B owned after the merger	Earnings per share Before merger	Earnings per share After merger
A's shareholders	5 000	4	4.67
B's shareholders	10 000	5	4.67
	15 000		

Since the total earnings are £70 000 and a total of 15 000 shares will remain after the merger is completed, the new earnings per share will be £4.67, an increase of 67p for A's shareholders and a decline of 33p for B's. The effect of the merger of the market value of the combined corporation is, however, more difficult to calculate.

A clearly identifiable synergy is an essential ingredient for success. Thus the merger plans between Beecham, a British company, and Smith Kline Beckman, an American company, found favour in most quarters. First, as research costs continue to increase, it becomes important to sell the resulting successful products quickly before patents run out. Smith Kline Beckman can offer Beecham 6000 additional salespeople to help achieve this. This is particularly important when effective selling time is reduced because the programmes for testing are continually becoming longer and more sophisticated. It now takes an average of twelve years before a drug is released on to the market-place, while in the early 1960s it took three years. The period covered by the patents in the UK and Europe has, however, remained fixed at 20 years, so companies now have only an average of eight years to recover their research and development costs with patent protection.

A second identifiable advantage of the merger is the pooling of research and development skill and experience in what is a very fragmented industry. The top ten companies account for only 26 per cent of the world market, while the largest company, Merck, has only 4 per cent of industry sales. Yet success when it happens is huge, the top two selling drugs having sales of US$2.5 billion.

APPENDIX 1

THE ESSENCE OF BUSINESS TAXATION

Introduction

The intricacies of business taxation are so complex that the following pages must be confined to providing a general overview of the subject. It is, however, important that managers should have adequate understanding of the tax effects of their decisions, and know when it is necessary to obtain expert advice before putting those decisions into action. It is also desirable that business people should have at least a broad comprehension of how the tax liabilities of their business as a whole are assessed.

In this context it is necessary to point out that the rates of tax and the system itself are subject to frequent amendment by the annual (and sometimes more frequent) Budget of the Chancellor of the Exchequer, and the subsequent Finance Act. The following discussion and illustrations have reference to the situation in the UK in 1989.

While taxation can often be legally minimized by certain courses of action indicated below, these notes rigorously exclude descriptions of tax avoidance devices which, apart from being usually illegal, are frequently overtaken by retrospective legislation.

Taxes Affecting Business

The three major forms of taxation levied on business profits are income tax, corporation tax and capital gains tax. In addition businesses are subject to the uniform business rate, customs and excise duties (including value added tax), and employers' national insurance. The total contribution to government expenditure by an individual business is therefore considerable, and all these charges must be taken into account when preparing budgets. Owners of businesses, and of shares in companies, should also make appropriate provisions for the inheritance tax which will be payable on the estate they leave on their death above a certain threshold.

Income tax is payable by individuals on their total income after charges and allowances. An individual's total taxable income includes the share of the profits he or she receives from an unincorporated business, such as one in sole ownership or a partnership. Corporate bodies such as limited companies pay corporation tax on their profits, but they are involved in income tax through the system of collection at source, such as by means of PAYE deductions from remuneration, income tax deductions from interest and 'imputed' tax on dividends.

Taxation Regulations and Administration

The statutory authority for the imposition of tax is now largely contained in the Income and Corporation Taxes Acts of 1970 and 1988, the latter being a consolidating Act. Particular aspects of the tax system are covered by the Taxes Management Act 1970, the Capital Allowances Act 1968, the Capital Gains Tax Act 1979, the Value Added Tax Act 1983 and the Inheritance Tax Act 1984. These enactments are amended by the annual (and sometimes biannual) Finance Acts, which follow the Budget. This voluminous legislation is interpreted by an even more extensive body of case law, decided in the courts and by the Commissioners for Taxes, by 'concessions' and by rules of practice issued by the Inland Revenue.

The proposed rates of tax and changes in the system are announced in the Budget, presented to Parliament by the Chancellor usually in March each year. These proposals, subject to amendments made by Parliament, refer to the next fiscal year, which runs from 5 April or, in the case of corporation tax, from 31 March.

Taxes on income and profits are imposed under six Schedules and Cases (or subdivisions of each Schedule). Assessments on business profits are largely covered by Schedule D, Case I regarding trades and Case II professions and vocations. However, a business is assessable for income on profits other than from trading, such as under Schedule A regarding rents, Schedule D, Case III regarding loan interest, Case IV and Case V regarding overseas income, Case VI regarding miscellaneous income, and Schedule F regarding income tax on dividends.

Overall management of the tax system is the responsibility of the Board of Inland Revenue. Assessments are made by Inspectors of Taxes, located in various districts and centres. The Inspectors have wide powers of negotiation and enquiry and can compel the production of relevant returns, accounts and documentation.

They can make estimated assessments when they have not received the accounts or information they require. The actual collection of assessed tax is undertaken by Collectors of Taxes.

Where the taxpayer does not agree with a decision of the Inspector, or with an actual assessment, an appeal can be made by either party to the General or Special Commissioners. The former are akin to magistrates and the latter are experts in taxation law and practice. Appeals from decisions of the Commissioners can be made to the courts.

Collection of Tax

Income tax, corporation tax and capital gains tax are collected on the basis of assessments on businesses. In the case of unincorporated businesses the assessments are normally based on the taxable profit derived from the accounts made up for a period ending in the tax year preceding the year of assessment. Thus a taxable profit made by an unincorporated business in the year to 31 December 1989 would be assessed in the tax year from 5 April 1990 to 5 April 1991. Special procedures apply in the years when an unincorporated business is first established and in the years when it is closed down. The income tax due would be payable by two equal instalments on 1 January in the year of assessment and on the following 1 July.

For a limited company the assessment for corporation tax is based on the taxable profit made for the accounts year ending in the tax year of assessment. Thus a limited company's taxable profit for the year ended 31 December 1989 would be assessed for the tax year 1989, which ends on 31 March 1990. Payment would be due in one amount nine months after the end of the accounting year.

A substantial amount of income tax is collected at source, i.e. from the payer of the taxable amount. This system notably applies under PAYE to remuneration, including salaries, wages and directors' fees, the tax deducted from the payment being remitted, normally at quarterly intervals, by the payer to the Inland Revenue. Interest, such as on loans, debentures and government stock, is normally paid subject to deduction of income tax at the basic rate; again the payer accounts to the Inland Revenue for the amount so deducted. In the case of dividends, basic rate income tax is said to be 'imputed' to the payment, meaning that for tax purposes the recipient is assumed to receive a dividend 'grossed up' at the basic rate. With a basic rate of income tax at 25 per cent dividends are grossed up by one third. Thus if a taxpayer received an actual dividend payment of £120, this would represent a grossed up amount of £160 so far as the taxpayer's taxable income was concerned. Higher rate would be payable if applicable on £160 subject to a 'tax credit' of the £40 basic rate tax imputed to the dividend.

The income tax imputed to dividends paid and received by a limited company, as well as that deducted from interest, is taken into account in the computation of a company's corporation tax liability.

Disallowances

The profit shown by the accounts of a business invariably needs adjustment for tax purposes. Certain items of expenditure are disallowed and, more rarely, some income may not be assessable. The major disallowance is for depreciation, which is replaced by capital allowances as described below. Other expenditure not allowable for tax purposes includes capital expenditure, appropriations of profit such as dividends, transfers to reserves and proprietors' drawings, entertainment expenses, personal expenditure and that not arising out of the trade, and general, but not specific, provisions. Capital profits on the sale of fixed assets are not assessable but enter into capital allowance computations.

The foregoing is a very brief summary and questions regarding whether particular expenses are or are not allowable are being continually referred to the Commissioners and the courts.

Capital Allowances

From the adjusted profits capital allowances are deducted. As mentioned above the statutory allowances for capital expenditure take the place of the depreciation in the accounts. Capital allowances called 'writing down allowances' apply to the cost of plant and machinery, of which the scope is very wide, and in 1989–90 were at 25 per cent each year, calculated on the reducing balance. In other words if a machine was bought for £1200 the allowance would be £300 in the year of purchase, leaving a balance of £900 on which an allowance of £225 could be claimed in the second year, and so on. The writing down allowance for industrial and agricultural buildings is 4 per cent. Allowances of the whole cost in the first year can be claimed for capital expenditure (but not buildings), for research and development, and for expenditure on new industrial and commercial buildings in Enterprise Zones. For private type cars used for business the maximum writing down allowance is £2000, i.e. on a cost of £8000.

The written down balances are amalgamated in separate 'pools' for plant and machinery, buildings and private cars. Each pool is increased by additions and reduced by sales each year and a single amount of writing down allowance is calculated on the balance. If this process produces a negative balance that amount is treated as a balancing charge to be added to profits, so as to ensure that no more than the cost of the assets is allowed. Where the proceeds of selling an asset are above cost a liability to capital gains tax will arise. Balancing allowances normally occur only on the closure or winding up of a business.

It should be appreciated that the system and rates of capital allowances are frequently altered by the annual Budgets and Finance Acts, and the foregoing refers to the rates current in 1989–90.

It is important to consider taxation implications when considering projects for capital expenditure. As explained in Chapter 8 these projects are usually appraised on the basis of the net cash flow, discounted to a present value, which they are likely to produce. In making these assessments the tax savings from capital allowances should be taken into account.

Where corporation tax is payable at 35 per cent and writing down allowances are 25 per cent, the annual tax saving will be 25 per cent of 35 per cent = 8.75 per cent of each year's written down balance, delayed for about a year when the corporation tax is payable. A business with a tax loss will obtain no cash flow advantage from the allowances.

The Computation

For an unincorporated business the taxable profit, adjusted as indicated in the section on disallowances above and less capital allowances, forms part of the taxable income of the proprietor or the partners. The profit is allocated to the partners in the agreed profit sharing ratios. It will be reduced by any previous loss carried forward, or that loss may be set off against other income of the proprietors, retrospectively for three years past in the case of a new business. The business income will be assessed under each applicable Schedule and Case.

For a limited company the following rules cover the main features of the computation.

1. The total taxable income under the various applicable Schedules and Cases, as well as capital gains, is assessed to corporation tax as a single figure, subject to the adjustments indicated below.
2. Dividends received from UK companies are excluded from the assessment, on the grounds that the profits from which they are paid have already been subject to corporation tax chargeable on the payer. Dividends paid by a company are not deductions from its profit chargeable to corporation tax.
3. Interest on loans made by a company (or investments in government stock) is received after

deduction of basic rate income tax. It is, however, the gross interest receivable which is included in profits for corporation tax purposes. Interest paid by a company on loans, such as debentures, is likewise subject to deduction of basic rate income tax, but the gross amount of the interest gives relief from corporation tax. The fact that loan interest paid is deductible and dividends are not is a significant factor in deciding on the relative merits of issuing shares or obtaining loans.

4. As part of the system of collecting income tax at source, wherever practical, a company provides the Inland Revenue with a quarterly account of (a) the income tax deducted from or imputed to interest and dividends paid, less (b) the income tax which it has suffered on interest and UK dividends received. The net amount is paid to the Inland Revenue with the quarterly account, and represents Advance Corporation Tax (ACT), which is accordingly deducted from the mainstream corporation tax eventually payable on the company's profits. The net effect of these rules is that the company does not pay income tax on interest and dividends received, nor does it obtain the benefit of income tax which it has deducted from, or is imputed to, interest and dividends paid.

These points are illustrated by the following specimen computation, for which 1989–90 rates of tax have been used, i.e. income tax basic rate: 25 per cent; corporation tax (for large companies): 35 per cent. Small companies with profits to £150 000 pay corporation tax at 25 per cent, and marginal relief applies to profits between £150 000 and £750 000 (subsequently increased).

		£
Trading profit as adjusted for disallowances etc.		1 000 000
Add: Interest received, gross		40 000
		1 040 000
Less: Debenture interest paid, gross		100 000
		940 000
Add: Capital gains		30 000
		970 000
Less: Capital allowances		70 000
		£900 000
Corporation tax at 35%		315 000
Less: Advance corporation tax		
	£	
Income tax imputed to dividends paid	40 000	
Income tax imputed to dividends received	3 000	
		37 000
		£278 000

A tax loss brought forward from previous years would have been deducted from the assessment of £900 000.

Capital Gains Tax

Capital gains occur where assets are sold (or otherwise disposed of) at a price above their cost. The value at 1/4/82 can be substituted for an earlier cost. The expenses of acquiring and selling the assets are allowable deductions from the surplus, and so is an indexation allowance based on movements in the Retail Price Index since 31/3/82. All kinds of assets are subject to the tax, including buildings and shares, except gains on the sale of UK government securities and certain national savings. Various exemptions are available to individuals, including the first £5000 of a year's gains, exemption for sales of chattels up to £6000 (1989–90) and the principal private residence, and relief on the sale of a business on retirement. Capital losses can be set off against capital gains in a particular year.

Capital gains tax applies to limited companies resident in the UK on gains arising both in the UK and overseas. As shown in the preceding section, the gains are included as part of taxable profit for the purpose of corporation tax.

Capital gains can be deferred by 'roll-over relief' when an asset is replaced. This means that the capital gain on the sale of a replaced asset can be set off against the cost of the new asset. The rate applies to land and buildings and to fixed plant.

Special provisions apply to the sale of leases of 50 years or less, and other wasting assets.

Capital gains tax can be minimized by setting off capital losses against capital gains, especially with investments in shares. The use of roll-over relief can also be of special importance where buildings are sold and replaced, since the rise in value of these assets normally outstrips the rate of inflation.

Value Added Tax (VAT)

Since 1979 up to the time of writing (1989–90) the rate of VAT has been 15 per cent. It is payable by businesses on the invoiced value of goods and services, subject to many exemptions, but the business recovers the VAT which it has suffered on purchases. The tax is therefore borne by the ultimate consumer.

Traders are exempt if their annual turnover is not more than £23 600 in 1989–90, but this threshold is increased each year. Exempted goods and services include, generally, interests in land, financial transactions, insurance, health, education, postal services, burial services, sporting activities and the activities of trade unions and professional bodies.

Zero-rated supplies are those which a trader invoices to his customers at a nil rate of VAT, but can recover the tax (if any) charged on relevant purchases. This category includes imported and exported goods, many foodstuffs, publications, fuel and power (but not petrol), private house construction, children's clothing, medicine and many medical appliances.

Returns of the net VAT payable by or refundable to a business are submitted to the local offices of the Customs and Excise, normally at quarterly intervals. Accurate records must therefore be maintained of the tax suffered on purchases and charged to customers. For registered (i.e. not exempt) traders the accounting statements, and the tax computations, will record income and expenditure excluding VAT. Nevertheless, the VAT payable or refundable each quarter will usually represent substantial amounts of cash outflow or inflow, and needs to be estimated in the cash forecast.

Business Expansion Scheme

The Business Expansion Scheme provides tax relief to individuals, not to businesses. It is, however, desirable for business executives to obtain a general understanding of the scheme because it facilitates the provision of capital to new businesses. The scheme gives relief from income tax to individuals of the amount they invest in the ordinary shares of newly set up and qualifying companies up to £40 000 a year, with a maximum investment of £1m, or £5m for ship chartering companies and those providing assured tenancies (1989). The shares must not be repaid within five years. The trades excluded from the scheme include property dealing, most farming, financial, insurance, legal and accountancy activities, and asset leasing. The companies issuing the shares must be unquoted and not be either subsidiaries or controlling companies. Investors do not qualify for the tax relief if they already own 30 per cent of the ordinary shares or loan capital of the company concerned.

The foregoing is a summary only of somewhat complex legislation.

Inheritance Tax

This is the tax on the value of any individual's estate at death and on gifts made within seven years of death; before 1986 it was known as the 'capital transfer tax' but was substantially amended in that year. The tax at 40 per cent applied to estates worth £118 000 in 1989–90, this limit being subject to annual increases. Many specific exemptions are also available, such as transfers between spouses and lifetime transfers up to £3000 a year (1989–90). Transfers of vacant agricultural land and businesses in sole ownership are relieved of 50 per cent of the tax, and there are reliefs for the transfer of interests in unquoted companies.

The tax does not therefore directly affect business. It is, however, important to those who own shares in companies, especially small unquoted companies, and to sole proprietors or partnerships of businesses. Those whose estates and transfers will be liable should make adequate provisions for funds to pay the tax on death. Arrangements for this purpose, and for minimizing the tax, need expert professional advice, but could include insurance of the estimated liability, transfers to spouses, transfers to trusts for dependants (subject to certain qualifications), and use of the annual lifetime transfer limit.

APPENDIX 2

FRANCHISING

Introduction to Franchising

Franchising is a marketing-oriented method of distribution in which one person, the franchisor, grants a licence or a franchise to another person, the franchisee, which permits the franchisee to use the franchisor's trade name, trade marks and business system in return for an initial payment and further regular payments.

The Parties

The franchisor is almost invariably a limited liability company.

The franchisee can, however, operate as a sole trader, a partnership or as a limited company. The franchisor will require the franchisee(s) to sign an agreement so as to guarantee the performance of the limited company.

Term and Option to Renew

The length of the agreement is likely to reflect not only the type of business but also the amount of the front-end fee.

Whilst five years might be said to be an average, agreements run from one year to 15 or more. However, many franchisors will offer an option to renew the agreement on certain conditions.

Territory

Franchisees have an exclusive territory in which to operate their franchise. This is, of course, a substantial advantage to the franchisees but a disadvantage to the franchisor, particularly if the franchisees do not work hard in the territory to exploit its potential upon which the franchisor depends as much for his income.

The franchisor might also reasonably require the franchisees to demonstrate their commitment by achieving a certain level of performance, failing which he may take back part of the territory or remove the exclusivity from the territory, and that might result in other franchisees offering the service in the same area.

Property

In some franchises the property from which the service or the products are offered can be of prime importance. The franchisor therefore may insist on controlling the property by taking a head lease and ensuring that the property reverts to him if for any reason the franchise should cease.

Exclusive Supply

The prime object of some franchisors is to distribute products which they themselves either manufacture or otherwise distribute. In these circumstances, the franchisee will be required to purchase the products exclusively from the franchisor. Provision should be made where the franchisor is unable to supply.

Fees

Most franchises provide for two or three payments to be made by the franchisee to the franchisor. The first is an initial fee to cover the expense of setting up the individual franchisee in his business and may include training, initial stock, shopfitting and a sum to reflect the existing reputation of the franchise.

Most franchisors, however, rely for their principal income upon regular payments for the continuing services they provide. These payments are made monthly or weekly and are normally calculated as a percentage of the gross income of the franchisee's business. Sometimes, however, where the franchisor exclusively provides products for sale in the business, he may derive his income from the usual mark-up on the sale of the products to the franchisee.

It is, of course, a matter of commercial judgment as to whether the amounts charged by the franchisor are reasonable in all the circumstances, bearing in mind the services which the franchisor provides to the franchisee both on an ongoing and special basis.

Sale or Assignment of Business

Unless the amount of capital invested in the business is small, or the term of the agreement is very short, most franchisors now permit the franchisee, subject of course to reasonable terms and conditions, to assign or sell the business.

The Franchise Manual

It is not only impossible but highly undesirable for the franchise agreement to try to set out all the details of the franchisor's business system. All franchisors, therefore, will have a separate Manual which specifies precisely how the business should be conducted. It will, together with the training course, impart the know-how and expertise so necessary if the franchisees are to succeed, and the franchisor therefore has an obligation to update the Manual as the business develops during the course of the agreement.

The Manual often contains a great deal of confidential information, and clauses restricting access to this information, and to prevent franchisees from passing on what they have learnt during the course of the Agreement, are both reasonable and desirable in order to protect the integrity of the franchise as a whole.

Franchisees benefit from the franchisor's proven business system and should therefore expect to follow the system precisely. The franchisor can react strongly to any breaches of obligations, as he has responsibilities to all franchisees.

Disputes

However fair and reasonable the terms of the agreement, however great the initial goodwill between the parties, from time to time differences will arise and these are always best resolved by direct discussions conducted with goodwill.

Some agreements provide for arbitration. The British Franchise Association is always prepared to assist when disputes arise between Members and their franchisees. Good franchisors will make the effort to communicate regularly with their franchisees as this provides one of the best ways of avoiding aggravations which can often become so contentious.

Franchising, whilst far from being a partnership in strictly legal terms, is very much a partnership in the everyday sense of the word, and depends for its success upon the commitment of each of the parties to comply both with the spirit and with the terms of the agreement.

The Franchise Contract

The franchise contract is the legal document in which the whole transaction is drawn together. It must accurately reflect the promises made and it must be fair, whilst at the same time ensuring that there are sufficient controls to protect the integrity of the system. In brief, the franchise contract should:

1. Deal correctly, in legal terms, with the various property rights owned by the franchisor.
2. Provide the operational details and controls.
3. Provide the franchisee with security in his operations and in his ability to develop and sell an asset.

The Franchisor's Proprietary Interests

This will clearly deal with such things as trade marks, trade names, copyright materials and the franchisor's business system and know-how.

The Rights Granted to the Franchisee

This will deal with areas of operation and the formal granting of rights to use trade marks, copyright material, etc.

Territorial Rights

It is relevant at this point to mention territorial rights, since these create practical problems. There are two aspects to the problem which arises when exclusive territorial rights are a feature.

First, there are the commercial considerations and these have caused many problems for franchisors over the years. It is very difficult to determine a territorial allocation which is fair to both parties, especially when the extent of the likely penetration of the market cannot be judged. Indeed, quite often, even the total size of the potential market cannot be estimated.

In the past, many franchisors who have chosen the exclusive territorial route have found that there was no effective way of ensuring that the potential of the area was fully exploited.

The effect of this is to harm the whole network. Quite apart from the fact that within the area a market and demand is being created by advertising and promotion which is not met by resources, the way is prepared for competition to move in and do better. Also, disgruntled or potential customers are not likely to look elsewhere within the same network for their requirements. The network thus gets a bad name.

The obvious response is to suggest that performance targets should be established. Since the assessment of fair performance targets is dependent upon the same factors as have to be considered in defining a territory, the problem remains basically the same. Additionally, if performance targets are set they should take into account the potential expansion of the business as well as inflationary factors. These are also difficult matters to deal with in a fair and equitable way.

Secondly, there are the legal considerations. The introduction of exclusive territorial rights is likely to trigger the operation of the Restrictive Trade Practices Act 1976.

The agreement is then required to be registered with the Office of Fair Trading. The restrictive provisions have to be considered in the light of the interests of consumers to the exclusion of what is in the interests of franchisor and franchisee. The provisions of the agreement in which the Office of Fair Trading usually expresses an interest are those provisions which are designed to protect the network and the integrity of the system from being copied and exploited by departing franchisees. The Act also allows for the continuous monitoring of the agreement, and for subsequent revival of interest by the Office of Fair Trading.

It is for these considerations that many franchisors do not offer exclusive territorial rights.

Term of Agreement

The contract will also specify the period of agreement. The basic principle to be adopted here is that the franchise relationship should be capable of subsisting on a long-term basis. There may be various reasons (including, where tied supply of products is involved, legal reasons) for a relatively short initial period, say five years, but most franchise schemes allow for the franchisee to be able to exercise a right of renewal.

Franchisor's Services

The nature and extent of the services to be provided by the franchisor to the franchisee, both initially and on a continuing basis, should be covered. This area of the contract will deal with the initial services, which enable the franchisee to be initiated, trained and equipped to open for trading.

On a continuing basis, the franchisor will be providing services which should be detailed in the agreement (see page 250 under the title 'Continuing Services') including the possibility of developing and introducing new ideas.

The Initial and Continuing Obligations of the Franchisees

These will range from accepting the financial burden of setting-up in compliance with the franchisor's requirements, to operating accounting and other administrative systems to ensure that essential information is available to both parties.

These systems will often be described in an operational manual to which the franchisee will be introduced in training and which he will have available as a reference guide after he has opened for business. The manual will be constantly updated as the system develops.

The Operational Controls Imposed upon the Franchisee

The controls are to ensure that operational standards are properly controlled – failure to maintain standards in one unit can harm the whole network. Franchisees will rightly be alarmed if any of their counterparts fail to maintain standards and the franchisor allows them to continue to do so. Often operational controls are very detailed with a cross-reference to the operational manual. The contract will contain the obligations and the manual will explain how the obligation is to be discharged.

Sale of the Business

One of the reasons for the success of franchising is the motivation it provides to the franchisee, which comes with self-employment and the incentive at the end of the day of making a capital gain. For this reason, the franchised business should be capable of being sold. However, there will always be controls. If there are none, it should be a matter for suspicion. After all, if a franchisor is highly selective when considering applications for franchises, there is every reason for him to be equally selective about those who want to join the network by buying a business from an established franchisee.

The criteria by which a prospective purchaser will be judged by the franchisor should be set out in the contract. The procedure to be followed should also be provided in the contract. Some franchisors insert into the contract an option to buy the business if the franchisee wishes to sell. If such a provision is inserted in the contract it should provide for the payment of at least the same price as is offered to the franchisee by a bona fide arm's length purchaser. Any artificial formula which might enable the franchisor to buy at less than market value should be resisted.

Death of the Franchisee

In order to give the franchisee peace of mind, provision should be made to demonstrate that the franchisor will provide assistance to enable the business to be preserved as an asset to be realized, or alternatively taken over by the franchisee's dependants.

Arbitration

Arbitration is in reality private litigation using an independent arbitrator chosen by the parties. It has advantages in that the proceedings are private; the arbitrator chosen can be selected because of his or her special knowledge of the business that is the subject of arbitration; the timing of the proceedings can be fixed to suit the parties' convenience; the parties may establish the rules for their arbitration and save time and expense in so doing.

There are disadvantages also. Not every dispute under a franchise contract will be resolved by the decision of an arbitrator, e.g. the franchisor will not want an arbitrator to judge whether his quality standards and system are being maintained. The franchisor's right to an injunction may be impaired if the arbitration agreement does not reserve those rights to him. The wrong choice of arbitrator may result in a compromise decision which will not satisfy either party.

Bearing in mind the long-term relationship involved, those areas where genuine misunderstandings can arise may be considered suitable for arbitration, e.g. fee calculations, rights of renewal.

Termination Provisions

Invariably, there will be express provision for the termination of the agreement in the event of a default by the franchisee. Usually, the franchisee will be given the opportunity to put right minor remediable breaches so as to avoid termination, providing that he does not persist in making such breaches.

The consequences of termination will usually involve the franchisee in taking steps to ensure that he ceases to display any association with the franchisor. The franchisee will no longer enjoy the use of the trade mark/trade name and other property rights, owned by the franchisor. In addition, the franchisee will be under an obligation for a period of time not to compete with the franchisor, or other franchisees, nor will he be allowed to make use of the franchisor's system, or other methods.

Financial Considerations for the Franchisee

It is important for the franchisor to provide the prospective franchisee with detailed financial information relating to the proposed franchise. One of the requirements for membership of the British Franchise Association is that a pilot site should have been operated for at least a period of one year. Consequently, as an absolute minimum, audited accounts should be available covering this operation. Longer-established franchise operations should have a wider range of historical financial information available relating to performance of existing franchisees.

Projected Profit and Loss Account

An essential requirement for the prospective franchisee is a cash flow projection of the timing of the costs associated with operating the franchise and the expected revenue from sales over the same periods. It would be helpful to see these projections for at least the first three years, preferably five. These statements will facilitate financial planning, because short-term finance may be required by the franchisee until sales revenue regularly exceeds the costs of running the business. Also it will allow the franchisee and his/her financial adviser to reach a judgment about the acceptability of the financial return from the investment of both labour and capital in the project.

Assuming that the prospective franchisee and his adviser/accountant are satisfied with the profit and loss account projections, they should have the opportunity to check the assumptions upon which the projections are based. This should take the form of actual evidence based on the original franchise and the results of market research. Costs and overheads are relatively easy to control and forecast, but sales are dependent upon a number of factors over which the franchisee has little influence.

However, market conditions, the propensity of consumers to purchase, the effect of competition, relative prices, the quality of the product or service and the effect of the franchisor's marketing and promotional activities can all be measured and quite accurately predicted by market research.

Projected Balance Sheet

This will be a useful document for estimating the future value of the business should the franchisee need to sell the concern before the term of the franchise expires. The projected balance sheet will identify the assets and likely liabilities of the business at various stages in the future and provide a useful indication of capital growth.

The Commitment Made by the Franchisor

In return for the initial franchise fee and a percentage of the franchisee's turnover (frequently 10 per cent) the franchisor will provide essentially three services:

1. *A protected business format* which may be used exclusively by the franchisee in the business area or territory. This may include:
   (a) A trade mark, or trade name, and the goodwill with which is it associated.
   (b) A business format – a system recorded in a manual, which will contain elements, some of which are possibly secret and confidential.
   (c) In some cases, formulae specifications, design drawings and operational documents.
   (d) Copyright in some of the above items which are in written form and capable of copyright protection.
2. *Initial services.* The nature of these services will vary, bearing in mind the type of business. The general principle is that the franchisor's initial services (including training) should be sufficiently comprehensive to set up a previously inexperienced person in business so that he can trade effectively, in accordance with his chosen franchise system, as soon as he opens.
3. *Continuing services.* Having established the franchisee in business, the franchisor now has the responsibility to sustain a continuing range of services to support him. These include:
   (a) Performance monitoring to help maintain standards and profitability.
   (b) Continuing update of methods and innovations.
   (c) Market research and new product development.
   (d) Promotion and advertising.
   (e) Benefit of bulk purchasing power.
   (f) The provision at head office of a specialist range of management services.
   In addition to the above, most franchise systems provide for advertising and promotion to be handled by the franchisor who will receive from franchisees a contribution for that purpose. The most common method of calculating the contribution is the same as for

franchise fees, namely as a percentage of the gross sales by the franchisee. Four per cent is a common figure.

In some cases a franchisor may include the advertising expenses in the franchise fee and undertake to spend a percentage of the fee on advertising and promotion. There are also cases where local advertising rather than national is more important and a franchisee may find the franchisor does not seek a contribution but imposes on the franchisee the obligation to spend a certain sum on approved local advertising.

APPENDIX 3

FINANCIAL TERMINOLOGY

Accrual. May be accrued income or accrued expense. Represents the proportion of a continuing receipt or payment which refers to the current period of account but is not yet due for payment, such as rent payable in arrear.

Amortization. Essentially synonymous with depreciation, i.e. the periodical reduction in the book value of an asset on some rational basis; particularly applied to leases.

Appropriation Account. The final section of the profit and loss account which shows how the profit for a period has been allocated to taxation, dividends, reserves, and the balance carried forward.

Assets. Everything owned by the business, generally divided into *Fixed assets*, *Current assets* and *Intangible assets* (qq.v.).

Authorized capital. The share capital which a limited company is authorized to issue by its memorandum and articles of association, or similar regulations for other incorporated bodies.

Balance sheet. The statement of the financial position of a business at a specific date. It is not a double-entry account. Comprises capital and reserves, assets and liabilities.

Bill of exchange. A negotiable instrument, payable on demand or at a specified future date, for a precise sum which may include interest. Frequently drawn on overseas customers and can normally be discounted or negotiated with a bank to obtain immediate payment.

Bonus shares. Additional shares issued to existing shareholders out of reserves.

Breakeven level. The volume of sales or output at which there is neither profit nor loss.

Calls on shares. The instalments required from shareholders on issued shares.

Capital. Variously interpreted as the issued shares; issued shares and reserves, with or without loan capital; the net assets after deducting current liabilities.

Capital employed. Usually equivalent to total assets less current liabilities, i.e. issued share capital, plus reserves, plus loan capital; sometimes interpreted as total assets.

Commitments. The financial commitments of a business are obligations to incur future expenditure, such as agreements to acquire fixed assets or trading supplies at a future date. Shown in notes to accounts.

Contingent liability. A possible future liability which will become payable on the occurrence of some event, such as the contingent liability under a guarantee. To be noted on the balance sheet but not included in the balance sheet totals.

Contribution. The surplus from deducting marginal or variable cost from income, representing the contribution towards the fixed costs and the profit.

Current assets. Assets comprising cash in hand and at bank, and assets due to be converted into cash within a year, such as debtors, temporary investments, bills of exchange receivable, stocks and work in progress.

Current cost. Historic cost revised to account for changes in money values.

Current liabilities. Amounts due to be paid within a year, including bank overdraft, creditors, bills of exchange payable, taxation liabilities, dividends recommended or due, and provisions other than for depreciation.

Debenture. A form of document in evidence of a loan, normally secured. Applied to secured loan capital. May be convertible, i.e. exchangeable into shares at a specified time.

Deferred charge. Expenditure which is temporarily treated as an asset, and thus withheld from being charged to the profit and loss account until it can be matched against the income it produces. An example is research and development expenditure of which the eventual recovery is assured. In strictness, depreciating fixed assets are also of the nature of deferred charges. Also used to apply to expenditure, such as on deposits, made before value is received.

Deferred shares. Shares of which the dividend is deferred to that of other shares, but normally entitled to the balance of available profit after ordinary shares have received a given rate of dividend. Known also as 'founders' shares'.

Differential cost. The difference between the cost of output at different levels. See also *Marginal cost.*

Direct cost. The cost which can be applied with reasonable precision and convenience to units of output, jobs, operations, cost centres, departments, etc. Normally includes direct labour and direct materials plus other direct expenditure.

Earnings. The profit after all prior charges (such as loan interest, preference dividends and tax) which is available for the ordinary shareholders, although not necessarily paid out as a dividend.

Equity. A term applied to the value of the ordinary shareholders' interests in a company.

Financial position. Various meanings, but specifically the position of a business shown by its balance sheet.

First in first out (FIFO). The method of valuing material issues which values the issues at the cost of the item longest in stock. See also *Last in first out.*

Fixed assets. Those assets which are held to assist in the earning of income and not for resale in the normal course of business. Includes premises for occupation (not for sale), working plant, fixtures, furniture, fittings and operating vehicles.

Fixed costs. Expenditure which does not vary in relation to activity *in the short term.* Examples include rent, other establishment expenses, depreciation (where not based on activity), and the cost of essential staff and services.

Floating charge. A charge on the whole undertaking of a business, usually created by a debenture, which entitles the lender to appoint a Receiver on default.

Gearing. Usually interpreted as the relation between (1) loan capital plus preference capital, and (2) equity capital or ordinary shareholders' interests.

Going concern principle. The general rule that a business is to be treated as a continuing enterprise unless a liquidation is imminent. Affects, in particular, the valuation of assets.

Goodwill. The value of a business above the value of its net assets; the value of its reputation and its ability to continue to attract customers. Can be calculated as the present value of expected future net cash inflows. In the case of another business acquired, goodwill is the excess of the consideration over the value of the net assets acquired.

Gross profit/loss.   The difference between sales income and the direct cost (including manufacturing overheads) incurred in producing the goods or services sold.

Historic cost.   The actual money spent in obtaining assets and services, not adjusted for changes in money values.

Increment.   The additional surplus gained by a given increase in sales; the marginal profit.

Indirect costs.   Those costs which cannot be attributed precisely to units of output. Generally synonymous with overheads. See also *Direct costs*.

Imputed cost.   The interest foregone on the funds applied to a project or operations. See also *Opportunity cost*.

Intangible assets.   Strictly those assets not susceptible to touch, but more practically the cost of obtaining rights such as copyrights, trade marks, licence agreements, and the value attributed to brands and goodwill.

Issued capital.   The shares which are actually issued to subscribers and for which the latter have a liability to pay.

Joint products.   Those products which emanate from a common source, as the various joints etc. of meat from a carcass, and the derivatives from coal and crude oil. The cost of each joint product cannot be precisely ascertained.

Last in first out (LIFO).   A system for valuing issues of material and goods at the price or cost of the purchase or output most recently placed in stores. See also *First in first out*.

Limiting factors.   The factors which limit the volume of production, sales or activity generally.

Liquidation.   The process of winding up a business, i.e. bringing it to an end.

Liquid capital.   Those current assets which are either available as cash or can be turned into cash in a short period, normally excluding stocks. Net liquid capital is liquid assets less current liabilities.

Manufacturing account.   An account showing the cost of producing goods in the factory, the cost of sales, and the cost of work in progress.

Marginal cost.   The additional outgoings incurred by producing one more unit of output. See also *Differential cost*.

Master budget.   The final summary of all the approved departmental budgets, usually in the form of the final projected accounts of a business.

Matching principle.   The general accounting rule that, so far as appropriate, related expenditure should be deducted from income in the period when that income arises.

Net assets.   The total assets less current liabilities, equivalent to capital employed.

Net current assets.   Current assets less current liabilities, often called (imprecisely) 'working capital'.

Oncost.   The overheads applied to direct costs by means of an overhead rate.

Operating account.   An account which records the direct cost of operations and the cost of sales. Generally applies to a non-fabricating or service activity, such as a mine, transport undertaking, maintenance workshop, etc.

Operating expenses and operating profit.   The emphasis is on 'expenses' as compared with direct costs of manufacture or purchase of goods. Those expenses of selling, distribution and administration deducted from gross profit to produce operating profit or loss.

Opportunity cost. The cost of the opportunity foregone; the additional profit which could have been made by an alternative course of action. Similar to *Imputed cost* (q.v.).

Ordinary shares. Shares, normally with full voting rights, entitled to a share of profit after prior rights, e.g. of preference shares. Otherwise known as 'equity capital', or risk-bearing shares.

Overheads. A generalized term synonymous with indirect costs of manufacture, and with operating expenses. Manufacturing or operating overheads form the basis of the overhead rate.

Paid-up capital. The shares on which the nominal value, plus any premium, has been paid or credited as paid.

Payback period. The time which elapses before rentals equal the original cost of the asset leased.

Period costs. Costs which move in relation to time rather than volume of output of sales, such as rent, rates and insurance.

Preference shares. Shares which are redeemable and are entitled to a fixed rate of dividend out of profits in priority to ordinary shares plus, possibly, further participating rights. Preference shares are normally 'cumulative'; that is, arrears of the fixed dividend are carried forward for subsequent payment.

Preferred shares. Shares which have rights of dividend up to a specified rate in priority to preference shares.

Premiums on shares. The amount subscribed on an issue of shares above their nominal value. Placed in a share premium account, which is a non-distributable reserve.

Prepayments. These may be of expenses or income. They represent the amount which has been paid in advance. Examples are rent payable in advance, rates and insurance premiums. Prepaid expenses are shown as assets and prepaid income as liabilities in the balance sheet.

Present value. The amount arrived at by discounting a future payment or receipt or a series of payments or receipts.

Price/earnings (P/E) ratio. The quoted price of a share divided by the profit available to the shareholder, whether distributed as a dividend or retained in the company.

Private company. A limited company which places a restriction on the transfer of its shares and is prohibited from issuing capital to the public at large.

Provision. An allowance in the accounts for an estimated expense or loss of which the precise amount cannot be determined with substantial accuracy. Typical examples are provisions for depreciation, bad debts, taxation, stock losses and exchange losses.

Public company. Any limited company which is not a private company. More particularly a company which can offer shares and debentures to the general public and can apply for a quotation on a stock exchange.

Quotations. Specifically the market price of shares and securities in a stock exchange. Applies only to public, not private companies, certain other incorporated bodies, and government stock.

Replacement cost. The cost of replacing assets, materials and services.

Reserves. Allocations (or 'retentions') of profit for general or specific purposes. They may be distributable or, such as share premiums and asset revaluations, not distributable as dividends, except in a winding up. Not to be confused with provisions or funds.

Residual income.   A term used in accounting for divisions and representing the amount of divisional profit remaining after deducting interest on capital.

Responsibility accounting.   The allocation to managers of income and expenditure within their control; associated with budgetary control.

Rights issue.   An issue of shares to existing shareholders giving them preferential rights over external investors.

Shareholders' interests.   Issued share capital plus reserves.

Sources and application of funds.   A statement showing the effect on available funds of changes in capital, assets and liabilities. The issued capital and reserves are also sometimes referred to as sources of funds, and the net assets as the application of the funds.

Standard costs.   Assessment of what the costs of an operation should be given reasonable efficiency and a level of output or activity.

Sunk costs.   Those costs which have been paid some time in the past, and may be carried forward in the balance sheet to be matched against future income. Examples are fixed assets subject to depreciation, and past expenditure on research and development and on launching a new product.

Super profits.   The profits above a reasonable return on capital. Used in assessments of the value of a business.

Tangible assets.   Real assets (susceptible to touch) which have material existence, as opposed to rights and intangibles such as goodwill.

Transfer pricing.   The notional price of goods or services transferred from one division to another.

Underwriting.   A form of insurance on the issue of capital whereby the underwriter undertakes to subscribe for those shares or debentures not taken up by the public or the stock market.

Variable cost.   The cost which varies more or less directly with activity, e.g. output or sales. Some costs are semi-variable or semi-fixed.

Variances.   Differences between standards or budgets and actual results.

Working capital.   A rather imprecise term for net current assets.

Work in progress.   The cost of partly completed production. The comparable American term is 'work in process'.

Yield.   The precentage the dividend bears to the quoted price. A redemption yield (as with redeemable government securities) takes into account the surplus, on an annual basis, to be obtained on redemption. The earnings yield is the percentage the earning per share bears to the price per share.

Selected Bibliography

Accounting Standards Committee, various Statements of Standard Accounting Practice (SSAPs), joint UK accounting bodies.

Annual Abstract of Statistics, HMSO, 1989.

Ansoff Igor, *Corporate Strategy*, McGraw-Hill, 1965, and Penguin, 1968.

Bierman, H. and Smidt, S., *The Capital Budgeting Decision*, Macmillan, New York, 1984.

Blackett, T. and Berry, C., *The Role of Brand Valuation in Marketing Strategy*, paper produced by Interbrand plc.

Bollan, J.F., *Guide to Investment in Enterprise Zones*, Longman, 1988.

Bull, R.J., *Accounting in Business*, 5th edn, Butterworth, 1984.

Chartered Association of Certified Accountants, *Cost and Management Accountancy*, Longman, 1989.

Chartered Institute of Marketing, examination papers.

Companies Acts 1985, 1988 and 1989, HMSO.

Crouch, Sunny, *Marketing Research for Managers*, Heinemann (hardback), 1984; Pan (paperback), 1985.

Dobbins, R. and Witt, S.F., *Practical Financial Management*, Blackwell, 1988.

Edwards, H., *Credit Management Handbook*, Gower, 1985.

Ernst & Young, *Acquisitions and Disposals: An Introduction to Buying and Selling Private Companies*, 1983.

Export Credit Guarantee Department booklet, *ECGD Services*, 1986 edn.

Gabor, A., *Pricing*, 2nd edn, Gower, 1988.

Goch, D., *Finance and Accounts for Managers*, Kogan Page, 1985.

Green, D., *Journal of Marketing Research*, Feb. 1973.

Horngren C.T. and Foster, G., *Cost Accounting: A Managerial Emphasis*, 6th edn, Prentice-Hall, 1987.

ICL, *New Salesman's Training Program Manual*, 1983. ICL plc.

Kotler, P., *Marketing Management, Analysis, Planning and Controls*, 5th edn, Prentice-Hall, 1984.

Lanzilloti, R., 'Pricing Objectives in Large Companies', *American Economic Review*, XLVIII, Dec. 1958.

Lee, T.E., *Cash Flow Accounting*, Van Nostrand Reinhold 1984.

Levy, H. and Sarnat, M., *Capital Investment and Financial Decisions*, 3rd edn, Prentice-Hall, 1986.

Long, L., *Computers in Business*, Prentice-Hall, 1987.

Market Research Society abstract, *Standard Questions*.

Marketing, various reports from the magazine published during 1988–9.

Mepham, M.J., *Accounting Models*, Pitman, 1984.

Michael Peters Brand Development Division (part of the Michael Peters Group) Survey, *New Product Development*, 1988.

Miller, E.L., *Inflation Accounting*, Van Nostrand Reinhold, 1980.

Mintel Report, *Pub Entertainment*, 1987. Mintel Publications, 7 Arundel Street, London WC2.

Pocock, M.A. and Taylor, A.H., (eds), *Financial Planning and Control*, 2nd edn, Gower, 1989.

Practical Guide to Company Acquisitions, Tolley, 1989.

Sullivan, M.F., *Financing International Trade*. Butterworth, 1989.

Sunday Times, The, Business section, various reports.

Taylor, A.H., *Costing for Managers*, Holt, Rinehart & Winston, 1984.

Taylor, A.H., *Taxation Simplified*, Lofthouse Publications, biannual Budget and Finance Act editions.

Taylor, A.H. and Shearing, H., *Financial and Cost Accounting for Management*, 8th edn, Macdonald & Evans, 1983.

Taylor, T.W., *The Finance of Industry and Commerce*, Heinemann, 1988.

Walsh, L.S., *International Marketing*, Pitman, 1981.

Wells, W., *Journal of Marketing Research*, May 1975.

Westwick, C.A., *How to Use Management Ratios*, Gower, 1987.

INDEX

accounting
    consistency 10
    consolidated 117
    development of 2
    objectives 3
    principles and conventions 9
accounts, interpretation of 12
accruals 37
acquisitions 228–35
activity, measures of 54
Advance Corporation Tax 241
appropriation account 42
articles of association 15
assets
    current 32
    disposal and replacement 48
    fixed 28
    intangible 30
    tangible 29

balance sheet 5, 13
    repair of 116
bills of exchange 34
brand names
    capitalization of 115–25
    profitability 120
    strength 121–3
    valuation 123–4
breakeven level 71
budgets 66
    capital 74, 103
    departmental 74
    revision 213
buy-outs 232, 233–4

C&F 162–4
capacity 63, 197
capital
    allotment 20
    authorized 18, 20
    employed 5, 12, 18
    equity 23
    loan 18, 21
    placings and offers for sale 17
capital budgeting 103–4
capital commitments 29, 37

capital gearing 23
capitalization methodology (of
    brands) 120–4
cash flow discounting 87, 103–14
cash forecasts 98–9
CIF 162–4
commissioning agent 170
companies
    private 15–16
    public 15–16
Companies Acts 2
complementary marketing 169
contract manufacture 167, 170
contribution concept 69–73, 151, 176–9,
    182, 199
control of salesforce 142–50
Corporation Tax 237
cost
    allowable 73
    direct 44, 50, 53
    fixed 53–5
    imputed 56
    indirect 44, 53
    marginal 55
    meaning of 49
    opportunity 56
    relevant 53
    of sales 40, 45
    standard 56
    variable 53–5
creditors 32
current assets 32
current liabilities 35

DCF 104–15
debentures 94
debtors 34–5
deferred charges 37
deferred income 37
deferred shares 21
deferred tax 37
depreciation 30, 46
development expenditure 195–7
direct costs 44
disposals 228–35
dividends
    cover 27
    policy 25

divisions, accounting for 75–7

earnings per share 213
ECGD 171–3
employers' share schemes 21
entity concept 9
equity interests 22
Export Credit Guarantee Department, *see*
    ECGD
export houses 169
exporting, financial aspects 162–75
    analyses 166–7
    direct 170
    indirect 169
    underwriting 172
ex-shop 162–4
extraordinary and exceptional items 42
ex-works 162–4

FAS 162–4
finance
    buyer credit 172
    supplier credit 172
financial position 5
financial resources 91
fixed assets 28
fixed costs 191–3, 196
FOB 162–4
FOR 162–4
forecasting potential sales 137–8
foreign exchange 173–5
FOT 162–4
forward market 174
forward rate 174
franchising 170, 244–51
    contract 246–9
    manual 245–6
franco
    domicile 162–4
    quay 162–4
    warehouse 162–4
funds
    availability of 87
    meaning of 87
funds flow 87

gearing of capital 23
'going concern' rule 10
goodwill 30, 116–18
government assistance 93, 171–3
gross profit 7

historical cost 13

income tax 237
incremental costs (NPV) 112
    control of 55
indirect cost 44, 53
inflation 13

Inheritance Tax 243
intangible assets 30
interest 23
internal rate of return 107, 108–14
inventories 80
investment
    appraisal 103
    evaluation of projects 103–14
    long-term 31

joint products 225
joint ventures 167, 170

labour costs 50
last in, first out (LIFO) 51
lead time 84
leasing 93
leveraged buy-outs 234
liabilities, current 32
limited auction 232
limited companies 15
limiting factors 194
liquid capital 32
liquidation 6
loan capital 5, 21, 94
loss leaders 224

make or buy decisions 220
management buy-outs 233–4
manufacturing account 43
marginal cost 55
market
    measurement 128
    objectives 229
    penetration 189
    potential 137
    segmentation 128
    skimming 190
marketing plan 176–85
marketing strategy 181–5
master budget 77
matching principle 10
material cost 51
memorandum of association 15
mergers 234–5
mission statement 176
mix-of-sales 222

net assets 13, 28
    current 32
net liabilities, current 32
net present value 104–14
net profit 42
new product development 155–61
nominal capital 19, 20

objectives
    accounting 3
    business 67, 176

operating account 43
operating expenses 41
operating profit 41
opportunity cost 56
order quantities, economic 83
ordinary shares 21, 95
organizations, business 14
overdraft 32
overheads
 rate 53
 recovery 45, 59
 variances 59
overseas manufacturing subsidiary 169, 171

Paciola, Luca 2
paid-up capital 16
partitioning the responsibility for sales 142–8
partly paid shares 16
partnership 14
patents 30
pay-back period of investment 107
placings of capital 17
potential buyers of a business 232
preference shares 21
preferred shares 21
premiums, on shares 17
prepayments 37
present value 106
price
 determination 188
 for export 162–5
 optimum 192
price/earnings ratio 213, 231, 234
pricing
 policy 188
 and product line 194
 standard cost method 189
 tactics 189, 191–3
principles of accounting 9
private companies 15
product
 abandonment 151–4
 development (new) 154–5
 launch 155–6
profit
 available 42
 and capital employed 201
 concept 9
 graph 71–2
 gross 40
 net 39
 operating 41
 planning of 218
 pre-tax 42
 retained 5, 42
 stages of 39
 target 67
profit and loss account 7, 249
projected balance sheet 250
projected profit and loss account 249

prospectus (selling) 232
provisions 36
prudence, concept of 10
private company 15, 228, 229
public company 15

quotations, for shares 16

reciprocal trading 167
recovery of overheads 60, 152–4
relevant cost 53
research and development, recovery of 195–7
reserves 5, 13, 18, 36
 revaluation of 13
residual income 76
responsibility accounting 66, 75
retained profit 7
revaluation of assets 31
risk and uncertainty 113

safety stock 84
sale of business 232–4, 248
sales
 analysis 177
 forecasting 128
 and lease-back 93
 planning sales areas 142
 revenue 176–9
 see also market
sales and marketing plan 176–85
sales channels 168
segmentation
 basis of 129–33
 measurement of 133–7
shareholders' interests 5, 22
shares
 bonus 26, 96
 issue of 16
 kinds of 21
 meaning of 19
 nominal value 19
 premium on 17
solvency 32
sources and applications of funds 88
standard costs variances 57
Statements of Standard Accounting Practice 2, 118
stock and work in progress 32, 80
Stock Exchange (London) 16
 City Code on Takeovers 228
subcontracting 198
'sunk' cost 195
super profits 31
SWOT analysis 180
synergy 235

tactics 189, 190
takeovers 228–35
tangible assets 29

targeting sales objectives 138
tariff barriers 166–7
taxation 24, 237–43
territory
    rights 246–7
    sales 142–50
territory management (sales) 148–50
time value of money 104–15
trade marks 30
transfer pricing 76
turnover of capital 212

underwriting 17
unissued shares 19

valuation of business 230
valuations
    fixed assets 31
    stock. 33
variable cost 53, 191–3, 196
variances
    budget 201
    standard cost 207
VAT 242 .

work in progress 33, 80
working capital 32, 117

yield on shares 213